Top Secret Exchange
The Tizard Mission and the Scientific War

The Tizard Mission was one of the key events in the forging of the Anglo-American alliance in World War II. Led by Sir Henry Tizard, the mission visited the United States and Canada in the summer of 1940 to make available virtually all of Britain's technical and scientific military secrets. Overwhelmed by British generosity, the U.S. reciprocated. David Zimmerman tells the story of that mission and examines the importance of technology in modern war and its crucial role in the defeat of the Axis powers.

Zimmerman traces the early development of the mission, including Britain's initial attempts at technical cooperation in World War I and unsuccessful efforts to restart cooperation in the late 1930s, highlighting Winston Churchill's prominent, yet remarkably inconsistent, role in the story and the often tumultuous diplomatic relations with the Roosevelt administration. He also shows how important the British contribution was. For instance, among the secrets Britain revealed was the cavity magnetron, which made microwave radar possible and marked the beginning of Anglo-American-Canadian cooperation on atomic energy.

The Tizard Mission established an effective system of teamwork for Allied technical and scientific cooperation, and it was this teamwork that proved to be a crucial factor in Allied technical superiority. It was also the beginning of the much longer story of Anglo-American scientific and technical cooperation. The Tizard Mission served as a model for the international technical cooperation that continues today in organizations such as NATO.

DAVID ZIMMERMAN is associate professor of military history, University of Victoria.

Top Secret Exchange

The Tizard Mission and the Scientific War

DAVID ZIMMERMAN

Alan Sutton Publishing Limited

McGill-Queen's University Press
Montreal & Kingston • Buffalo

ISBN 0-7735-1401-5

Legal deposit second quarter 1996
Bibliothèque nationale du Québec

First published in the United Kingdom in 1996
Alan Sutton Publishing Limited
Phoenix Mill • Far Thrupp • Stroud • Gloucestershire

ISBN 0-7509-1242-1

Canadian Cataloguing in Publication Data

Zimmerman, David, 1959–
Top secret exchange : the Tizard mission and the scientific war
Includes bibliographical references and index.
ISBN 0-7735-1401-5
1. World War, 1939–1945 – Military intelligence – Great Britain.
2. World War, 1939–1945 – Military intelligence – United States.
3. World War, 1939–1945 – Military intelligence – Canada.
4. World War, 1939–1945 – Technology. 5. World War, 1939–1945 – Science. 6. Tizard, Henry Thomas, Sir, 1885–1959.
I. Title.
D810.S2Z55 1996 940.54'86 C96-900102-9

British Library Cataloguing in Publication Data

A catalogue record for this book is available from the British Library.

This book has been published with the help of a grant from the Social Science Federation of Canada, using funds provided by the Social Sciences and Humanities Research Council of Canada.

McGill-Queen's University Press is grateful to the Canada Council for support of its publishing program.

Typeset in Palatino 10.5/13
by Caractéra inc., Quebec City, Canada
Printed in Canada by Friesens

This book is dedicated to my grandparents,
Edith and Murray Green

Contents

Abbreviations

AI	airborne interceptor
ASV	air to surface vessel (radar)
ASW	anti-submarine warfare
AVHLI	A.V. Hill Papers
BATM	British Admiralty Technical Mission
CC	Churchill College, Cambridge
DSIR	Department of Scientific and Industrial Research
GEE	grid-reference radio navigation device
HLRO	House of Lords Record Office
HTT	Tizard Papers
IFF	identification of friend or foe
IWM	Imperial War Museum
LORAN	long-range navigation system
NAC	National Archives of Canada
NACA	National Advisory Committee for Aeronautics
NARS	National Archives, Washington
NAS	National Academy of Sciences
NDRC	National Defense Research Committee
NHC	National Historical Center, Washington
NRC	National Research Council
NRL	Naval Research Laboratory
PRO	Public Record Office
RDF	radar

Acknowledgments

In a study of this scope there were, of course, numerous people who assisted me along the way. I would like to make a special mention of the late Dr E.G. "Taffy" Bowen, who provided the inspiration for this work. It was Dr Bowen's eloquent plea for someone to write the history of the Tizard Mission that initiated this project in 1987. Although poor health prevented him from taking an active part in the study, his memoirs proved to be the single most important personal account of the mission.

I would like to thank all the archivists who helped me, and I especially wish to single out the staff of Churchill College, Cambridge, for their cheerful assistance during my two briefs stays there. Also tireless in their assistance were the overworked, underpaid staff of the National Archives of the United States. Working in deplorable conditions that are no less than a national disgrace, they were able to find for me the main American records of the mission. Unfortunately, as a result of mismanagement and carelessness in the past, most of the individual army divisional and navy bureau records of the mission have been lost or destroyed.

David Hall provided invaluable assistance in guiding me to the appropriate Air Ministry records on British efforts to acquire the Norden bombsight. Wesley Wark kindly gave me the primary lead I required to gain access into the main U.S. Army intelligence records on the mission. I would also like to express my appreciation to Ted Wooley for providing me with notes of the letters of Frank Aydellotte which refer to the Tizard Mission.

Michael Hadley, George Davison, Jim Boutilier, and Paul Mackenzie made a great contribution by helping me transform my often inarticulate prose into a smooth-flowing manuscript. Their voluntary editorial work took many hours, for which I can only offer my profound gratitude.

Funding for this project has been provided by a variety of sources, including the department of National Defence's postdoctoral fellowship in military history, the Social Sciences and Humanity Research Council's postdoctoral and general grants programs, a University of Victoria research grant, and a grant from the Department of National Defence's Military and Strategic Studies Program.

This study was only made possible by the numerous people who gave me accommodation. They include Simon and Carolyn Chenery, Ray Winn, Anne Winn, Bobbi and Milt Greene-Goldman, Roger Sarty, and Barb and Kelly DeVries. I owe a great debt to you all.

I would like to thank all those at McGill-Queen's University Press who have seen the manuscript through its lengthy and often tortuous route towards publication. In this regard, I would like to single out Philip Cercone and Joan McGilvray. A special thanks to Carlotta Lemieux for her extraordinary skill as a copy editor.

I would like thank Adam Hilger Press and Edward Bowen for permission to quote and use photographs from E.G. Bowen's *Radar Days*.

Last but not least, I must express my infinite appreciation to my entire family – Elaine, Michael, Peter, Edith, Gaye, Emily, Nathan, Max, and Martin – for their never-ending support and love.

Sir Henry Tizard (Godfrey Argent)

Professor A.V. Hill (Godfrey Argent)

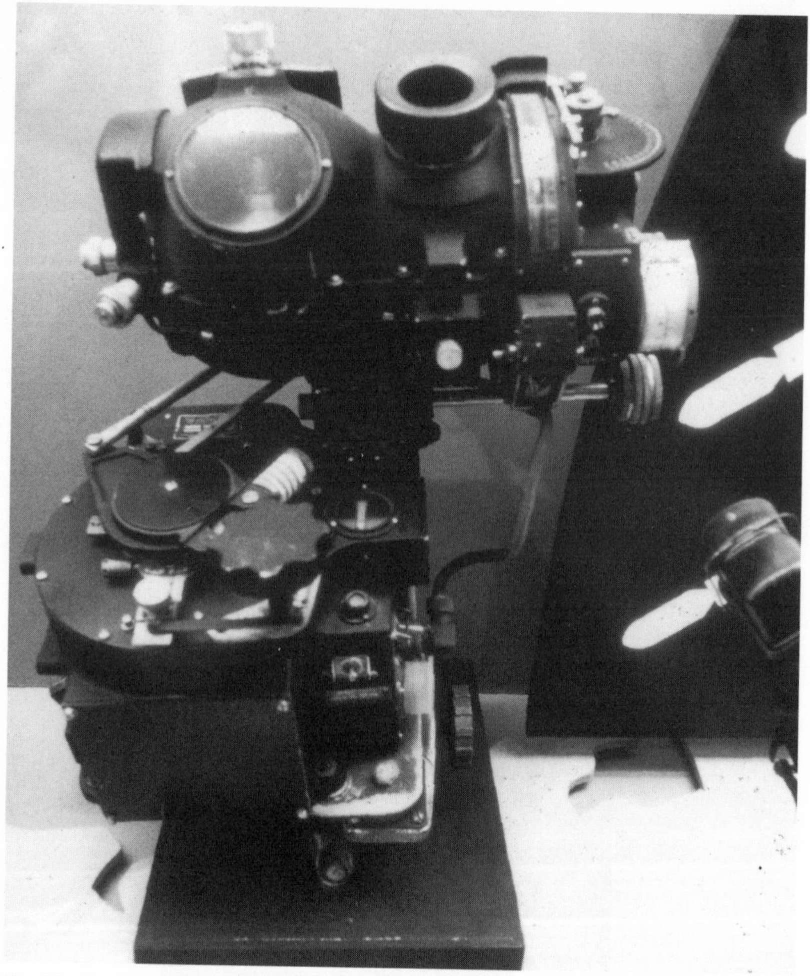

The Norden bombsight (David Zimmerman)

The Tizard Mission in August 1940. *Back row, left to right:* Brigadier Charles Lindemann, the army attaché; Sir Henry Tizard; and George Pirie, the air attaché. *Front row, left:* Professor R.H. Fowler (Imperial War Museum)

American scientific administrators. *Left to right:* Robert Oppenheimer, director of the Los Alamos Laboratory; James Conant, who succeeded Bush as chair of the NDRC; and Vannevar Bush, chairman of the NDRC in 1940 and later head of the Office of Scientific Research and Development (Harvard University News Office)

Left to right: Professor Frederick Lindemann, Sir Charles Portal, Sir Dudley Pound, Winston Churchill, and General Sir Alan Brooke at a Home Guard weapon demonstration in June 1941 (Imperial War Museum)

Alfred Loomis, the father of American microwave radar research (E.G. Bowen)

Planning for the Radiation Laboratory. Outside Alfred Loomis's house at Tuxedo Park, 12 October 1940. *Left to right:* Carol Wilson, Frank Lewis, Professor Edward Bowles, E.G. ("Taffy") Bowen, Professor Ernest Lawrence, and Alfred Loomis. This photograph was taken by Professor Cockcroft, the other member of the mission at this meeting (E.G. Bowen)

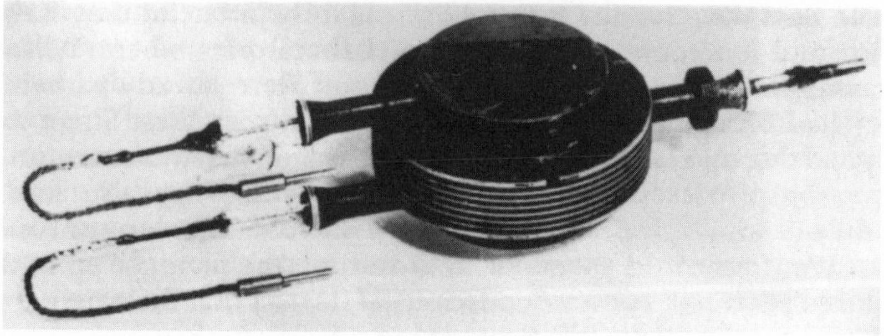

"The most valuable cargo" ever brought to American shores – cavity magnetron no. 12, which was taken to the United States by the mission. This device made microwave radar possible (E.G. Bowen)

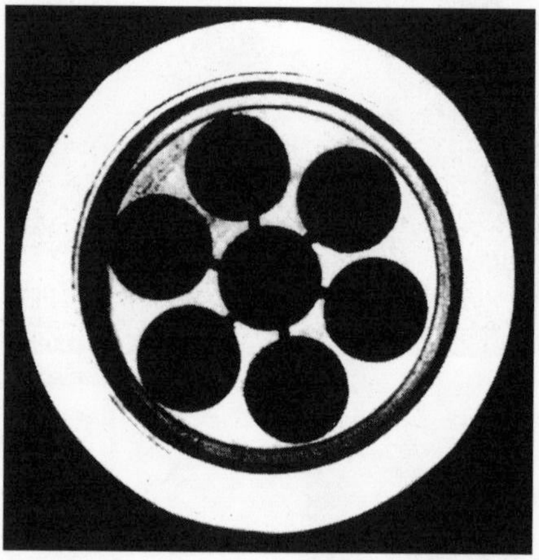

The core of Boot and Randall's original cavity magnetron. It formed the basis for ten of the twelve first production models (E.G. Bowen)

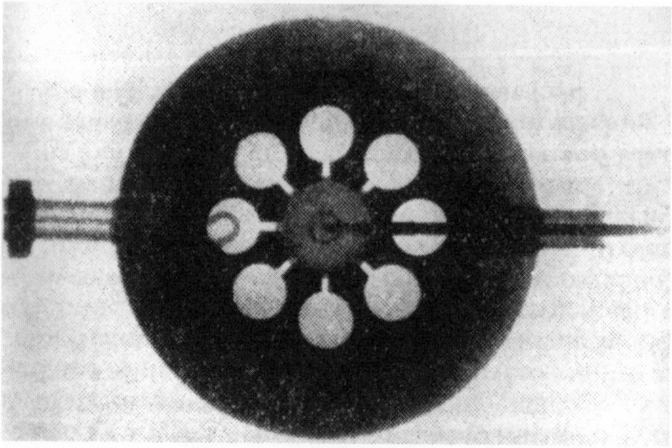

An x-ray picture of magnetron no. 12. Note the difference in the number of cavities from those in the previous photograph (courtesy of Bell Telephone Laboratories)

Examining the magnetron. *Left to right:* Dr Lee DuBridge, director of the Radiation Laboratory *(standing)*, E.G. ("Taffy") Bowen, and Professor I.I. Rabi. Note the small size of the magnetron in Rabi's right hand (E.G. Bowen)

The first American aircraft fitted with radar. This PBY Catilina aircraft was fitted with the ASV Mark II radar in December 1940. Note the antenna array along the side of the aircraft (E.G. Bowen)

The Conant Mission leaving for Great Britain. *Left to right:* Frederick Hovde, James Conant, and Carol Wilson (World Wide Photo)

Top Secret Exchange

Introduction

The Tizard Mission was one of the most important events of the Second World War. This study of the mission is an account of technology and its importance for war, and also of diplomacy and the emergence of the great Anglo-American alliance. It is an account of the changing role of the scientist in the military and political decision-making process. The mission was central to the beginning of the story of technological cooperation between the United States, Great Britain, and Canada, which played a crucial role in the defeat of the Axis powers and had ramifications far beyond the end of the war. Yet Sir Henry Tizard's name and the name of the British Technical Mission, which he led to North America in August 1940, have been obscured by the passing of more than fifty years. Since the publication of a then excellent but now dated biography of Tizard by Ronald W. Clark in the early 1960s, no one has examined the history of the Tizard Mission in detail or used the large amount of documentation that has become available in British, American, and Canadian archives. This is the first major study of the mission.

The Tizard Mission was of central importance in the history of the Allied scientific war. The war of the scientists was won by the Allies despite notable successes by the Axis powers in such areas as rocketry and torpedo technology. The tactical and strategic advantages that accrued to the Allied armed forces are too numerous to mention, but the most important must be in the field of microwave radar technology and the best known the construction of the atomic bombs. In almost all aspects of this war, either directly or indirectly, some mention must by made of the mission.

The scientific war was won in large measure by the Allies because they were more successful than their enemies in mobilizing their scientific, technical, and engineering expertise without subverting the basic principles that allowed for the effective use of this talent. As much as possible, they kept external ideological or security considerations to a minimum and did not allow them to hamper the effective pursuit of research. One of the critical factors was the free flow of ideas between scientists in all the countries of the Western Alliance. This was done not as it had been during peacetime, when information was disseminated in journal articles and scholarly conferences, but by a carefully established system of international scientific and technical liaison. The Tizard Mission marked the beginning of scientific and technical cooperation between the United States and Great Britain. The arrival of the mission inaugurated the free and open exchange of top secret military technology to the great benefit of both countries.[1]

This exchange was unique in history. Great Britain was at war with Germany and Italy, but the United States was still at peace. There was no formal alliance between Britain and the United States, and the two countries harboured a great deal of mutual suspicion about one another's goals and capabilities. Despite this, they agreed to swap virtually all of their most carefully guarded military technical secrets. Each nation had to overcome deeply ingrained instincts to protect the security of its key weapon systems and research projects. Before the mission, attempts to cooperate had generally been frustrated by mutual fears of lax security and by a chauvinistic belief in the superiority of their respective items of equipment.

Also distinctive was the vital role played by scientists in the United States and Great Britain in bringing about the policy decisions that allowed the mission to proceed and prosper. Before the Second World War, scientists were not traditionally members of the policy-making teams of governments, especially when discussions concerned fundamental issues of national security. But in the 1930s the Tizard-led Committee for the Scientific Survey of

Air Defence changed all this in Great Britain. This committee provided the answer to the bomber menace by developing the Chain Home radar defence system. In doing so, it opened the corridors of power to scientists. The mission played an important role in allowing American civilian scientists, particularly Vannevar Bush, the chairman of the American National Defense Research Committee, to establish a similar influence in their government's decision-making process.

Above all, this is a story of technology and its importance in modern war. The attempts to trade technological secrets before the war foundered because of the U.S. Navy's obsession with preserving the secrecy of the Norden bombsight and the almost equal fixation of the Royal Air Force on obtaining it. The most consequential result of the mission was that the British government provided the United States with perhaps the most significant piece of technology of the war: one of the first of its cavity magnetrons. This in turn led to the development in the United States – well before Pearl Harbor – of the scientific and industrial infrastructure needed to mass-produce the microwave radar sets which the magnetron had made possible. Significantly, mission members worked closely with American scientific colleagues to plan the establishment of the famous Radiation Laboratory, which developed these sets.

This book traces the origins of the Tizard Mission back to the later part of the First World War, which was the first time that international military technical cooperation was attempted between the United States and its European allies. Although this cooperation ceased shortly after the war, it had important implications for the next war. One of the major discoveries of this book is its linking of the Tizard Mission to the prewar and early wartime policy of exchanging information on a *quid pro quo* basis. My examination of the two years before the mission was established offers an intriguing case study of British and American decision-making processes during this crucial period. Before the war, attempts to trade technical secrets on a *quid pro quo* basis had failed. But in the autumn of 1939, British scientists, soldiers, politicians, diplomats, and bureaucrats began to discuss whether or not to proceed with open technical cooperation with the United States. It was a lengthy and frequently confusing debate, which was carried on during the first year of the war.

As a result of the significant implications for Anglo-American relations, this study is also a diplomatic history. By the summer of 1940, people in both countries saw the Tizard Mission as an exceptional way of improving the strained relations between the world's most important democracies. By removing years of deep mistrust and ignorance, the mission played a critical part in building the special relationship that characterized the Western Alliance. Although the most significant impact of the mission concerned Anglo-American diplomatic relations and military preparedness, it also had important ramifications for Canada. The Canadian side of the story has never been told before. An entire new industry was created in Canada to manufacture radar for the Allies. Close connections were developed with both Great Britain and the United States which had a direct bearing on the nature of Canada's involvement in the scientific war.

In view of the mission's great importance to the Western Alliance, it is surprising that no one has previously undertaken a detailed study of it. With the exception of one chapter on the subject in Clark's biography of Tizard, no attempt has been made to do so. The absence of a study of this important event is indicative of the need to re-evaluate the entire scientific war. As yet, except for a few modern studies that have focused on individual aspects of war research, we have been forced to rely on an indifferent collection of memoirs and official histories for our appreciation of Allied scientific cooperation.

The Tizard Mission had a profound impact on the history of the Second World War. The lack of a detailed study has meant that our understanding of the war work of scientists has been incomplete at best. A broader understanding of the mission is nevertheless not a definitive history of the scientist's war. It is only a beginning of the major reinterpretation of the scientific war. This reinterpretation must be set in the broadest possible context and be based on new investigations using primary documentation. Only then will we have a better understanding of the role of science and technology in determining the course of the war and of the war's impact on science and technology.

1 Scientists and Soldiers

The origins of the Tizard Mission can be traced back to the First World War, for it was in that conflict that scientists began to have a central role in the development of new ways to manufacture raw materials and in the design and development of revolutionary new weapon systems. Germany provided the first examples of the importance of science to total war. The most terrifying symbol of the military utility of science was Germany's use of poison chlorine gas in 1915. Chlorine led to the development of gas defences and to even deadlier substances to defeat them. More significant to the German war effort was the prewar work of Professors Fritz Haber and Walther Nernst, who discovered the process of fixating nitrogen from the air. This process provided supplies of ammonia nitrate, a vital chemical for the manufacture of munitions at a time when imported stockpiles were running low.[1]

It was not long before the major belligerents grasped a central truth: only by harnessing the intellectual skills of their scientists could they hope to stay ahead in the technological war. However, this axiom was not accepted immediately by the army and navy establishments. They tended to believe more in the innate abilities of civilian and military inventors and engineering staff to solve complex technical problems. This reliance worked in some situations, but the inventors found the solution to certain vital problems, such as the detection of submerged submarines, beyond their grasp. Academically trained scientists were much more capable of solving these problems because of their skills based on the accumulated experience of experimental and theoretical science.

In 1915 organizations were established in France and Great Britain to sift through the thousands of mainly impractical, if not idiotic, proposals for new weapons that had been made by overly patriotic citizens. These organizations were also given the much more useful task of supervising and coordinating scientific research. In Britain, the Admiralty established the Board of Invention and Research, while the Department of Munitions formed the Munitions Inventions Department. Their French counterpart was the Direction des inventions intéressant la défense nationale.

Science had, of course, always been more effective when researchers could exchange ideas across institutional and national boundaries. The free exchange of information, however, directly contradicted the most fundamental principles of military security. Traditionally, the military had gone to great lengths to hide its technical equipment, not only from the enemy but also from its allies. It was suspicious of even a friend's ability to keep its secrets or to remain a defence partner forever. Thus, scientists and sympathetic officers often found it difficult to break the barriers of service conservatism and establish secure liaison channels with other countries. Nevertheless, wartime expediency eventually overcame the opposition of the most intransigent bureaucracies, and exchanges of information became common between the two Western allies.

It was not until April 1916 that the Munitions Inventions Department exchanged a liaison officer with the Direction des inventions. But ever distrustful of imparting confidential information on any organization not under its control, the Admiralty continued to deny technical exchanges on naval matters until October. Shortly thereafter, a reasonably effective system of information sharing was created, based on the exchange of research reports, visits to each other's laboratories, and the establishment of permanent liaison offices. The Admiralty quickly appreciated the value of this type of cooperation. It discovered that the French had made important improvements in hydrophones for the passive detection of submarines. More significant for the long term was the fact that a team of scientists in Paris had developed the first primitive prototypes of sonar. Sonar transmits high-frequency sound waves that reflect off submerged objects. These reflected waves are detected to provide an indication of a target's depth, range, and distance. By the end of the war, a British scientific team, led by the Canadian physicist R.W. Boyle, was able to build on this work and develop the first practical sonar, known in Admiralty parlance as asdic.[2]

Even before the United States entered the war in the spring of 1917, American scientists, aware of the important role their European counterparts were playing in the conflict, had taken steps to organize themselves for war research. In June 1916 the National Academy of Sciences had formed the National Research Council (NRC) to manage war research. The NRC was not a government agency and had no direct access to government funding. Initially, much of its money came from private donations. A competing organization, the Naval Consulting Board, had been established somewhat earlier under the leadership of Thomas Edison. This board deliberately limited the influence of academic scientists, viewing them as impractical theoreticians. By the spring of 1917, the consulting board had established a research station at Nahant, Massachusetts, in an effort to convert a device originally designed to send Morse code through the water into a submarine detector. As a reflection of the board's discrimination against university-based scientists, the Nahant group deliberately excluded them, ostensively to avoid complications regarding the ownership of any patents that might develop from this research. The staff consisted of industrial engineers and inventors.

On 31 March 1917, just two days before President Wilson asked Congress to declare war on Germany, the National Research Council authorized the dispatch of a scientific mission to Great Britain, France, and Italy. The mission was to obtain all possible information "on the present status of scientific developments in aid of war." In early April seven scientists and medical doctors, headed by Professor Joseph Ames of Johns Hopkins University, set off for Europe.[3]

As soon as the French and British learned of the Ames Committee, they began organizing a reciprocal mission. On 28 May 1917 an Anglo-French team of technical experts and scientists arrived in New York. Manchester University physicist Sir Ernest

Rutherford led the British delegation. Rutherford was already familiar with North American scientific capabilities from his work earlier in the century at McGill University in Montreal. Accompanying Rutherford was Commander Cyprian Bridge, the chairman of the Allied Invention Board. The larger French delegation was headed by Professor Charles Fabry, a physicist at the University of Marseilles. Other members included Professor Henri Abraham, physicist at the University of Paris and an expert in wireless and anti-submarine devices; the Duc De Guiche, a pilot and a specialist in aeronautical research; Lieutenant M. Paternot, a naval wireless expert; and Captain Doupoue of the army. They were joined on 15 June by Professor Victor Grignard, a chemist at the University of Nancy, and Captain Capart of the French army. Both men were specialists in gas warfare.[4] At the end the month Professor Georgio Abetti arrived, representing the Italian government.[5]

The mission's main business was conducted during two conferences in June. On 1–2 June the Anglo-French team met with a group of American army and naval officers, as well as with senior NRC scientists and industrial researchers from the Naval Consulting Boards' Nahant Station. The Allied scientists briefed the Americans on current military technical research programs. They focused on methods of submarine detection – an increasingly crucial issue because the German U-boat campaign posed a very serious threat to the Allies' supply lifelines.[6] The information and samples of equipment provided by the Anglo-French team demonstrated "the insignificance of the efforts" which had "thus far been made in the United States to utilize the scientific resources and the powers of the country to combat the submarine menace." The Allied scientists urged the Americans to launch "a comprehensive attack upon the scientific side of submarine detection."[7]

As a result, Professor Robert Millikan organized a larger conference focusing on anti-submarine issues. Millikan was the United States' leading experimental physicist. He taught at the University of Chicago and was both a member of the NRC's Executive Council and chairman of its General Anti-Submarine Committee. Using funds provided by a private donor, Millikan invited more than fifty scientists, including one Canadian, to come to Washington to meet with the Anglo-French mission. The three-day conference sponsored by the NRC opened on 14 June. Also in attendence were members of the consulting board and some American and British naval officers.[8]

Extensive briefings were provided on the latest submarine-detection devices. Rutherford outlined various passive listening devices, or hydrophones, that were under development in Great Britain. Abraham and Fabry outlined French hydrophone development and provided the first details of the supersonic transmitting and receiving system that eventually became sonar. Millikan later wrote that "out of this conference grew a very large part of the experimental work on submarine detection and other new applications of science to warfare which was thereafter undertaken by the American groups."[9]

To utilize this new information, the American scientists left the meeting determined to organize their own research centres, separate from those of the consulting board. The British and French equipment displayed was far superior to the apparatus being developed at Nahant. The research council argued that it was now necessary for the navy to emulate the British and French and allow academic scientists to play a central role in anti-submarine research. By the end of June, the research council had won approval from the navy to establish its own submarine detection laboratory at New London, Connecticut. By the beginning of 1918, the Americans had made several important technical improvements on the French and British hydrophones provided in June 1917 and had begun the mass production of several different types.

Meanwhile, a group of scientists in New York, under the leadership of Dr Michael Pupin of Columbia University, had been working on submarine-detection problems since mid-May. Using private funding and with limited guidance from the navy, they had had little success, but after the conference Pupin seized on the idea of developing ultrasonic detection apparatus. In August, scientists based on the West Coast founded a research station at San Pedro, to work on supersonic submarine detection devices as well.[10]

The Anglo-French mission influenced many other aspects of American scientific mobilization. Fabry and Abraham provided guidance for the establishment of a U.S. Army gun sound-ranging unit. Sound ranging had been introduced to provide an acoustical means of locating enemy artillery hidden behind the impenetrable wall of the trench system. The techniques and equipment were complex and thus required the formation of a unit consisting of scientific experts. According to the American electronics and radio expert Lee de Forest, the information provided by Fabry and Abraham saved him "much time and useless duplication" in developing American sound-ranging equipment.[11] Grignard, Fabry, and Capart also advised on the organization of an American gas warfare service. This led directly to the formation of "a special committee to make recommendations concerning the proper organization of gas warfare." Millikan became the NRC's representative on this committee.[12]

In addition, members of the mission furnished information on aviation technology, range finders, and a host of other devices, production techniques, and organizational issues. One of the predominant concerns of the Allied scientists was that the United States might squander its scientific resources. At the beginning of the war, scientists in Britain were not considered to possess uniquely valuable skills, and consequently many of the best young scientists had been allowed to enlist and had been killed in the trenches. On 11 June 1917 George Hale, the chairman of the NRC, had sent to the secretary of war a memorandum by Rutherford in which the British scientist argued that scientific men should not be conscripted into the armed forces indiscriminately. In early July the army, while refusing to exempt scientists from the draft, did agree that special consideration was needed in determining the nature of their employment.[13]

The Anglo-French mission began to wind down in July 1917. By the middle of that month the British delegation had returned to London. Fabry and Abraham, the last two remaining members of the mission, left for France on 11 August. Even before their departure, steps were being taken to ensure that the mission's work would continue. On 20 July, when reporting the results of the mission to the panel of the Board of Invention and Research, Rutherford stated: "Enormous and hitherto unutilized scientific and technical resources are available in America to an extent at present quite unobtainable in England or France. These resources comprise not only large numbers of highly skilled scientists and assistants with numerous large and well equipped labs, but also practically unlimited mechanical assistance for the manufacture of experimental apparatus."[14] The Board of Invention and Research decided that maintaining cooperation with the Americans was crucial and that it should facilitate intercommunication.[15] However, it took no steps to establish a formal liaison system. Instead, scientific information was exchanged by a series of uncoordinated visits and by personal correspondence. This system of information transfer was neither efficient nor comprehensive. In one extreme example, an air board request for information was rejected because it was the seventh such application from American sources.[16]

Meanwhile, some British scientists working for the Munitions Invention Department were proposing a permanent liaison structure. On their own initiative, two Cambridge University scientists working on improving anti-aircraft gunnery wrote to several prominent NRC officials, including Hale and Millikan, proposing their own scheme. They were unaware of the Anglo-French mission – an example of the inadequate cooperation between the Munitions Invention Department and the Borad of Invention and Research. They suggested that young, intelligent, and well-trained American scientists be sent to work side by side with their British and French counterparts; and that once these Americans had become well versed in all aspects of military scientific research, they could return home to begin their own research or could join the U.S. Army in France as technical experts. By the end of August, this unofficial suggestion was endorsed by the Ministry of Munitions and was made into a formal request to the American government.[17]

There had been heated discussion in Washington since the beginning of August on the nature of Allied liaison. Attempts to establish an agency to administer international scientific cooperation foundered because of conflict between the military and the NRC over who would control the agency. The Ministry of Munitions' request galvanized both sides to seek a solution, and in November the Military Committee of the NRC met to discuss the British proposal. This committee consisted of senior army and navy technical officers and leading government scientists, with Millikan and Hale representing the civilian scientists. They decided that the major problem with the proposal of the Munitions Invention Department was that it did not go far enough, so they created a special panel to make recommendations concerning an extensive liaison network.

By 3 December the Military Committee had approved the creation of the Research Information Service, which was to have its European headquarters in Paris, with subsidary offices in London and Rome. In all three cities uniformed NRC scientists, attached to the army and navy attachés' offices, would gather technical and scientific information for transmission to the United States. The Research Information Service would act as a central coordinating agency for all information and for all scientific and technical visitors to and from Europe. By the spring of 1918, Dr W.F. Durand and Dr Karl Compton had opened the Paris office, and Dr H.A. Bumstead the London one. They were soon sending to the United States weekly summaries of the latest Allied research, development, and operational results.[18]

Given the very late start of international scientific cooperation in the First World War, it did not have a decisive influence on the course of the war. For instance, the U-boat offensive was defeated by a tactical innovation – the introduction of an effective convoy system – rather than by any technical breakthrough. But there had been impressive technological progress by the end of the war. Using the information supplied by the Anglo-French mission, American scientists had developed hydrophones of reasonable effectiveness. These devices were just entering service use when the hostilities ceased. As well, the Americans had joined the British in creating an effective sonar system, a development that had been greatly assisted by ongoing technical cooperation between research teams in all Allied countries. The first primitive sonar prototypes were just being tested in the autumn of 1918. Although these groups did not produce a sonar set for service use in the First World War, their work became the basis of American and British sonar technology in the Second World War.

Unfortunatley, this international cooperation did not long outlast the cessation of hostilities. All the prewar nationalistic, commercial, and bureaucratic jealousies re-emerged, no doubt assisted by strong public sentiment against involvement in another war. Within a few years, Anglo-American military scientific and technical research cooperation came to an end. In 1921 the U.S. Navy refused an Admiralty request to exchange information on sonar or asdic equipment, and the following year the British naval attaché was instructed to compile a report on American sonar but not to offer any information on a reciprocal basis.[19] Throughout the 1920s, technical cooperation was replaced by competition and conflict. There was a series of disputes concerning patent rights and royalty payments to the inventors of many of the technological devices exchanged during the war.[20] No more technical cooperation would be contemplated between the two nations' armed forces until just before the next world conflict.

Although Anglo-American military-technical cooperation ceased shortly after the end of hostilities, the First World War did result in a major long-term transformation of the role of scientists in the defence establishments of both nations. Even before November 1918 the armed forces had begun to assimilate scientific research organizations into their bureaucracies. In 1918 the Board of Invention and Research was transformed into the Admiralty's Directorate of Scientific Research, while, in the United States, the New London anti-submarine station was transferred to the direct control of the Department of the Navy. In the immediate postwar period, permanent scientific research centres were established, such as the American Naval Research Laboratory (formed in 1923) and the British army's Air Defence Experimental Establishment (created in 1924). Other existing technical bodies, such as the Royal Aircraft Establishment (formerly the Royal Aircraft Factory), were given scientific staff and research facilities.

Direct contact between these new defence scientific establishments and academic science was inhibited by three factors: the re-emergence of military security regulations; a strong belief by many scientists and the general public that defence research was immoral; and the desire of academic scientists to return to pure scientific research. Aeronautical research remained the one major exception to this, for close contact was maintained through joint civilian-military research advisory boards, the American National Advisory Committee for Aeronautics, and the British Aeronautical Research Committee. In all fields, however, military scientists tended to have a closer relationship with their counterparts in industry than with those in the universities. Military scientific research between the world wars suffered from its isolation from academe and from the control exercised over it by the defence bureaucracy. The compartmentalization of research, whereby one group of investigators was isolated from others, was quite normal. Avenues of investigation were often directed by nontechnically trained officers and laboratory management rather than by scientists, and this usually resulted in very conservative and narrowly focused research.

Despite these obstacles, the defence scientists in these permanent research institutions did achieve some remarkable technical breakthroughs. In the autumn of 1922, two radio scientists began research on "the properties and propagation characteristics" of radio waves of five-metre wavelength. They were Albert Hoyt Taylor and Leo Clifford Young of the U.S. Naval Aircraft Radio Laboratory – which was soon to be merged with other facilities to form the Naval Research Laboratory (NRL) in Washington. One property on which they reported was the ability of a solid object, such as a ship, to reflect these waves. They were not the first scientists to observe the reflective properties of radio waves – Hertz had noticed it in the late nineteenth century – nor were they the first to suggest that this had practical applications. But they were the first defence scientists to do so. Their report to the Bureau of Engineering stated: "Possibly an arrangement could be worked out whereby destroyers located on a line a number of miles apart could be immediately aware of the passage of an enemy vessel between any two destroyers of the line, irrespective of fog, darkness or smoke screen." They proposed to continue to work on this idea, but the navy did not make funds available, and the project ceased. It was not revived for another eight years.[21]

In 1930 Lawrence H. Hyland, another NRL staff member, noticed that aircraft reflected radio waves. He realized that this might make it possible to detect aircraft accurately at long range. Leo Young, who was now a senior NRL administrator, proposed something even more effective: the development of a radio-pulse system, whereby radio waves would be sent out in regular long intervals. The time it took for the reflections of these radio waves to return would determine the target's distance, while the bearing of the reflected wave would provide its direction.

Young had sketched out the basic outline for modern radar, but the technology had to be developed for high-frequency pulse transmitters and receivers. The importance of his idea was not realized immediately by either the NRL administrators or the Navy Department. Instead, the NRL spent most of its limited budget on doing ordinary testing of equipment already in service, and Young's work was given very low priority. Not until 1935 had enough progress been made for Congress to authorize a special

$100,000 appropriation. In 1936 aircraft were being detected at a range of two and a half miles, and two years later a radar set was ready for operational trials. Only in 1939 was the first American naval radar tested successfully at sea.

Progress was hampered in part by security regulations that went to ridiculous extremes. It was not until 1936 that the Army Signal Corps learned by chance of naval radar research; this was the result of a visit by an army scientist to the NRL on another matter. The army then began its own independent research program, but at one point the navy ceased sending it research reports because it had raised the project's security classification from classified to secret. Apparently the navy did not even trust its sister service. As a result, at the beginning of the Second World War in 1939, American radar was not yet fully integrated into the nation's defence systems.[22]

It was not always possible to overcome the difficulties of conducting research in military laboratories. In one extreme example, the British War Office's Air Defence Experimental Establishment spent nearly twenty years trying to perfect a device for the long-range location of aircraft by means of highly sensitive sound detection systems, using concrete acoustical mirrors. These experiments failed to produce consistent satisfactory results. In 1935 the Air Ministry, although fully aware of the limitations of the acoustical mirrors, authorized the construction of a full-scale acoustical detection system to defend the Thames Estuary. The rationale for proceeding on such a dubious venture was that no other government laboratory had anything better to offer. It is doubtful that this research would have been allowed to continue for so long if it had been subject to independent scrutiny.

This failure had profound consequences, for it caused a change in the way in which military scientific research was carried out and in the status of the scientist in the defence establishment. At the end of the First World War, the military in most countries recognized that scientists were required for new equipment to be developed for the armed forces, but the scientists were given a very small role in deciding which research projects to pursue and how new equipment should be used. The defence scientists also had virtually no place in the upper echelons of the military decision-making process. However, unfounded fears of the abilities of strategic bombers to destroy entire cities, coupled with the more realistic evaluation that the Royal Air Force could not prevent enemy aircraft from violating British airspace, created the political climate in which the status of the scientist was to change for ever.

On 12 November 1932 the British politician Stanley Baldwin warned the nation that "the bomber would always get through." Baldwin's warning was confirmed in a series of air exercises during the summer of 1934, when standing patrols of RAF fighters failed to intercept more than 40 per cent of the attacking Bomber Command aircraft. With both Parliament and the Air Ministry theoretically destroyed in one night and with growing evidence that Germany was creating a large air force, there was serious cause for worry. A special subcommittee of the Committee of Imperial Defence, consisting of senior officers led by Air Marshal Sir Robert Brooke-Popham, was formed to investigate improving the air defences of London. Without a technological breakthrough, however, no improvement seemed possible.

The apparent inaction of the government allowed a group of individuals, led by Winston Churchill – the voice from the wilderness – to create a public furore over the sobering results of the summer tests. On 8 August 1934, Frederick Lindemann, professor of experimental philosophy at Oxford University and a confidant of Churchill, wrote to the *Times* decrying the Royal Air Force's attitude, which, he said, seemed to stress building up bomber forces rather than defensive fighters simply because the service believed there was no effective protection from aerial assault. Lindemann warned that this mind-set would lead to the temptation to be "the quickest on the draw" and to strike first with conventional, incendiary, chemical, and bacteriological bombs. He called on the government not to adopt a defeatist attitude "until it has definitely been shown that all the resources of science and invention had been exhausted." No single individual or department could find the solution, he maintained, but in order to achieve this, "no effort and no sacrifice" would be too great.[23]

Lindemann's concerns were already being acted on by one group within the Air Ministry. There, H.E. Wimperis, the director of scientific research, and A.P. Rowe, his able assistant, had begun a detailed survey of the ministry's effort to develop defences against bombers. They concluded that scientists had never been consulted despite the fact that a scientific solution to the bomber threat was the only one possible. On 12 November 1934 Wimperis, who usually acted as an administrator rather than a policy maker, took the initiative. He wrote to Lord Londonderry (the secretary of state for air), Air Marshal Sir Edward Ellington (the chief of air staff), and Sir Hugh Dowding (the air member for Research and Development), proposing a radical change in procedures. Wimperis reminded them of the "stupendous technical advances of the last 50 years" and the possibilities of further progress being applied to air defence. He mentioned that the Air Ministry had extensive files on rays of energy being used to destroy engines or to explode the plane's bombs, proposals made by unscrupulous or ignorant inventors. Wimperis discounted these possibilities because of the ease of shielding metal components, but he did not discount the possible effect of this radiation on human beings.

Wimperis suggested that a subcommittee of the Committee of Imperial Defence be formed, composed of independent and government scientists. His terms of reference were prophetic: "'To consider how far recent advances in scientific and technical knowledge can be used to strengthen the present methods of defence against hostile aircraft.' The committee should be at liberty to consult other experts (for example in radio technology) when they deem this to be necessary."[24] The independent scientific members of the committee were to be Professor A.V. Hill, a Nobel Prize–winning physiologist, who would advise on the effects of death rays on air crews; Professor P.M.S. Blackett, a leading experimental physicist; and Henry Tizard, to act as the chairman.

The choice of Tizard, a second-rate experimental scientist, might appear unusual on the surface. He had not published a single scientific paper for seven years and had stopped pursuing active research even earlier. Tizard later admitted that he had ended his research career because "[I] would never be outstanding as a pure scientist – younger men were coming on – all with greater ability in that respect."[25] Outwardly, nothing indicated that he had the natural qualities of leadership required to head one of the most important committees ever established by a British government. Of medium height, medium build, and looking very much like the stereotypic English bourgeois bureaucrat, Tizard did not have a particularly commanding presence. At times, according to his good friend C.P. Snow, "he looked like a highly sensitive and intelligent frog."[26]

Tizard, however, transcended the limitations of his pure science abilities; his ordinary exterior hid one of the great scientific leaders of this century. Tizard was one of the best of a type of scientist that was new to this century – the scientific manager and administrator. Scientific administrators have proven to be as important to the development of science in the twentieth century as the inspirational theoreticians such as Einstein or the brilliant experimenters such as Rutherford. This century has seen the development of "big science," where some of the most important work is done by huge research programs involving hundreds and sometimes thousands of individuals working collectively towards a common goal. No individual or small group could hope to equal the collective abilities of these large research groups, nor could they provide the usually expensive equipment so easily. Some scientists – for instance, Ernest Lawrence and Robert Oppenheimer – had the ability to be both managers and experimenters or theoreticians. Others, such as James Conant and Vannevar Bush, turned into successful administrators after ending productive research careers. Few, however, had as profound an impact on the history of science as Tizard.

Henry Tizard was born in Kent on 23 August 1885. His father was a captain in the Royal Navy at the time and was soon to become the assistant hydrographer of the Admiralty and an elected fellow of the Royal Society. His mother was the daughter of a prominent civil engineer. If it had not been for his poor eyesight, Tizard would have followed his father into the navy. With this avenue closed to him, he won a scholarship to Westminster, one of the more prestigious British public schools, where he soon showed an excellent ability in mathematics and science. In 1904 he went to Magdalen College, Oxford, where he had been awarded yet another scholarship. He graduated in 1908 with a coveted first-class degree in mathematics and chemistry, and that autumn he was admitted to the University of Berlin as a postgraduate student in chemistry with Professor Walther Nernst. However, because of financial limitations, Tizard was forced to leave Berlin after one year, having undertaken no publishable research. This was mainly the fault of Nernst, who instructed him to undertake several unproductive research projects. It was in Berlin that Tizard first met Frederick Lindemann, an Englishman of Alsatian and American parents, who was a fellow postgraduate student. At first a close though not intimate friend, Lindemann was destined to become Tizard's most bitter enemy.

After a year as a researcher at the Davy Faraday Laboratory at the Royal Institution in London, in 1911 Tizard was offered a fellowship to be a resident tutor at Oriel College, Oxford, and a demonstrator and lecturer at the university's Electrical Laboratory. But his time there was comparatively brief. The First World War interrupted his career, changing his life forever by removing him from the serenity of Oxford. For the first time, Tizard became aware of the need for scientists to play a role in military research. "The war did me a great deal of good," he later observed. "It pulled me out of the rock of Oxford. It forced me to do things which I should never have done of my own accord in peacetime, but which I found in practice much easier than I imagined. It brought me into close and friendly contact with all sorts and conditions of men and it made me realize that a purely scientific education was of value for men who had to deal with the practical affairs of life. Of course I was one of the lucky ones."[27]

Tizard began his war service in the army, enlisting in 1914. Since the nation placed no special value on scientific skills at the beginning of the war, he seemed destined for service in France. Unlike other scientists, however, he never risked his life in the trenches. Soon after enlisting, he was persuaded to volunteer for the Royal Flying Corps, and he joined the Experimental Flight of the Central Flying School at Upavon aerodrome. As aviation was becoming increasingly important to the military, there was a growing need to speed technical advancement. Here, too, improvement by empirical invention was not good enough. Tizard, along with a handful of other scientists, was assigned by the Royal Flying Corps to develop scientific methods of analysis for aviation, and he soon became one of the pioneers of the new science of aeronautics.

Soon after his arrival at Upavon in 1915, Tizard decided that the only way he could understand aircraft was to learn to fly them. This he did at the age of thirty, despite intense opposition from the station commander, who only agreed to allow a scientist flight time if it was confined to days when the weather was too bad for combat pilot training. Similar bureaucratic intransigence limited scientific work until a separate airfield for scientific testing was established in early 1917 at Martlesham Heath near Woodbridge.

Tizard was appointed the scientific officer in charge. By the end of 1917 he had established methods of accurately measuring aircraft performance in various weather and service conditions, and had developed a variety of new flying techniques. It was here that he developed his particular expertise of getting operational personnel to work closely with scientists. So successful was he that when the Royal Air Force was established in 1918, he was appointed assistant controller of research and experiments at the new Air Ministry. He became the acting controller in the last three months of the war, after his superior died in an air crash.

Although Tizard returned to Oxford briefly at the end of the war, his future career was focused on government scientific administration. In 1920 he accepted the position of assistant secretary to three boards that were being established at the Department of Scientific and Industrial Research (DSIR) to coordinate the defence research of all three services. Tizard's responsibilities included coordinating the work of the three boards, which dealt with physics, chemistry, and engineering, and he took executive action on the decisions made by them. Tizard's administrative abilities quickly led him to the most senior positions in the DSIR; in 1927 he was appointed the permanent secretary and thus the leading scientific administrator in the British government.

Financial worries caused Tizard to leave the DSIR in 1929 and accept the position of rector at the Imperial College of Science and Technology. However, he remained heavily involved in government research. He had been a member of the Aeronautical Research Committee since 1920, and in 1933 he was appointed chairman, a post he held for the next ten years. The Aeronautical Research Committee was a unique institution because only here did the armed forces continue to have close contact with civilian scientists. Its membership consisted of four representatives from the Air Ministry, two from Imperial College, one each from the Royal Aeronautical Society and the DSIR, and seven independent academic or industrial scientists. The committee had broad powers to advise both government and industry on aeronautical problems, to supervise the aviation research of the Air Ministry and other government departments, and to promote aeronautical education. It was through this body that Tizard remained a leading authority on aviation research.

During his lengthy public career, Tizard developed an extraordinary ability to communicate to any audience. Whether he was talking to senior civil servants, air marshals, politicans, scientists, fighter pilots, or lowly office messengers, he was able to bridge the often huge gap in language and understanding when he discussed complex technical problems. "He was a master of the searching question," able to analyse a complicated problem, break it down into its simplest components, and then find the right question to put to the right expert.[28] Tizard was a team player, running his committees by consensus. He listened carefully to all sides before making a decision. His honesty and clear thinking inspired immense loyalty among most of those who worked with him. If he had a serious flaw it was his inability to understand those who did not meet his own high standards, a trait that was to cost him greatly during the war. His strong personality and administrative talents made him an ideal choice to chair H.E. Wimperis's proposed subcommittee on aerial defence in 1934.[29]

Wimperis's proposal for a scientific committee to investigate air defence was approved by Lord Londonderry, the secretary of state for air, in November 1934, but it did not to hold its first meeting until January 1935. In the meantime, Wimperis pursued his own investigation on death rays. He asked Dr Robert Watson-Watt, superintendent of the National Physical Laboratory's Radio Research Station at Slough, about the theoretical possibilities of a death ray, whereupon Watson-Watt asked his assistant, A.F. Wilkins, to calculate the amount of power required for such a ray. When simple calculations proved its impracticality, the two men offered an alternative proposal to Wimperis: instead of harnessing death rays to kill the air crew, perhaps reflected radio waves could be used to detect aircraft at long range.

Thus, when the Committee for the Scientific Survey of Air Defence met for the first time on 28 January 1935, the principal theoretical concept that was to solve Britain's air defence problem already existed. In a little more than four years, the committee's brilliance transformed Watson-Watt's theoretical idea into a fully effective air defence system, using radar to detect enemy bombers and to vector fighters of the Royal Air Force to attack positions. Against every form of bureaucratic, political, and financial opposition, the committee supervised the program through each stage.

Tizard led the organization and pioneered new ground in the scientist's relationship with the defence establishment.[30]

Tizard was able to convince even the most conservative RAF officers that from this point onwards scientists had an important role to play at the most senior levels of military policy making. They were to have a major voice in deciding which research projects should be pursued and how new technologies would be utilized operationally. Symbolic of this change was the fact that shortly after war was declared, Tizard was appointed to be the first scientific adviser to the chief of air staff, a post that gave him great powers to influence and guide almost any technical aspect of Air Ministry policy. The RAF's practice was soon emulated by the other services. Thus, by late 1939, science was fully integrated into every level of the British defence establishment. This close scientific-military cooperation was the secret weapon that the British and their allies would exploit to its fullest extent in the six years of war. It was an important factor in the eventual defeat of the Axis powers.

2 The Problem with *Quid Pro Quo*

Until the beginning of the Second World War, the British and American defence, diplomatic, and political establishments gave scientists little opportunity to influence policy. Thus, scientists were virtually excluded from the efforts made to restart Anglo-American military technical and scientific cooperation in the months leading up to the war. The scientists were excluded despite the fact that in many ways they were far more qualified than the military and diplomatic personnel who evaluated the technical capabilities of other nations' armed forces. They were less likely to subscribe to notions of national technical superiority. This was not solely because of superior technical knowledge. Science in the twentieth century has been an international affair, with scientific ideas transferred across national boundaries in scholarly journals and at international conferences. Close professional contacts and friendships have been established, and many scientists travelled widely long before it was common to venture overseas. As a group, they were more aware of the worsening international situation in the 1930s than most people were. Many had first-hand contact with colleagues who were already fleeing Nazi and fascist repression. They understood the need for an international effort to deal with the emergence of fascism, and a large number became leading advocates for action.

Despite the enhanced status of scientists within the British military establishment, they did not have the power to call for international defence technical cooperation. In 1937 Tizard proposed that a scientific attaché be assigned to the embassy in Washington to investigate American technical resources and perhaps to restart Anglo-American cooperation. This proposal was rejected by the Air Staff because of fears that the Americans would want to send their own scientific attaché to London and that he might uncover Britain's most closely guarded technical secrets[1] – an example of the British penchant for secrecy. It was not until September 1939, when Tizard became the scientific adviser to the chief of the Air Staff, that British scientists were given the opportunity to influence decision making at senior staff levels.

Scientists in the United States had even less influence on prewar discussions. The separation of academic science from military research at the end of the First World War excluded most politically influential scientists from the inner circle of defence policy making. Not until the summer of 1940, when Vannevar Bush was given the authority by President Roosevelt to establish the National Defense Research Committee, were scientists able to influence defence policy.[2] Scientists employed by the various army and navy research centres also had little power beyond answering strictly technical questions. Paradoxically, as the international situation worsened, the American armed forces spent less on research. The average annual army and air corps research expenditures between 1924 and 1933 was a paltry $4 million. By 1936, increased fiscal appropriations under the Roosevelt administration allowed this figure to grow to $9 million. In that year, however, the army General Staff re-examined the need for research as war grew near, and concluded: "The Army needs large quantities of excellent equipment that has already been developed. The amount of funds allocated to Research and Development in former years is in excess of the proper proportion for the items in consideration of the rearmament program."[3] The General Staff therefore recommended that the research budget of the army and air corps be cut to between $5 million and $7 million per year. This response, wrote A. Hunter Dupree, illustrates the army's belief that "the crisis was much too serious to wait for research. This understandable response reflected clearly the assumption that the coming war would not be dominated by technological change based on scientific research."[4]

The immediate origins of Anglo-American technical cooperation in the Second World War must therefore be traced through traditional diplomatic and defence policy channels. The great Atlantic alliance of English-speaking democracies was not yet in existence, for the British and American governments were suspicious of each other's motives and goals in the years before the war. This resulted in a general failure of joint diplomatic efforts to prevent Axis aggression. Prime Minister Neville Chamberlain believed that the Roosevelt administration was unreliable and that it was unwilling or unable to provide concrete support for British diplomatic initiatives in Europe. Roosevelt could not even control the isolationist elements in Congress, as was demonstrated by the passage of neutrality legislation in 1935 and the president's subsequent failure to amend this act. For his part, Roosevelt viewed Chamberlain's policy of appeasement with growing alarm, particularly after the prime minister's refusal to respond to the purge of conservative elements from the German government and the subsequent resignation of Anthony Eden as British foreign secretary in February 1938. Chamberlain's reluctance to confront Hitler led Roosevelt to conclude that Britain could not be relied on to deter aggression. Economic conflicts over issues such as imperial preferential tariffs increased the mutual apprehension. Although the diplomatic disagreements did not directly prevent effective prewar technical cooperation, they certainly did not lead to an atmosphere that was conducive to it.[5] Not until the German annexation of Czechoslovakia in March 1939 did American and British "vital interests" begin "to coincide."[6]

Meanwhile, technical cooperation was recommenced as a result of one of the first attempts to coordinate British and American military responses to Axis belligerence. On 31 December 1937, Captain Royal E. Ingersoll of the U.S. Navy arrived in London under orders from President Roosevelt to discuss with Admiralty planners the coordination of any potential Anglo-American response to Japanese aggression in China. Throughout January 1938, Ingersoll met with Captain T.S.V. Phillips at the Admiralty. They agreed that the two navies would divide responsibilities in the Pacific and that technical information on fleet communications would be exchanged to facilitate cooperation.[7] As a consequence of Ingersoll's visit, Captain Russell Wilson, the American naval attaché, approached the Admiralty in January 1938 to reopen the exchange of technical information between the two navies that had been terminated shortly after the end of the First World War. Wilson initially requested information on communications equipment. Later that month he suggested that information might also be traded on boom-defence equipment and damage-control procedures. At the end of April he expanded his request to include data on high-speed minesweeping.[8]

It was comparatively easy to make a secret agreement in principle on how the fleets might cooperate if the political decision was taken to respond to the Japanese, but it was quite another matter to effect the exchange of classified technical information that would make this cooperation feasible. As Wilson and others soon discovered, it was no easy task to re-establish technical cooperation. Wilson's initiative and others like it before the summer of 1940 either failed or had only limited success. The failure of prewar and early wartime technological collaboration can be traced to several causes. Undoubtedly the diplomatic differences between the two nations were an important factor. Chamberlain's policy of appeasement and Roosevelt's inability to circumvent the isolationists greatly limited diplomatic and military cooperation. The inability to coordinate diplomatic policy meant that the staff talks begun by Ingersoll were not resumed to any significant degree until the summer of 1940. The absence of coordinated defence planning meant that there was no requirement for the armed forces of the two nations to share technology. Efforts to establish technical information sharing did in fact continue, but they did so without staff talks or diplomatic cooperation, and without a diplomatic catalyst it was impossible to overcome the other obstacles to effective technical exchanges.

In the late 1930s, British and American politicians, diplomats, generals, and admirals shared a strong chauvinistic belief that the other country's defence technology was inferior and therefore of little value. In part, these opinions were formulated because, until the war was underway, information on each other's technical competence frequently came from ill-informed and untrained military attachés or from occasional visits by equally unqualified operational officers. Technical chauvinism continued to hamper technical cooperation until the dispatch of the Tizard Mission in the summer of 1940.

Even the best attachés could not penetrate the veil that shrouded military secrets. In the autumn of 1938, Captain Wilson investigated Admiralty anti-submarine warfare (ASW) capabilities, but he was unable to furnish any information on submarine-detection equipment; all he could provide were details of the large number of personnel involved in anti-submarine operations and research. Wilson's sources were public documents such as the Navy List and Treasury estimates. Yet he concluded that the quantity of resources devoted to ASW "indicates the importance attached to the subject and their apparent large-scale, and apparently successful efforts to attain effectiveness therein."[9] Similarly, British attachés could provide no details on American sonar development. Until the spring of 1940, neither British nor American military attachés gave credence to evidence that both nations had developed radar independently (see below and chapter 3).

The technical chauvinism and ignorance were combined with the fear of surrendering top secret information. One of the principal reasons for the failure to establish international liaison was the obsessive military concern with secrecy. The British government was reluctant to provide technical information even to its allies, and the United States was not an ally. The dominions, for example, were not informed of the existence of radar until the spring of 1939, and the French not until the summer, less than two months before the commencement of hostilities.[10] As we shall see, the U.S. Navy's determination not to divulge the secrets of the Norden bombsight was the single biggest obstacle to technical cooperation. The attitude that prevailed until the Tizard Mission arrived in Washington in late August 1940 was that no classified information should be shared unless something of equal value was offered in return. This *quid pro quo* mentality and the lack of any unbiased or accurate intelligence evaluations of technical capabilities doomed any prewar attempt to establish Anglo-American technical cooperation.

The Admiralty's response to Wilson's requests in 1938 for information on communications, boom defence, high-speed mine-sweeping equipment, and damage-control procedures illustrates all of these problems. A heated debate raged between the technical and policy directorates within the Admiralty. The former opposed an exchange on boom defences and damage control, while the latter favoured it for political reasons. Lord Chatfield, the first sea lord, supported the policy divisions, agreeing that "the closer we get to the United States Navy the better."[11] The advantages were strictly political to Chatfield. Like most British officers, he believed that American technology was generally inferior, though he did not think the Americans were as far behind as some did.

Duff Cooper, the first lord of the Admiralty, threw his weight behind Chatfield. After Anthony Eden's resignation in February, Cooper was the leading exponent in the cabinet of improving Anglo-American relations. He characterized the general attitude in the Admiralty as being "in favour of exchanging information with the Americans, but against giving anything away." On 12 March he told the Admiralty, "There seems to be some scepticism as to the value of anything they may have to offer. I suspect that this scepticism may be exaggerated. Their FAA [Fleet Air Arm] for instance is supposed to be the best in the world whereas ours is a source of grave anxiety. These conversations will be of no use if they are entered into the spirit of 'you show me first' – but I believe a frank exchange of information would be useful from more points of view than one."[12] Soon after this, Chatfield ordered the technical departments to prepare lists of the information they would like from the Americans. They were also to list what they were prepared to give in return and on what subjects no exchange would be allowed. The technical departments listed seventy matters that were open to reciprocal information and a further twenty-five on which information was desired from the Americans but for which nothing could be offered in exchange.[13]

On 12 May 1938 the Board of the Admiralty agreed that "the United States should be treated exceptionally." The board realized that no formal agreement could be reached because it might become public knowledge and indicate that a defence alliance existed, something the American electorate would not tolerate. So the board decided that if the U.S. Navy asked for information on any subject it would, if possible, be granted, but the Admiralty would demand "as a *quid pro quo* information that we ourselves desired, possibly on some different subject." Certain highly classified data would be denied, but if the right *quid pro quo* could be found, all exchanges would be as frank as possible.[14]

The technical exchanges went well at first. On 24 May, Wilson was given complete specifications and drawings of the Admiralty's two-speed destroyer minesweeping gear. Wilson in turn provided details on the U.S. Navy's minesweeping equipment and arranged for the British naval attaché in Washington to visit two ships equipped with experimental minesweeping apparatus.[15] However, problems soon emerged. In part these were the result of Wilson's attempting to increase Anglo-American naval cooperation too quickly and over too many areas. In May, without authority from Washington, he proposed that exchanges move beyond the technical and strategic areas, which had been agreed to by Ingersoll and Phillips, into the area of fleet tactics. In return for an exchange on tactics, he offered technical information on the U.S. Navy's air forces.

This proposal triggered strenuous objections at the Admiralty. The director of naval intelligence doubted that, once detailed tactical discussions had been started, it would be possible to limit the subjects covered. Others argued that Wilson's offer to provide details on naval aviation was worthless, because recent missions to the United States had reported that American technology in this area was only marginally better than British equipment. The director of naval intelligence also pointed out that the Fleet Air Arm was still the responsibility of the Air Ministry and thus the Admiralty could expect no direct advantage from this exchange. Ultimately, the Admiralty would only agree to allow Wilson to meet with the head of the Tactical Division for discussions "on the general nature of tactics." Nothing specific would be discussed because it was "impossible to draw a line of demarcation once details" were provided.[16]

The situation worsened progressively during the rest of 1938. After having surveyed American minesweeping equipment, the British naval attaché in Washington reported in September that in this particular exchange "the gain is entirely to the advantage of the United States." He found that the arrangement was "in no way an ample *quid pro quo*" for the British information provided.[17] The Admiralty also had difficulty in arranging an adequate trade for its information on boom defences. The Americans did not have any data on boom defences to exchange, and thus alternative information on another type of equipment had to be provided. Twice the U.S. Navy rejected the Admiralty's suggestions of acceptable alternative technologies. The American's did not even make a counter offer.

By December the director of naval intelligence was convinced of the necessity of a complete review of technical cooperation with the Americans. He felt that the U.S. Navy was abusing its special relationship and was gaining far more information than the Admiralty. As a result, technical cooperation had degenerated into "haggling," which was counterproductive to the establishment of good relations. Much of this haggling, it was believed, was caused by the lack of coordination between the different bureaus within the American navy. For instance, the Admiralty had requested information on aircraft carrier arresting gear in return for details of boom defences. This request had apparently been rejected because the U.S. Navy's Bureau of Aeronautics had seen no direct advantage in the exchange. There were two possible solutions. The Admiralty could either tell Wilson frankly that the policy of reciprocal exchange would cease unless the Navy Department was more forthcoming, or they could revert immediately to exchanging information strictly on a reciprocal basis.[18] On 9 January the director of naval intelligence met with Wilson and confronted him with the Admiralty's growing sense of frustration concerning the technical exchanges. The two agreed that the difficulties were confined to technical transfers while intelligence cooperation on subjects such as information on Japanese capital ships was proceeding smoothly. Wilson was sympathetic to the complaints, and since he was due to return to Washington, he agreed to pursue the matter at the Navy Department. The British gave him an *aide-mémoire* outlining their complaints.[19]

Wilson was able to get the Navy Department to agree to provide the details of the carrier landing systems, and the new naval attaché, Captain Alan G. Kirk, was provided with details of boom defences in March.[20] But it had taken more than a year of time-consuming discussions at the most senior level to arrange this relatively minor technical exchange. This caused growing frustration on both sides. By the beginning of 1939 the two leading champions of naval technical cooperation at the Admiralty were gone. Duff Cooper, disgusted with the policy of appeasement, had resigned over the Munich Agreement. He was replaced by the Earl of Stanhope, a loyal supporter of Chamberlain, and a man unlikely to encourage technical exchanges with the Americans.

Chatfield had retired in late 1938. His successor as first sea lord, Admiral Sir Roger Backhouse, was far less willing to be flexible with the Americans because of political concerns – an attitude that closely reflected those of other senior officers and the new first lord of the Admiralty. On 27 March, Backhouse told his colleagues: "It is not that I wish to be 'sticky' with the Americans, but hitherto they have been very much the reverse of helpful in this matter of exchanges. Therefore, I consider we should proceed with great caution."[21]

Matters remained essentially unchanged until the summer of 1939. A few minor naval technical exchanges continued, but only if a direct *quid pro quo* could be found. There was little advantage to this sort of exchange, and it did more harm than good to Anglo-American naval relations. This situation might have continued had not the Royal Air Force (RAF) requested Admiralty assistance in acquiring a piece of American technology that it coveted above all else.

When RAF officers had surveyed the aviation industry in the United States prior to the war, they had been just as willing as their naval colleagues to belittle American technology. RAF-sponsored missions by industrial experts and intelligence and operational officers had been frequent in the last few years of peace. The members of these missions went to the United States to evaluate any potentially useful technology or the capacity of American manufacturers to make up any shortfall in the British rearmament program – but they carried their biases against American technology across the Atlantic.[22] In the reports that reached London from these missions, little praise or interest was expressed in American aviation technology. Even the latest aircraft, such as the Boeing B-17 bomber, failed to impress the overly critical British observers. On viewing the early models of the so-called Flying Fortress, they repeatedly pointed out the complete absence of power-operated turrets, which they believed were the only way to mount defensive guns effectively. Even the diplomatic and sophisticated George Pirie, the British air attaché in Washington, found little of vital interest in American aviation technology. With the notable exception of Pirie, many of these observers were biased by a deep-seated dislike of all that was American. Air Commodore Arthur Harris, who visited the United States in early 1939, spent almost as much time composing biting satire on American habits and lifestyles as he did on technical reporting. He humorously derided the American obsession with air-conditioning (which, he said, allowed the Americans to avoid breathing fresh air) and their appalling half-hour lunch breaks taken at hamburger stands.[23]

One piece of American aviation technology, however, could not be belittled, and by mid-1938 it was considered vital for the RAF to acquire it. Unfortunately, it was also the one piece of aviation equipment that the RAF could not have. This was the Norden bombsight – a major breakthrough in bombsight technology. Since 1920, the American inventor C.L. Norden had been developing bombsights for the American navy. He had gradually improved his device so that by 1932 its accuracy and versatility far surpassed anything else in the American inventory. In that year the Army Air Corps ordered its first Mark XV Norden sights, subsequently known as the M-1 in army service. Like all bombsights, the Norden was a sophisticated mechanical computer attached to an equally complex optical sighting mechanism. Once the bombardier had located the target, information such as air speed, altitude, and wind velocity was automatically calculated to determine the optimum drop-point. What made the Norden unique was its use of gyroscopes to stabilize the sight automatically and its development of an autopilot as the third element in the system. A bombardier using the Norden was able to find a target at a considerable distance ahead of the aircraft and lock on the sight. Once locked onto its target, the gyrostabilizers automatically kept the fix by cancelling out the effects that turbulence, air speed, and wind would have on the sight. The bombardier was able to turn over control of the aircraft to the stabilized bombing approach equipment (SBAE), which in effect was an automatic pilot. The SBAE then automatically steered the aircraft to the bomb drop-point.[24] It was technically far superior to anything the RAF possessed, since a gyroscopically stabilized sight was only just then being discussed by British designers, and production of an equivalent device was not anticipated until 1940 at the earliest. Moreover, there were no plans to build a British bombsight linked to an automatic pilot.

Information on the great accuracy of the Norden bombsight led the RAF in the spring of 1938 to ask the U.S. Navy about the possibility of acquiring it. The navy replied that the Norden was not for sale. This was not acceptable to the RAF because of the great importance placed on strategic bombing, which was seen as the primary role of the service. Any device that would greatly improve the accuracy of bombing and therefore the effectiveness of the main striking force was considered vital. Thus, on 17 June, Air Chief Marshal Sir Edgar Ludlow-Hewitt, the commander-in-chief of Bomber Command, insisted that the Air Ministry pursue all available avenues to secure details on the American sight.[25]

One month later Major A.R. Boyle, assistant director of air intelligence, ordered Pirie to approach the U.S. Army and offer an exchange of bombsight technology.[26] The air attaché replied on 9 August that he had already approached the army about the sight, because it was usually more cooperative than the navy, only to discover that, although they were using the Norden, the rights to the device were controlled by the navy. The army could not reveal any details without the navy's permission. The situation was made worse because, two days after the first request for technical details of the sight, a major espionage scandal had broken involving the leaking of classified material to foreign attachés. As a result, even unofficial inquiries were rejected. It would be at least six more months, when changes in personnel were scheduled to take place in the navy's Bureau of Aeronautics, before any information might be forthcoming.[27]

Boyle dutifully waited six months before pursuing the matter further. Then, on 8 March 1939, he instructed Pirie to offer the Americans, in addition to information on British bombsights, data on power-operated gun turrets and on modifications made to the Browning machine gun to improve its reliability. Turrets were of particular importance because the RAF believed that only bombers equipped with them could battle their way, unescorted, through defending fighters and thus reach their targets. The British had seen no evidence of turret development in the United States, and they believed that since American air doctrine was similar to the RAF's, the Americans would jump at the opportunity to acquire this information.[28]

Pirie dismissed Boyle's unfounded optimism and believed that he could not pry the Norden secret from the U.S. Navy. In the last few months, he informed Boyle, the bombsight had become a "political" piece of equipment. Its virtues, though not any technical details, were being flaunted almost weekly in the press and in

Congress. The Norden was "the United States' most closely guarded secret," and Pirie believed that it would be almost impossible to secure it. Only direct diplomatic intervention by the British ambassador to the State Department might work, said Pirie, but the ambassador was reluctant to take this step because he would likely be rebuffed. Diplomatic overtures would ultimately involve President Roosevelt, and he was not anxious to trade any secret technical information, because of an "unfortunate incident."

Pirie might well have expanded on this point to Boyle. The "unfortunate incident" involved the crash of a prototype of the latest Douglas light bomber in late January. Pulled from the wreckage just before it burst into flames was a man whom the Douglas Company identified as a mechanic named Smithin. Reporters soon discovered that Smithin was in fact Captain Paul Chemidlin, a French military observer. Several isolationist congressmen turned the incident into a major political scandal when it was revealed that Roosevelt had personally ordered that Chemidlin be given permission to view the plane, despite the objections of the Army Air Corps. The isolationists accused Roosevelt of wanting to get the United States involved in war and of willingly selling the country's military secrets regardless of the cost to national security. It took the administration the entire month of February to weather this political storm. Roosevelt was forced to make a pledge not to sell any classified technology to any foreign powers.[29] Pirie summed up the administration's attitude after this scandal: "The smallest exchange is most grudgingly made and requires much more servile bargaining than I would ever have believed possible two years ago."[30]

Pirie and Arthur Harris, who was in Washington at this time, could think of only one course of action that might make the Americans provide details of the bombsight. They proposed that an expert be dispatched to Washington with the latest RAF bombsight, with the intention of convincing the U.S. Navy that it had much to learn from British technology. An American naval officer would be given an hour or so to examine it. Only then might the navy be induced to allow an exchange of bombsight technology.[31] It was a proposal that illustrates the remarkable technical ignorance of the officers assigned to carry out technical liaison at this time. Pirie and Harris did not seem to realize that there was no equivalent to the Norden in the RAF's arsenal. No British bombsight used gyrostabilization – either in production or on the drawing board. The Royal Aircraft Establishment was scheduled to start designing such a sight sometime in the future but not before 1940 at the earliest. This is why the Air Ministry was so desperate to acquire the American bombsight.[32]

Before the Air Ministry could respond to Pirie and Harris's suggestion, several reports were received which provided more details of the performance of the Norden bombsight and made the Air Ministry even more determined to arrange an exchange. On 13 April, Pirie attended an air demonstration at Fort Benning, Georgia. The results of four B-17s bombing a target of a battleship outlined on the ground from an altitude of 12,000 feet were impressive. "The first B-17 was due to drop its bombs at 1:27 pm," Pirie reported. "About 1:26 pm everyone started to look and listen for it. Nothing was seen or heard. At 1:27 while everyone was still searching the sky six 300-pound bombs suddenly burst at split second intervals on the deck of the battleship, and it was at least thirty seconds later before someone spotted the B-17 at 12,000 feet." It was a remarkable display, even if the weather conditions were perfect. And the result was no accident. The next three B-17s all hit the target. After this, a group of twelve B-18As each carrying twelve 100-pound bombs attacked a target 600 by 600 yards square from 10,000 feet. All but one of these planes hit its target successfully.[33]

Pirie's report and that of Wing Commander D.F. Anderson and Air Commodore Arthur Harris, who were touring American aviation establishments in the spring of 1939, convinced the most senior officers in the Air Ministry that they had to have the Norden. W.S. Douglas, the assistant chief of air staff, believed that the RAF should be prepared "to pay a good price for it."[34] The deputy director of intelligence went even further; he told the director of operational requirements that they "should leave no stone unturned" to get the American bombsight.[35]

Pirie was once again urged to pursue every possible means of securing information on the bombsight. But neither direct overtures nor espionage proved successful. While visiting Mitchell Field, Anderson found the American officers very helpful on every subject but the bombsights – they had been issued very strict orders not to talk on this subject with any foreigner. Anderson was able to get only a brief long-distance view of what he believed to be the sight, and this was of little value.[36]

Harris was "resolutely prevented from catching even a surreptitious glimpse of it" during his tour of American facilities. When direct methods proved unsuccessful, he turned to subterfuge:

> By leading on some of the officers in one of their Boeing "fortress" squadrons, under the influence of several high balls, I gathered the following. I suspect they only bomb directly up or down wind with this sight. It is used in a sitting position. It has a gyro stabilized vertical and the sighting can be optically projected forward as far as the horizon or as far as the target can be seen. The operation of "bringing back" the optical projection towards the vertical, when following the target, guided either the pilot or the aircraft direct through the automatic control, onto the target.[37]

Despite these alcohol-induced indiscretions, no detailed technical data was provided.

The hope that a change in personnel at the Bureau of Aeronautics might improve the situation proved to be equally fruitless. Rear-Admiral Jack Towers, who took over the bureau in the spring of 1939, was a close friend of Pirie, but he did not have the authority to give information on the sight. Pirie discovered that the device was controlled by Admiral W.R. Furlong, head of the Bureau of the Ordnance. According to Pirie, Furlong was "rather stubborn, narrow-minded, jealous and nationalistic." Although both Towers and Admiral Leahy, the chief of naval operations, appeared sympathetic, neither was willing to risk a bureaucratic battle to please the British. Nor was anyone overly enthusiastic about the prospect of allowing any foreign power the opportunity to acquire such an effective weapon. The navy feared that its ships would be endangered if it was faced with an enemy that possessed such an accurate bombsight. Although the Americans did not see the British as potential enemies, they did argue that the British were more likely to go to war before they did and that, once at war, it was inevitable that the sight would fall into the wrong hands. Supplying the British with the sight, it was believed, would hurt them more than it would help, since the Norden was particularly effective against maritime targets. If the

Norden fell into the hands of the Germans, it would be disastrous for the Royal Navy.[38]

Thus, despite the Air Ministry's persistent demands that Pirie find a way to acquire the bombsight, he informed London in late May that it was impossible for him to succeed. Any future approaches to the Americans must come from Sir Ronald Lindsay, British ambassador to the United States. Lindsay said that he was willing to try, but only if the Air Ministry considered the matter "one of vital importance to the defence of the country." The Norden had to be worth a great deal, he warned, because any further overtures to the Americans about it might involve "serious political considerations."[39]

Lindsay's warnings did not deter the Air Ministry, which continued to pursue the one piece of equipment that the United States would not supply under any conditions. The reason for the continuing British effort was that many senior RAF officers believed that the Americans could be persuaded to trade anything if the price was right; the Air Ministry had just not found the right bargaining chip yet. Also, the RAF's single-minded emphasis on strategic bombing meant that the Air Staff considered the Norden of such vital importance that efforts to acquire it had to continue, no matter what the cost.[40] In a memorandum of 5 June, W.S. Douglas informed Air Chief Marshal Sir Cyril Newall, the chief of air staff, that the bombing results using Norden sights were three to four times as good as the RAF's and that it was therefore of the "utmost importance" that the British government "should try to obtain from the Americans, if it [was] humanly possible to do so, specimens of their latest bombsights." He urged Newall to approach the Foreign Office to pursue the matter through the most senior diplomatic channels.[41]

It took some time for Douglas's proposal to win Air Ministry approval. This delay may partly have been caused by the failure of an attempt in early May to broaden the scope of Anglo-American technical cooperation. On 1 May, Joseph Kennedy, the American ambassador to Britain, met with Kingsley Wood, the secretary of state for air, at the Air Ministry. Kingsley Wood proposed that there be a mutual exchange of information on radar technology, observing that in some areas the British felt they were ahead and in others that the Americans were.[42] Kingsley Wood's offer was a remarkable development. Radar was Britain's most closely guarded technical secret, and the British believed that the Americans really had very little to offer in exchange for this information. Unfortunately, British records concerning this proposal have not been located. But it is apparent from Kennedy's telegrams to Washington that Kingsley Wood's proposal came more in the form of a private rather than official offer. It may very well have been the air minister's personal attempt to encourage the Americans to remove restrictions on technical cooperation, and thus to secure a trade for the Norden. It is also more than likely that Tizard, whose influence at the Air Ministry was increasing daily, suggested that this private offer be made.

Whatever the origins of Kingsley Wood's proposal, it did not matter in the long term, because the American government rejected it outright. Not realizing that the navy dominated research in this area, the State Department consulted the War Department about a possible exchange of information on aircraft detectors. When Joseph Green, the State Department's chief of the Division of Controls, arrived at the War Department, the senior officers whom he wished to consult – including General George C. Marshall, the chief of staff – were absent. So Green was ushered into the office of Harry Woodring, the secretary of war. Woodring was remarkably uninformed on radar, but this did not prevent him from belittling the British proposal. Green reported to the State Department:

> [Mr Woodring] thought it *extremely* unlikely that the War Department would be willing to exchange information in regard to the apparatus in question with *any* other government. He said that the detector which had been developed by the Army was considered by the War Department to be the most important military secret in its possession. He said that from what he had heard, he felt sure that the British had developed nothing comparable to it; that the British undoubtedly knew of its existence and desired to obtain it, but that he did not believe it possible that they could give in exchange anything which could be considered of even approximate equal value.

Even had he wished to provide the information, Woodring added, he could not do so. He was prevented by the promises made by Roosevelt after the incident involving the French air force observer in the Douglas bomber.[43] As a result of Woodring's objections, the British proposal was rejected. Thus, a golden opportunity to advance Anglo-American technical cooperation was lost.

The rejection of Kingsley Wood's radar proposal and the continuing failure by Pirie to obtain the Norden bombsight finally convinced the Air Ministry that it needed to have the ambassador make an official request for the device. Thus, on 17 August 1939, the Foreign Office was requested to attempt to secure the sight by diplomatic means. Growing international tension had made it "essential" to double the efficiency of the RAF's bombers.[44] However, Lord Halifax, the foreign secretary, decided that the matter was too urgent and the international situation too critical for an ambassadorial approach. He decided that it should be taken up at the highest levels of government. As a result, on 25 August, Prime Minister Chamberlain wrote directly to President Roosevelt requesting the Norden bombsight. Chamberlain told the American president:

> I make this urgent personal request to you because Great Britain today faces the possibility of entering on a tremendous struggle confronted as she is with a challenge to her fundamental values and ideals. Moreover, I believe they are values and ideals which our two countries share in common …
>
> Should the war break out, my advisers tell me that we would obtain a greater immediate increase in our effective power if we had the Norden bombsight at our disposal than by any other means we can foresee. Air power is, of course, a relatively new weapon which is so far untried on a large scale; there is the danger of unrestricted air attack which we for our part would never initiate. I am however most anxious to do all in my power to lessen the practical difficulties which may arise in operations against legitimate military targets, and feel that in air bombardment accuracy and humanity really go together. For this reason again I am certain that you would render the greatest service if you could enable us to make use of the magnificent apparatus which your Services have developed.[45]

This emotional request was designed to appeal to Roosevelt strong sense of democratic values and humanity. Yet Chamberlain carefully avoided the domestic political realities with which the American president had to cope.

On 31 August, just three days before Great Britain declared war on Germany, Roosevelt rejected Chamberlain's request. The president's brief note stated that under existing neutrality and security legislation, the only way the sight could be provided was if the technology was made available to all other foreign powers. Since this was obviously undesirable, the bombsight could not be given or traded to Great Britain. However, Roosevelt unwittingly left the door open for future British attempts to acquire the sight. He told Chamberlain that he would undertake "continued consideration to the request you have made and to the possibility of acceding to it either under the present conditions or under such new conditions as may arise."[46]

The British government refused to accept the president's legalistic arguments. Roosevelt was, after all, in the process of orchestrating amendments to the Neutrality Act to allow for the purchase of military equipment on a cash-and-carry basis. The act had banned the sale of all armaments to any belligerent. Lord Lothian, the new British ambassador to the United States, believed that what lay behind Roosevelt's rejection of Chamberlain's request was the opposition of the navy, the department whose advice Roosevelt "invariably" followed. Lothian speculated that the navy might drop its objections if the RAF could develop a device that would guarantee the destruction of the Norden sight when a bomber crashed behind enemy lines. Alternatively, Lothian suggested that the RAF might promise to restrict the bombsight's use to attacks on naval targets. Any bomber that was shot down would then crash into the sea, taking its precious bombsight with it to the bottom.[47]

Ronald Lindsay, who had now returned to London from his Washington ambassadorial post, made another recommendation. He informed Lord Halifax that he believed the problem was that the RAF did not have the right *quid pro quo* to trade with the American navy. Perhaps, Lindsay suggested, the Admiralty might have a suitable item to tempt the American sailors.[48]

These suggestions were pursued to no avail throughout the rest of 1939. The process revealed Britian's extraordinary failure to grasp the nature of American opposition. The U.S. Navy could simply not be bribed. Senior American naval officers believed it vital to national security that this technology not be risked, no matter how good the intentions of those who wanted it. And

Roosevelt was unwilling to face the political consequences of the public learning that this technology had been provided to a foreign power. In part, Roosevelt was protecting British interests, for he did not wish to jeopardize the careful political balancing act that would assist the Allies by altering the neutrality legislation.[49] In fact, the amendment of the neutrality laws, rather than discouraging the British requests for the Norden bombsight, actually led to further attempts to secure it. The Air Ministry believed that the changes to the legislation, which passed Congress on 4 November, meant that Roosevelt's legal arguments against providing the bombsight were now null and void. All that was needed was to find the right *quid* for the American *quo*. Taking up Lindsay's suggestion, the Admiralty was asked to offer its asdic or sonar in return for the American bombsight.[50]

However, the new first lord of the Admiralty, Winston Churchill, had already offered asdic to the Americans. Since June, Admiralty efforts to continue technical exchanges with the U.S. Navy had foundered as a result of mutual suspicions and recriminations over the unsatisfactory nature of the early trades. Concern had also been expressed about the ability of the Americans to protect British secrets. On 16 October, however, Churchill, in the third of his famous "naval person" letters to Roosevelt, had offered to reopen naval technical cooperation. Apparently without consulting his colleagues on the Board of the Admiralty, he had offered the closely guarded asdic secrets to the American navy – and he had done so without directly implying that any American technology was expected in return. There was only one precondition: the U.S. Navy must ensure that information on asdic was protected.[51]

Roosevelt informed his navy of Churchill's offer, and Rear-Admiral W.S. Anderson, the director of naval intelligence, instructed Captain Alan G. Kirk, the naval attaché, to begin negotiations. Anderson's instructions to Kirk reveal the American attitude to the *quid pro quo* method of exchange and show why the arrangement bred mutual suspicion rather than encouraging technical transfers. Kirk was ordered to get whatever the British were willing to give, and at the lowest possible price. He was authorized to trade information on American submarine-detection systems on a reciprocal basis, but only if a better bargain could not be secured. Before giving the Admiralty anything of substance,

Kirk was to assure himself that what the British were offering was worthwhile. This implied that American technology was probably far superior.[52] The Admiralty had precisely the same negotiating strategy and a similar attitude on the capabilities of American technology. As a result, this round of talks proved no more fruitful than previous ones.

On 9 November, Kirk met with Admiral John Godfrey, the new director of naval intelligence at the Admiralty, and broached the subject of receiving information on asdic. Godfrey was visibly surprised by Kirk's inquiry, for apparently he had been given "no intimation that this subject might be open" for discussion. He told Kirk that asdic was "still a very secret matter." This suggested to Kirk that in order to secure the required information he must be able to offer a full exchange of American sonar.[53] But by 27 November, when he was finally authorized to provide information on U.S. naval sonar, the British government had decided what it wanted in return for its asdic secret: the Norden bombsight. At least two weeks earlier, the Admiralty had agreed with the Air Ministry that asdic technology should be traded only for the bombsight. The Air Ministry now believed that it could sway the American navy by offering it submarine-detection equipment and information on a device that would destroy a Norden sight if a bomber was shot down. Once again, these plans show a complete lack of appreciation of the depth of the U.S. Navy's obsession with preserving the Norden secret.

In early November, while the Air Ministry and Admiralty were trying to sweeten the deal for the bombsight, the American navy was taking steps to deter any further leaks about the device's capabilities. A number of articles had appeared in *Time*, *Colliers*, and *Popular Aviation Magazine* lauding the bombsight's accuracy and versatility, and the navy had discovered that the journalists had been briefed by the Army Air Corps publicity office. This infuriated the navy; it was appalled by the "notorious" laxity of the Army Air Corps security and, paradoxically, by its attempt to take credit for developing the device. The air corps publicity office, complained one naval officer, was larger than the navy's. "Until the army policy changes," he added, "we should not give them anything without a prior public release – since they would release it anyhow themselves as their own."[54] Admiral Furlong, of the Bureau of Ordnance, demanded that the army "stop this publicity … as it only makes foreign agents try harder to steal the sight from our various stations."[55]

Despite the U.S. Navy's attitude, Lord Lothian was instructed on 5 December to approach Roosevelt with the two-pronged British offer. Lothian was told that the Admiralty did not consider the American offer of exchanging information on submarine-detection equipment an adequate *quid pro quo*. Meanwhile, in late November, Kingsley Wood had held discussions about the exchange with Joseph Kennedy, the American ambassador, and Kennedy had apparently said that he supported the British proposal and had promised to take up the issue with the president when he returned to the United States for a short visit in early December.[56]

On 9 December the War Cabinet heard Churchill summarize the current state of negotiations. It was agreed that the American offer of a reciprocal trade of asdic technology was unacceptable. In a classic example of technological chauvinism, the War Cabinet accepted that the U.S. Navy had "no weapons of special value for the purpose." This conclusion was reached despite the fact that asdic had originally been developed at the end of the First World War when all technological secrets had been shared by the Allied powers. Inexplicably, it was assumed that while the Royal Navy had greatly improved asdic, the Americans had made no valuable technological progress in this field. The members of the War Cabinet decided that no formal rejection should be sent; instead, they would wait for a formal response from the Americans about the British proposal. It proved to be a long wait.

On 13 December, Lothian had a private interview with Roosevelt at the White House, during which he informed the president of the British offer. Roosevelt was deliberately noncommittal. While he was intrigued by the existence of a device that could destroy the bombsight and prevent it from falling into enemy hands, he was still not prepared to reveal details of the bombsight itself. Roosevelt was not interested in taking the political risk of giving the British any information on this now very public "secret technology," and he seems to have been waiting for a response to the U.S. Navy's proposal of a reciprocal trade of asdic technology. Consequently, he never responded to Lothian's proposal. And since the British did not reply to the American counter offer, a diplomatic stalemate resulted.[57] An alternative to the *quid pro quo* bargaining system would have to be found, otherwise it would continue to be a major stumbling block to better Anglo-American military technical relations.

The stalemate that resulted from the *quid pro quo* negotiations did not, however, mean a sudden end to efforts to trade technical information on this basis. In a few areas of minor importance, technical exchanges continued. Thus, it was not immediately apparent to those involved in negotiations that attempts to secure more vital information had reached an impasse. Lothian tried several more times between February and July 1940 to arrange for the acquisition of the Norden, but he met with no more success than on previous occasions. In early February, for example, he suggested to Roosevelt that a provisional order might be placed for a quantity of the sights "pending their definite release." The president approved of the idea in principle, and the Foreign Office instructed Lothian to order one thousand of the devices, but nothing more was heard of this scheme. Apparently, it was scuttled by the continuing reluctance of the American navy to release any information on the bombsight.[58]

Captain Kirk, the U.S. naval attaché, was perplexed by the Admiralty's failure to respond to the American offer of a direct exchange for sonar and by his own navy's reluctance to trade for the bombsight. On 5 January 1940 he wrote to Admiral Anderson, the director of naval intelligence, pointing out that the Air Ministry was so desperate for the bombsight that if the U.S. Navy released it, a very hard bargain could be made with the British. Kirk advocated trading the sight for full details on a number of vital areas: German magnetic mines and corresponding British countermeasures; the use of the bombsight in operations; radio and sound aircraft-detection apparatus and the organization developed to utilize it; and information on aircraft design, armament, and tactics. It was necessary, he argued, to receive information on all these points because there was little to be learned from British technology itself. But one could gain knowledge of British operational procedures and organization.[59]

Despite Kirk's recommendations, the bombsight was not forthcoming. The disappointment of the British over the American intransigence concerning technology, and their anger about the restrictions imposed by the neutrality legislation, created an atmosphere of growing mistrust. The scope of this mistrust was reported by Kirk to his superiors in Washington at the end of January. He told them that various Admiralty directorates would no longer approve any information exchanges because of a mistaken belief that technical secrets would be leaked to the Germans by the U.S. Navy. Kirk was sympathetic to the anxieties of the British, though not to their specific complaints. He wrote: "A serious war is being waged, and we must realize the natural and proper anxiety of the Admiralty not to risk anything that might be of benefit to the enemy."

In early February, Kirk met with Admiral Godfrey to discuss the Admiralty's growing anti-Americanism. Kirk argued forcefully that it was in Great Britain's best interest to provide the U.S. Navy with intelligence on German war methods, material, and operations, and to do so without demanding a *quid pro quo*. Godfrey responded that, given the present attitudes, it was highly unlikely that his government would agree to this. Kirk then demanded to know if the British had any evidence of a single incident in which information had been leaked to the Germans by the U.S. Navy. The reply was an emphatic "No!" But although Godfrey was sensitive to Kirk's complaints, he felt that there was nothing he could do to alter the situation – unless the Americans could give something concrete to the Admiralty to change attitudes. Godfrey did not state what this "something" was, but it is obvious he was alluding to the Norden bombsight.[60]

Kirk's observations are confirmed in Admiralty documents. On 26 February 1940, Godfrey wrote a lengthy memorandum on the subject, which he said he was "keeping constantly under review." He reported that Kirk had been visiting the Admiralty nearly every week asking for information on British asdic (sonar) and on Germany's new magnetic mines and torpedoes. The Americans, he noted, were particularly anxious to receive information on the damage that these weapons were inflicting on British warships, for they wanted to be sure that their new ship designs would be better able to "resist this latest form of menace." Kirk had argued that it was to Britain's advantage to give him the information, since the Americans would ultimately come into the war against Germany and had to be prepared to deal with German weapons.

Godfrey outlined the failure of the prewar *quid pro quo* basis of exchange, blaming it on the American navy and the war departments. In his view, they had been rather "sticky" about a fair exchange and had even been embarrassed about any clear British superiority in technology. He argued, however, that the exchange of technical information should begin without the guarantee of a *quid pro quo*. The Americans, he explained, had already assisted the British by transferring their fleet to the Pacific, and they were passing on intelligence from their Berlin and other European attachés, as well as information concerning the Japanese navy.[61]

Godfrey's report generated a debate within the Admiralty on whether or not to continue to insist on reciprocal technical exchanges.[62] There was no consensus of opinion. Some members of the Admiralty had even hardened their views against any form of information trade. But the issue was not destined to be decided on the basis of *quid pro quo*. Even as this debate was taking place, a radically different concept of technical cooperation with the United States was being formulated. The shift of attitude was triggered by a scientific intelligence-gathering expedition to the United States by Professor A.V. Hill.

3 Hill's Mission

Archibald Vivian Hill was Britain's most respected physiologist; he was the joint secretary of the Royal Society and the society's Foulerton research professor. In 1922 he shared the Nobel Prize in Physiology and Medicine with German scientist Otto Meyerhof "for his discovery relating to the production of heat in muscles." Hill's Nobel made him well know both personally and professionally to the American scientific elite.[1]

Hill was intimately familiar with military research. He had a flexible and inquisitive mind that allowed him to apply his scientific knowledge to any technical field. During the First World War he had used this talent as head of the Anti-Aircraft Experimental Section, dubbed Hill's Bandits. The Bandits used statistical analysis and experimental science. Their aim was to improve the accuracy of anti-aircraft gunnery by examining such things as the effect of high-altitude winds on shells and the accuracy of range tables. Hill later claimed that, in the process, the experimental section created the science of operational research.[2] In the 1930s Hill served on Tizard's Committee for the Scientific Survey of Air Defence, the committee responsible for the creation of Britain's radar defence chain. At the beginning of the Second World War, Hill and Professor A.C. Egerton, the other co-secretary of the Royal Society, lobbied the government to improve scientific liaison with the National Research Council of Canada.[3]

Ronald W. Clark, Tizard's official biographer, claims that Hill's mission took place because of Tizard's desire to bring "American scientists into the war before their Government." Tizard was scientific adviser to the chief of air staff in November 1939, and he proposed that Hill be sent to Washington to work as a scientific adviser to the air attaché, George Pirie.[4] There can little doubt, of course, that Tizard played a key role in the choice of Hill and in structuring his mission. Yet Clark's assertion that Tizard alone was responsible for Hill being sent to the United States is typical of the inaccurate characterization of Tizard in the literature on Anglo-American technical exchange.

Most of the literature on the mission has been written by scientists or by the biographers of scientists, and the various works take a similar approach. Tizard is repeatably portrayed as the omnipotent scientist, the central figure in whose fertile mind the idea of the exchange originated, who by sheer force of will convinced hostile political and military leaders of the necessity of carrying it out. Tizard, it is claimed, did this despite the hostility of Lindemann, who, as Churchill's scientific consultant, forced Tizard to resign as scientific adviser to the chief of air staff in June 1940. The novelist and physicist C.P. Snow described Tizard's role as follows: "He had arranged for A.V. Hill to be sent to Washington, and both of them had become convinced that there were overwhelming arguments for telling the American scientists the whole of our radar and other military scientific secrets. Nearly all the English scientists agreed – Cockcroft, Oliphant, Blackett all pressed the matter. Nearly everyone else disagreed."[5]

The accounts of scientists and their biographers should not always be trusted. As we have seen, it was not Tizard who first proposed having technical exchanges with the Americans. Although the concept of sending a scientific attaché originated with Tizard, the Air Ministry approved the mission because it had its own agenda. This was quite different from Tizard's idealistic concept of "bringing American scientists into the war before their government." The Air Ministry was still anxious for supplies of the Norden bombsight, and it believed that a new approach was necessary. Thus, the new attaché was not sent to the United States to trade military secrets; his role was to investigate the viability of a future technical exchange by undertaking the first scientific survey of U.S. technical capabilities.

In late October 1939, Tizard had revived his 1937 proposal for sending a scientific attaché to Washington. At first, he recommended Professor P.M.S. Blackett for the role, but by early December Blackett had been replaced by Hill. Although the documents do not make clear just why this change took place, it is probable that Blackett, like most physicists, was already considered indispensable. Hill's technical skills as a physiologist were considered less vital, and he was arguably the most qualified available person in Great Britain to go on a scientific intelligence mission. He was, therefore, a better choice to be sent overseas. The Air Ministry approved Tizard's proposal in less than a week. Yet a further four months passed before Hill's departure.[6]

The causes of the delay were twofold. First, until early January 1940 the Foreign Office, the Treasury, and the Air Ministry were engaged in a lengthy bureaucratic battle over whether or not to allow the new attaché diplomatic privileges, how he was to be paid, and who would be his superior at the British Embassy in Washington. Once these problems had been settled, there were still further concerns. There were serious worries about letting Hill negotiate with the Americans, who might not have anything to trade, and there were fears that British secrets might be leaked to the Germans. In order to alleviate these anxieties and to gain final approval for the mission, Tizard and Hill made a suggestion to Sir Cyril Newall, the chief of air staff, on 5 January 1940, "that if there is trouble over a definite appointment [for Hill] and if the thing cannot be settled soon, it might be wise to send him over specially, for three months, then let him come back and report, and on the basis of the report decide whether to replace him with anyone else."[7] Newall agreed and ordered the mission to proceed.

When this lengthy wrangling had finally spent itself, all the arrangements were undone when Hill decided in early 1940 to run as an Independent Conservative for one of the Cambridge University seats in the House of Commons. When he won on 25 February, the Treasury, which had agreed to provide him with a salary, balked, holding that it was illegal to provide an additional stipend to serving members of Parliament. The Foreign Office also changed its mind. It no longer wanted Hill to be sent to Washington, for he had become a political figure and was therefore unsuitable as a diplomat. Only in early March was a compromise reached: Hill's salary would be paid by the Royal

Society, and he agreed not to assume his seat in the House until his return from North America.[8]

This lengthy delay had its distinct advantages, for Hill was able to use the time to establish the goals of his mission. After consultation with the Air Ministry, it was agreed that he would investigate the attitudes of America's political, scientific, and military elite towards the war. He was also to serve as a secret agent, evaluating the usefulness of American technology and industry to the British war effort; and he was to determine whether the Americans knew anything about radar or any of the other secret devices in the British arsenal. All of this was to be done discreetly so as not to arouse isolationist opposition. Officially, Hill was simply to be a "supernumerary Air Attaché technically on loan from the Royal Society."[9]

Hill began laying the groundwork for his American trip in January 1940 by writing to leading British scientists who had knowledge of the United States. He asked them to supply him with a list of contacts, their positions, addresses, and, most importantly, their attitude towards the war. From this and from Air Ministry and Foreign Office sources, Hill compiled an eleven-page list of people to meet in the United States and Canada. On the list were almost all the men who were destined to lead the United States' scientific war effort. They included Vannevar Bush, who at the time was chairman of the National Advisory Committee for Aeronautics and president of the Carnegie Foundation; Lyman Briggs, head of the Bureau of Standards; James Conant, president of Harvard University; and Arthur Holly Compton, president of the California Institute of Technology. Hill was also advised to see leading physicists such as the expatriates Enrico Fermi and Leo Szilard, both of whom were trying to convince the American government to begin work on the atomic bomb. The list contained the names of important politicians, generals, and admirals – all of whom Hill would endeavour to interview on their attitude towards a general technical exchange. Also provided were names of high-technology companies, such as Kodak and Sperry Electronics, whose facilities he was expected to investigate if possible.[10] Hill was no doubt briefed on the persistent though unsubstantiated rumours that the Americans did in fact have a form of radar. From his correspondence, he developed a revealing cross section of British scientific opinion on the United

States. Some of the scientists were openly supportive of increasing cooperation, while others opposed it. Most held views similar to that of F.G. Bartlett of the Cambridge Psychological Laboratory, who wrote: "I am most glad that you are going on the mission and think nothing but good can come of it, although to be frank, my view is that the American public attitude of world affairs is disgusting."[11]

No itinerary or diary of Hill's mission to the United States has survived, and it is only with great difficulty that any part of his visit can be reconstructed. When Tizard was gathering information for his never-begun memoirs in 1957, he wrote to Hill asking him for any recollections of his time in the United States. Hill remembered few of the details, recalling only his date of arrival at Halifax. This he remembered because it had taken place the day after he had observed the vernal equinox. Hill wrote apologetically to his old friend: "It is a pity that my records are so scanty and my memory (except for odd things like equinoxes) so dim." What is certain is that Hill left Liverpool on 9 March 1940, landed in Halifax on the nineteenth, and arrived in Washington on either the twenty-first or twenty-second.[12] For the next two months, he held meetings with as many important North Americans as possible, travelling widely throughout the eastern United States and Canada. His visit was public, although its purpose was secret, and on 12 April he gave a lecture to the American Philosophical Society in Philadelphia. Hill's most important contact and supporter in the United States turned out to be the British ambassador, Lord Lothian.

Philip Kerr, the eleventh marquis of Lothian, had been appointed ambassador to Washington in August 1939. Lord Halifax, the foreign secretary, had foreseen Anglo-American relations entering a much more dynamic phase in which the United States, the ever-reluctant world power, would have to be wooed to join the struggle against fascism. Halifax wanted as ambassador a dynamic individual who was familiar with the Americans and their "peculiar" system of government, and was sensitive to their fears of foreign entanglement, but would be able to sell Britain's position without appearing to be spreading propaganda. Halifax looked outside the ranks of professional diplomats to find the most suitable candidate, and he chose Lothian because of the marquis's extensive contacts with influential Americans. This circle included the journalists

Walter Lippmann and William Allen White, the banker Thomas Lamont, and Felix Frankfurter, a Roosevelt appointee to the Supreme Court. Lothian's extensive contacts with Americans came about in part because of his "deep commitment" to Christian Science and his work as secretary to the Rhodes Trust. Lothian had made fourteen trips to the United States, during which he had visited forty-four states. He had met Roosevelt several times, including during the Paris peace conference in 1919, where he served as Lloyd George's private secretary. His cousin, Mark Kerr, was an old friend of the American president.[13] An equally important factor in the selection of Lothian as ambassador was his firm commitment to the idea of closer relations between the United States and Great Britain. Since the First World War, Lothian had believed that this was "the essential foundation of world peace." His ultimate goal was the establishment of a world government modelled on "a truly federal British Commonwealth." However, in the 1930s he had sought "isolation from European commitments and cooperation with the Empire and the United States to promote world peace."[14]

As we have seen, Lothian had tried unsuccessfully to secure a supply of Norden bombsights prior to Hill's arrival in Washington. Using Lothian's extensive connections, Hill was able to have conversations with leading political, military, and scientific figures. These included an important meeting on 27 March with Justice Felix Frankfurter. Frankfurter told Hill that he thought that President Roosevelt would support an open and frank technical exchange, and he promised to assist the British in securing the president's approval. Meetings with Vannevar Bush brought a similar response. From these meetings, Hill was able to ascertain that most leading Americans supported the British and disproved of Hitler's regime.

Hill was also able to gather a great deal of technical information, some of which came as quite a surprise to British officials. Most astonishing of all, Hill concluded that the Americans had developed their own radar systems, the existence of which had been undetected by any of the service attachés in Washington. His information came from a variety of sources: conversations with academics; inferences gained from visits to industrial laboratories; congressional leaks to the press about the existence of aircraft-detection devices; and mysterious anonymous letters received by the British Embassy about the possibility of using reflected radio waves to locate aircraft.

Most intriguing was the tight American military security around radio research facilities. This security, Hill inferred, would only have been necessary to protect some new military technology such as radar. Hill was denied access to RCA's research centre in Camden, New Jersey, and he was accompanied on his visits to the facilities of General Electric and Bell Telephone Laboratories by a naval officer "to see that I did not obtain information I shouldn't." Hill requested Edgar S. Bloom, a member of the British Purchasing Commission and former president of Western Electric to contact Dr Frank Jewett, the current head of the Bell Laboratories and president of the National Academy of Sciences. Hill wished to discuss with Jewett "the possibility of providing" the British with American aircraft-detection information and equipment. Jewett, while not denying that such devices existed, declined to discuss them because he had been "absolutely prevented" from doing so by a ban placed on him and his company by the navy. American service personnel simply refused to discuss the secret radar work, and Hill found that most industrial scientists were equally tight-lipped.

However, Hill discovered that academic scientists had somewhat less respect for military security. At one point he met with Dr Frank Aydellotte, who was president of Swarthmore College, American secretary of the Rhodes Trustees, and a member of the pro-British Century Club. Hill believed him to have close connections with the American army. Without any prompting, Aydellotte asked him, "What are you people doing with radio waves reflected from aircraft for directing anti-aircraft gunfire?" When Hill looked dumbfounded, Aydellotte added, "Don't tell me if you think you ought not to."[15] Although Hill believed that British radar technology was largely superior to the American, he found evidence that the Americans might be ahead in certain areas. He discussed high-power microwave technology with Bush, Alfred Loomis, and Dr Mel Tuve, and they left him with the impression that the Americans had radio tubes that could generate far more power then similar British equipment. Hill knew that this equipment would greatly improve radar, particularly small aircraft-mounted sets of the sort being designed in Great Britain.[16]

By the third week of April, Hill was convinced that a totally open technical exchange had to take place with the Americans, without any preconditions. He wrote to Lord Lothian, advising him that "it might be of major importance to offer a very frank interchange of technical knowledge and experience as a basis for the indirect co-operation which promises to be so valuable and so unlikely to arouse political objections."[17] In the British ambassador Hill found a receptive listener, who would became one of the most important supporters of a technical and scientific exchange between the United States and Great Britain. In a telegram Lothian sent to the Foreign Office on 23 April, he summarized Hill's preliminary findings and gave his wholehearted endorsement of an immediate technical exchange on radar. Lothian told London: "Our present bargaining position is strong owing to [our] earlier start and service use. If we wait the USA will probably discover the essential for themselves. I suggest that we offer full information on RDF [radar] and its developments in exchange for similar information on their systems and for complete facilities to obtain the latest types of instruments and equipment to our specifications and requirements from firms now working on United States Government contracts."[18]

While Lothian emphasized the possibility of cooperation with the Americans on radar technology, he did not discount the prospect of expanding the exchange to include other forms of equipment. With an eye towards continuing American sensitivity to the Norden bombsight, the ambassador informed London that he "would try to get the release of the bomb sight [*sic*] as part of the exchange though as a method of negotiation it might be wiser not to [do] this at first."[19] Lothian argued that while an exchange of military information and equipment was desirable on technical grounds, as Hill and Pirie now believed, it was no less important in improving Anglo-American diplomatic relations. It would bring "the services of the two countries into closer liaison and sympathy [on] war preparation." If London approved of the exchange, he said, he would "make the proposal to the President personally."[20]

Lothian's telegram had a strong impact on London. The Foreign Office had been searching for a way to obtain supplies of the Norden bombsight ever since the failure of Lothian's proposal to Roosevelt in early February. It had hoped to discuss technical cooperation with Sumner Wells, the American undersecretary of state, who was sent to Europe in the winter of 1940 to discuss an American-mediated peace settlement, but the discussions that were held in London with Wells from 11 to 14 March had focused on the peace initiative and did not involve a technical exchange.[21] Thus, the Foreign Office enthusiastically endorsed Lothian's and Hill's proposal. On 24 April, John Balfour, the head of the Foreign Office's American Department, told the Air Ministry, "We are all in favour of such an exchange of information especially as the Ambassador seems to think there is some chance of getting the Norden bomb sight as part of the exchange."[22] The next day Lord Halifax met with Joseph Kennedy, the American ambassador, and the issue of a technical exchange was discussed. Kennedy claimed, erroneously, that the United States had already given the British all its military secrets except two – one of which was the Norden bombsight.[23]

On 26 April, Halifax brought the issue of technical exchange before the War Cabinet; this was the first time the issue had been considered by Cabinet since December 1939. Predictably, the discussion centred on the acquisition of the bombsight. Halifax believed that another personal appeal to Roosevelt might work in securing information on the device, whereas Chamberlain thought that giving the Americans information on radar might "persuade" them to provide details on the bombsight. Radar, after all, was a technology in which Britain "had more to give" than to receive. Only Sir Samuel Hoare, the secretary of state for air, argued that an exchange of radar information might be useful by itself. To his mind, it would foster "closer cooperation" between American and British scientists. A mutual exchange of radar information had the potential of leading to great improvements in radar equipment, he argued, because "we were very short of expert research workers in this field, and we should try to get as many American scientists as possible to work on these problems for us."[24]

The discussion ended with the issue still unresolved. It might have remained so if the Air Ministry had not determined that Anglo-American technical cooperation was an important matter to pursue. On the same day that Lothian had sent his telegram to the Foreign Office, Pirie, the air attaché in Washington, had sent his own telegram to the Air Ministry, advising the chief of air staff to press for the adoption of the ambassador's proposal and to allow Hill to begin immediate discussions with the Americans.[25] The chief of air staff was also lobbied by Tizard, his scientific adviser, to press for an Anglo-American technical exchange. Tizard was encouraged by many of his fellow government scientists to ensure the implementation of Lothian's proposal. The names of these scientists sound like a "Who's Who" of the contemporary high-level technical experts: Sir Frank Appleton of the Department of Scientific and Industrial Research, Robert Watson-Watt of the Air Ministry, C.S. Wright, the Admiralty's director of scientific research, and H.J. Gough, director of scientific research at the Ministry of Supply. All urged Tizard to use his connections to encourage the Air Ministry to push for the dispatch of a technical mission to the United States. Moreover, Appleton recommended that Tizard should head the mission.[26]

On 30 April, Tizard told the chief of air staff that he was "definitely in favour of a frank interchange of all technical information with the American Navy and Army Departments." While admitting that there might be a risk of secret information being revealed to the enemy, Tizard argued that "we should gain more than we should lose by taking this risk." He wanted the latest scientific discoveries in service use as soon as possible, and he held that American manufactures could greatly accelerate this process. Radar secrets should be provided because it was Britain's "best bargaining counter." Tizard concluded by telling the chief of air staff – who, he knew, still wanted the bombsights – that the Americans might cooperate in other ways if handled properly.[27]

Tizard was likely preaching to the converted. It is therefore impossible to assess his influence on the Air Ministry's decision to begin discussions on implementing technical and scientific cooperation with the Americans. A meeting was called at the Air Ministry on the afternoon of 3 May to begin this process. In attendance were several senior Royal Air Force officers, including Air Vice-Marshal R.H. Peck and Air Marshal Sir P.B. Joubert de la Ferté. Also attending were Tizard, Watson-Watt, Sir George Lee, director of communication development [radar], Vice-Admiral Sir James Somerville, representing the Admiralty, and Major General K.M. Loch of the War Office. Tizard presented the Air Ministry's position and strongly supported giving the Americans radar information in return for potential technical data. He held that even if the Americans were still unwilling – or had no equipment of equivalent technical value – the British "should get their goodwill and co-operation which meant a great deal considering their facilities for applied research and production."[28]

The unpredictable Watson-Watt and Lee, while not against the principle of technical cooperation with the Americans, disagreed with Tizard's evaluation of the possible benefits. They insisted "that the Americans could not teach us anything, and, that we should get the worst of the bargain." Watson-Watt added chauvinistically that the production argument was invalid since, by the end of the year, British electronic production facilities would be larger than the American ones – whereupon Tizard observed that if this actually occurred, "it would be the first time in history."[29] While effectively dismissing Watson-Watt's objections, Tizard had less success with those of Admiral Somerville. Somerville's doubts were based on a growing belief at the Admiralty "that anything told to the American Navy went straight to Germany."[30] Tizard asked to see direct evidence of lax American security or collaboration with the Nazis, and Somerville promised to provide it. On this inconclusive note, the meeting ended. It had achieved little more than authorizing the preparation of a report "setting out the pros and cons of the suggested interchange."[31]

The report that followed was written by Tizard, using information from those who had attended the meeting. It laid out in some detail all the viewpoints that had been expressed, both for and against technical exchanges with the Americans. But as Tizard worked over several drafts, he slanted them increasingly in favour of sending a technical mission. He examined the political, diplomatic, technical, scientific, and industrial advantages, and he also examined the evidence of poor American security. As he had suspected, the Admiralty's case was a weak one. It was supported only by "the past experiences of naval attachés in Washington" and by comments made by an American naval officer while visiting the bomb-damaged HMS *Southhampton* in Rosyth on 10 October 1939. The American officer had "volunteered not to report to his own government a certain deficiency which was apparent in the enemy's bombs." This was because he had considered that "it should not be communicated to the Germans which, he said, 'it was almost certain to do' if he reported home." But even if the chances that information given to the Americans would find its way into German hands were minimal, the report pointed out the grave consequences that might result. These included enabling the Germans to circumvent Britain's radar air-defence system or to make the radar stations their first target in an aerial campaign. Even without American information reaching Germany, this section of the report concluded, the secret of radar would certainly become known to the enemy. The general theory behind it was common knowledge among scientists, and if the Americans had developed radar independently, why not the Germans? The French had been provided with technical details, and at least one aircraft carrying an air-to-surface-vessel radar might have been recovered by the enemy already.[32]

The Tizard report concluded that the committee could not make a decision based on the available evidence. Thus, Tizard requested that "higher authority" consider the arguments. Nevertheless, the report had a strong bias in favour of sending a technical mission to the United States, and even though Tizard could not endorse one, he did outline its possible composition. He suggested that it "should be headed by a senior Royal Air Force officer and should include service representatives of the Admiralty and of the War Office as well as civilian experts." Furthermore, in order to remove the risk of security leaks in the United States, the mission should be armed with evidence of past breaches to "be laid before the President." Assurances should be requested in order to prevent future breaches of security, stated Tizard, and the mission should only proceed if it was "reasonably satisfied that the steps to be taken would prove to be effective."[33]

Like the meeting itself, the discussions on Tizard's report were inconclusive, and it was not until July that technical exchanges with the Unites States were again examined by the "higher authority" of the War Cabinet. There were several reasons for this delay, which worked against a swift approval of the Air Ministry's proposal. The first and perhaps most important reason was the most obvious – the rapid and disastrous change of fortune that befell the Allies just days after Lothian's telegram was dispatched, and the ensuing political upheaval when Neville Chamberlain resigned as prime minister. Even before the meeting of the War Cabinet on 26 April, Norway seemed lost. Two weeks later, on 10 May, the German army began its assault on France and Belgium, and within two more weeks it had surrounded not only the

British Expeditionary Force at Dunkirk but the Belgium army and a sizable part of the French army. Anglo-American relations, to which a technical exchange was now inextricably linked, went through a period of rapid readjustment. This was because American assistance was now no longer merely desirable; it was vital if the British Empire was to survive. Thus, technical exchange with the United States became just one small part of a much bigger picture. A technical mission would not proceed unless progress was made on other more substantive issues, such as the pressing need for American destroyers or for some further relaxation of the neutrality laws. The connection between an Anglo-American technical exchange and these other matters was emphasized by the new prime minister, Winston Churchill, throughout the summer of 1940.

Before he became prime minister on 10 May, Churchill's attitude to Anglo-American technical and scientific cooperation had been ambiguous at best. Even as late as 1 May, although Churchill saw some benefit from this type of cooperation, he did not believe it was of any great consequence. In the first draft of his response to Lothian's proposal, while admitting that there could be some advantage from sharing radar secrets if American security arrangements could be trusted, Churchill wrote that the Americans were "probably only six or eight months behind us and will make up the leeway anyhow." The much-desired Norden bombsight, he argued, was not "worth making any great sacrifice to discover the design, as it is almost certain that there is no great novelty in it, and the same results can be obtained with any stabilized bomb-sight of reasonable type." Churchill saw only one advantage in the American bombsight – that it was already in production and that the immediate delivery of "some thousands" would tide Bomber Command over until British production of similar equipment could begin in about six months' time.[34] However, ten days later, in one of his last acts as first lord of the Admiralty, Churchill altered his position dramatically. In the final draft of this letter, one of Churchill's private secretaries wrote: "Mr. Churchill is not in favour of an interchange of information about RDF [radar] with the American Government unless we can get some very definite advantage in return." Churchill was not prepared to approve Lothian's proposal unless the Americans agreed to supply Norden bombsights immediately.[35]

What changed the tone of Churchill's letter so dramatically was probably the anxiety of several senior Admiralty officials, most notably Admiral John Godfrey, the director of naval intelligence. Godfrey stated that it would be "most unwise" to give the Americans any details of secret equipment. "Their security arrangements are rudimentary," he observed, "and they are notoriously bad at keeping things to themselves." Indeed, Godfrey doubted Hill's contention that all American officers were pro-Ally. Some of them, he suspected, were Nazi sympathizers willing to reveal British secrets. Godfrey's apparent about-face requires some explanation. According to Captain Kirk, Godfrey had continued to support Anglo-American naval cooperation throughout the spring of 1940, but his memorandum had apparently been written in order to summarize the views of the majority at the Admiralty. They were not his own views. This conclusion is supported by Godfrey's action in backing American requests for information both before and after he wrote the memorandum.[36]

Whatever his reasons for making these statements, Godfrey influenced Churchill to alter his attitude to Anglo-American technical cooperation. However, as suggested, Godfrey did not represent the views of everyone at the Admiralty. C.S. Wright, the director of scientific research, remained an enthusiastic proponent of cooperation. On 2 May he stated that he was in favour of a technical exchange with the Americans and claimed that the further the British went towards "*complete* frankness the better."[37] Wright criticized the *quid pro quo* negotiations of the past. He struck at the heart of the distrust between the two countries: "Discussions in which both sides are trying to get a little bit more than they give will surely not encourage the kind of feelings which we would like the U.S. Navy to have; the effect is more likely to be the reverse."[38]

Wright maintained that Godfrey's and Somerville's concern about poor American security were not all that significant. Even if the allegations were true, he argued, most technical secrets "must become known to the enemy" in wartime anyway. He also pointed out that if Britain shared its secrets even if American material assistance was not forthcoming immediately, a great "moral" gain would be achieved and Anglo-American goodwill enhanced. Besides, it was in everyone's interest to see that the U.S. Navy was strong. This could only be accomplished by providing it with "the knowledge which we have gained and are now gaining by costly experience."[39]

Wright was no doubt echoing Tizard's arguments. Throughout the remainder of his tenure as scientific adviser to the chief of air staff, Tizard waged a diligent behind-the-scenes battle for swift approval of a comprehensive technical exchange. Just after the meeting on 3 May, he had checked the validity of Somerville's allegations with Group Captain R.W. Chappell of the Air Ministry's Directorate of Military Intelligence, and Chappell had assured him that there was no evidence of Americans leaking information to the Germans. This was corroborated a few days later when Air Vice-Marshal Peck informed Tizard that the Admiralty had provided the Air Ministry with no specific evidence of American security lapses.[40] Tizard made sure that people in high places were aware of the apparently spurious nature of the Admiralty's claims. As he asked one senior Air Ministry official, "Are we to assume that our intelligence service is quite incapable of extracting information from America and that the German intelligence service finds it quite easy?"[41]

It is difficult to assess how great a part scientists such as Tizard and Wright played in continuing the discussion on Anglo-American technical cooperation. It has already been shown that – with or without Tizard – the Air Ministry had a continuing interest in acquiring the Norden bombsight and in developing a more broadly based scientific and technical exchange. The flagging fortunes of the Allies in France, and the concurrent increase in the importance of the United States to Britain's survival, was undoubtedly a major factor. Certainly, interest was maintained at senior policy-making levels, despite the new prime minister's opposition.

At a meeting of the chiefs of staff on 18 May 1940, Sir Dudley Pound, the first sea lord, raised the issue of an exchange with the Americans. Pound disagreed with Godfrey's assessment of the risks involved in dealing with the United States, and he told the other service chiefs that recent information indicated that the Americans had important information on microwave radio tubes. Newall pressed for approval of a technical mission, but he was unable to arouse the interest of the army. General Sir Edmund Ironside, chief of the Imperial General Staff, stated that the army had no interest in the mission because it had no secrets to provide. This was no surprise, since the War Office had little interest in any American technology that was not already available. What was shocking was the reversal of the Admiralty's position. This meeting also was inconclusive, its only result being to ask Newall "to examine the proposal to pool secret information with the United States, and to report his conclusions."[42]

Pound was not satisfied with such indecision, and he decided to seek immediate political approval for the long-sought technical exchange. In his strong desire for this exchange, he was almost certainly influenced by C.S. Wright's memorandum of 2 May. On the same day as the meeting of the chiefs of staff, he prepared a note to A.V. Alexander, the new first lord of the Admiralty, on an Anglo-American technical exchange. This document closely followed Wright's earlier correspondence, both in wording and in the supporting arguments. Pound told his minister that a full and open exchange was necessary on all technical matters, including asdic, radar, anti-mining technology, bombsights, and radios, and he proposed that the best way to accomplish this "would be a definite proposal by the Prime Minister to President Roosevelt to pool all knowledge on naval technical matters."[43]

Alexander approved Pound's proposal the next day and ordered the drafting of a letter to Churchill.[44] This letter, sent on 20 May, followed Pound's ideas closely. It asked Churchill to make a direct appeal to Roosevelt for an "unrestricted offer to pool technical information" without appearing to "bargain."[45] But Churchill dismissed the Admiralty's proposal. He told Alexander on 21 May:

> I do of course appreciate very forcibly the importance of retaining the good will of the United States authorities and of extracting from them all the material they can give; but I should prefer to wait a few days before reaching a decision upon the proposal you make. I do not think that a wholesale offer of military secrets will count for much at the moment. I made an offer previously to give them the secret of the Asdics [*sic*] in exchange for their bomber sight, but it was not accepted. However, I will keep this new suggestion in mind until the moment is ripe.[46]

Churchill had made an Anglo-American technical exchange one of his bargaining chips for securing military assistance from the United States. For him, the question was no longer whether or not an exchange had any intrinsic value; that was irrelevant. What was important was that an exchange might encourage greater American support. Churchill was using a stick-and-carrot approach with the Americans. The stick came first, for Churchill hoped to bring Roosevelt to a more open and concrete commitment by refusing to provide assurances on the fate of the British fleet if the Germans invaded. The British fleet in Nazi hands would pose a major security threat to the United States. Churchill believed that a carrot could be offered to the Americans in a "few days," because he anticipated that they would offer some form of assistance in return for assurances that the British fleet would remain out of German hands. When the Americans refused to play Churchill's game – deciding that instead of offering aid, they would wait and see if the British survived – Churchill's position on giving military secrets to the Americans hardened. Even his closest confidants could not sway the stubborn prime minister.

Frederick Lindemann, Churchill's close friend and his scientific adviser, had long remained silent on the issue of technical cooperation with the United States. Although his attitude at this time to an Anglo-American technical exchange is unknown, he could not have given it his unequivocal support. Had he done so, Churchill would never have been so strident in his opposition. It is likely that Lindemann's silence stemmed from his reluctance to support one of Tizard's principal goals. Lindemann loathed Tizard because of his embarrassing expulsion from the Committee for the Scientific Survey of Air Defence in 1936. Tizard had been chairman of the committee, but he had resigned because of Lindemann's disruptive and ungentlemanly tactics in pressing for a policy that would have seen a more broad-based approach to aircraft detection, rather than concentrating only on the rapid development of radar technology, a course favoured by the majority of the committee. When every other member of the committee followed Tizard's lead, the committee had been reconstituted without Lindemann.

Lindemann had returned from the wilderness with Churchill in September 1939 and had followed his patron's meteoric rise to Downing Street. In May 1940, Churchill overhauled the organization of the Air Ministry, creating the Ministry of Aircraft Production to handle aircraft acquisition and development. As a result, much of the responsibility for scientific and technical development was stripped away from the Air Ministry, where Tizard remained as scientific adviser to the chief of air staff. Both the new minister of aircraft production, Lord Beaverbrook, and the new secretary of state for air, Sir Archibald Sinclair, were longtime political associates of Churchill. Increasingly, they turned to Lindemann for scientific advice.

By early June, Tizard was finding himself thwarted in his efforts to get any policies approved. Like other scientists, he was worried about Lindemann's growing power. Lindemann appeared to be the only one allowed to give technical and scientific advice to the War Cabinet. In early June, Tizard was informed by Watson-Watt about a meeting to be held at the Air Ministry on 7 June concerning future research and development work. Tizard had not been invited to this meeting. When he made inquiries, he was told by a senior ministry official that the meeting was of minor consequence and there was therefore no need for him to attend. Tizard attended anyway and was "very surprised to find a formal meeting at a very high plane with Professor Lindemann" as Sinclair's principal scientific adviser.

On 19 June, after a second meeting at the Air Ministry in which Lindemann was involved and from which he himself was deliberately excluded, Tizard felt that his position was becoming untenable. Not only was he outraged that Sinclair had created a parallel system of decision making that excluded him, but since he clearly could not command the confidence of the air minister, the minister of aircraft production, or the prime minister, he considered himself useless as a scientific adviser. The issue that finally forced him to resign was his opposition to the findings of R.V. Jones, a young physicist involved in scientific intelligence work for the Air Ministry. Jones had concluded that the Germans had developed a radio navigation system for accurate night bombing. This was the device known as *Knickebein*. Tizard, who was already deeply upset by his declining influence, disagreed with Jones's conclusions despite a considerable amount of evidence to the contrary. Tizard's judgment may have been affected by Lindemann's support of Jones's theory. At all events, when it became apparent that his advice concerning the beams was being ignored, he felt compelled to resign. As he told Sinclair, "Too many cooks spoil the broth … I feel, therefore, that I should resign my position and thus rid you of one of the spoiling cooks."[47] It was a bitter parting, especially as Jones was proved correct a few days later. The German beams were detected at exactly the place and frequency where Jones had said they would be. It did not matter that this was one of the few times that Tizard was ever wrong about a major technical policy decision. The incident simply accelerated his departure from the Air Ministry.[48]

Meanwhile, Lindemann had an apparent change of heart and began to support the idea of a technical exchange with the Americans. This was probably because now that his efforts to remove Tizard were meeting with success, he felt free to promote a good idea even if it was one that Tizard had championed. Thus, on 5 June, Lindemann told Churchill that a technical exchange with the Americans should go forward because of the urgent need for one thousand Norden bombsights, "which would be installed in our machines, since there seems little prospect of stabilizing our own sights this summer." Lindemann added that the ability to "hit our targets from a greater height might make all the difference."[49] But still Churchill could not be swayed – even by Lindemann. The day before receiving Lindemann's message, Churchill had shown the depths of his anger towards the Americans in a message sent to the Canadian prime minister, William Lyon Mackenzie King. King had asked Churchill whether or not the fleet would be transferred to the United States if the Germans invaded Great Britain, and Churchill told King why he would not provide these assurances: "Although the President is our friend, no practical help has been forthcoming from the United States. We have not expected them to send military aid, but they have not even sent any worthy contribution in destroyers or planes, or by a visit of their fleet to Southern Irish ports."[50] Churchill dismissed Lindemann's request in a similar fashion. He told his old friend that he was "not inclined" to pursue technical exchanges because he was "waiting for further developments of the American attitude."[51]

Rebuffed, Lindemann was unwilling to press Churchill further. Now that Tizard, one of the main advocates of the concept, was isolated, it seemed unlikely that an Anglo-American technical exchange would take place. With no one to pursue the matter, it might very well have been forgotten as Churchill tried to come to grips with the defeat of France and the risks of continuing to fight without a major ally. Although the Americans' failure to become actively involved had been Churchill's reason for refusing to approve an information exchange, no progress was made towards sending a British technical and scientific mission to the United States even when Roosevelt authorized the first major shipments of arms to Great Britain on 12 June.

The situation might have remained unchanged if A.V. Hill had not hurried back to England on 13 June because of the official silence that had greeted Lord Lothian's telegram of 23 April. Tizard and other scientists had been keeping Hill informed of the opposition to the idea of technical cooperation, and Hill returned because of his fervent belief that the exchange was crucial if Britain was to survive.[52] On 18 June he completed two reports on his mission. He outlined his appreciation of American technical capabilities and drafted a carefully crafted plan for improving Anglo-American technical relations. The plan had been worked out by Hill with the help of Felix Frankfurter.[53] Hill warned that the British "assumption of superiority, and a failure to appreciate the easy terms on which closer American collaboration could be secured may help to lose the war." The Americans, he argued, had a "strong desire" to help, but "the same fetish of secrecy exists in the service departments in the USA as in Great Britain." Hill believed that American resources would be made available only "by a frank offer to exchange information and experience." He dismissed any concerns that the Americans might leak secrets to the enemy. If the Americans entered the war in any foreseeable situation, they would do so in support of Great Britain, and it would therefore "not be in their interest to pass that information to the enemy."[54]

As a first step, Hill envisioned sending a scientific attaché to Ottawa. The attaché would not only assist the Canadians in their scientific and advanced-technology industrial mobilization, but he would begin to lay the groundwork for Anglo-American technical cooperation. Hill believed that his successor should be based in Ottawa, for he had been warned by American friends that placing a permanent scientific liaison officer in Washington might cause political problems with isolationists. The scientific attaché could set the stage for a technical mission in the near future.[55]

Hill ensured that his reports were circulated widely. Among those who received a copy of them was Lindemann. Hill also sent him a formal proposal of how a technical exchange should be implemented. Like others before him, he called for a direct appeal to Roosevelt. The British government should offer the American government, "without condition," all "scientific and technical information in connection with the war, and any service experience relating to it." In return, it was hoped that all the "restrictions on information or purchases" that existed in the United States would be modified.[56] Like the other scientists who supported the mission, Hill was obviously unaware of recent developments at the senior levels of government. The question at the Cabinet level was not whether a mission should take place but when it should proceed. Hill, therefore, brought nothing original to the debate, his main contribution being the contents of Lothian's telegram of 23 April, but what he did do was to act as a catalyst to ensure that the concept of a technical exchange was not forgotten.

Hill's reports were read with great interest by Archibald Sinclair, the secretary of state for air, who met with him on 22 June. Sinclair at first refused to support Hill's proposal unreservedly; but three days later, after a meeting with Air Marshal Joubert, he changed his mind.[57] Joubert was the member of the Air Staff responsible for radar, and in June, as Tizard's influence had begun to wane, he had taken a leading role in promoting the mission. Joubert had at first attempted to solicit approval directly from 10 Downing Street, and when this failed he had tried to persuade his minister to intervene with Churchill. Joubert had briefed Sinclair on new intelligence indicating that the radar secret was already compromised.[58]

As early as 14 May, senior Air Ministry officials had believed that Germany had its own radar system, and information supporting this conclusion had appeared in that month's "Air Ministry Scientific Intelligence, Monthly Summary." According to the article, a refugee German scientist had reported that in 1931 a Bremen radio company had demonstrated the detection of reflected radio waves. The report added that "a German prisoner whose scientific enthusiasm outweighs his discretion, [had] stated that the Germans now have a coastal chain of stations which detect British aircraft by reflection methods."[59] Joubert believed these reports and thus argued that "we might as well make a virtue of a necessity and let the Americans have [radar] while it has some value."[60]

Sinclair agreed to approach Churchill once more, and on 25 June he wrote to the prime minister, asking if he felt that the time was now "ripe" to make the offer of a technical exchange with the Americans. Sinclair outlined once again all the now familiar arguments for the exchange. He pointed out the increasing American support, Hill's belief that the Americans had much to offer both technically and industrially, and the fact that the Germans already possessed most British technical secrets.[61] Churchill, who for the moment was pleased with the state of Anglo-American relations, finally agreed that technical cooperation could proceed forthwith. On 30 June he told Sinclair that a technical mission could be sent to the United States, "provided the specific secrets and items of exchange are reported beforehand."[62] Although Churchill would later regret his decision, it could not be undone. In less than a week, steps were taken that made the Anglo-American technical exchange inevitable.

4 An Irrevocable Decision

On 8 July 1940, Lord Lothian was finally able to proceed with his long-delayed proposal to begin technical cooperation with the United States. On that day he sent an *aide-mémoire* to President Roosevelt informing him that the British government had decided on "an immediate and general interchange of secret technical information." Significantly, the policy of *quid pro quo* had come to an end, for Lothian explained that the proposal was not to be "the subject of a bargain of any description." Instead, he said, the British government, "in order to show their readiness for the fullest cooperation, [wished] to be perfectly open with you [the president] and to give you full details of any equipment or devices in which you are interested without in any way pressing you beforehand to give specific undertakings on your side, although they would hope you would reciprocate by discussing certain secret information of a technical nature which they are anxious to have urgently." If this was agreeable, said Lothian, a small technical mission "of two or three service officers and service scientists" would be sent immediately to discuss a variety of technical issues. The discussions would focus on radio applications, particularly radar (this was the first time a representative of the British government had officially given the Americans any confirmation of the existence of this top secret device). The only specific request Lothian made was for access to the U.S. radio industry, particulary in getting information on ultrashort-wave technology. In order to give the Americans no reason to reject the British proposal, no mention was made of the Norden bombsight. This was as Lothian had first proposed to London in April.[1]

The decision to exclude the Norden bombsight from the exchange was specifically designed to prevent it from once again derailing Anglo-American technical cooperation. The situation had altered so much since the beginning of the war that the Norden secret, while still desirable, was no longer considered of vital importance to Britain. It is impossible to state exactly when this transformation in British attitudes occurred, but it undoubtedly started with Hill's mission in the spring. It can also be tied to the fact that daylight strategic bombing by the Royal Air Force had failed to play a decisive role in fighting Germany. Instead of being invincible, the RAF bombers had proved to be highly vulnerable to the German defences. The war had shown that other technologies, particularly radar, were far more significant. The German conquest of France was another major factor. In the summer of 1940, it had become much more important to galvanize American support for the overall British war effort than to keep on demanding the bombsight. Thus, in July 1940, no one in Britain, with one major exception, considered American obstinacy over this matter to be of any great consequence. It was only hoped that British technological largesse might alter the American attitude, but no preconditions were demanded.

Lothian's proposal to Roosevelt came after a week of rapid decision making by the British government, following Churchill's tentative approval on 30 June of an Anglo-American technical exchange. Even before Churchill approved the measure, bureaucrats and senior officers had been coming round to the view that a mission to North America would be of great benefit. This quick response was the result of their general consensus. The pressure from Lothian for action on his April telegram was another contributing factor. On receiving no reply to his initial proposal, he had become increasingly frustrated, for he believed that an offer to exchange technical information was an ideal medium for improving Anglo-American relations. It was Lothian who encouraged Hill to return to England in June to lobby for a technical mission to the United States; and when Hill failed to make immediate progress, Lothian telegraphed the Foreign Office to express his disappointment that he had still received no reply to his April proposal. In this telegram of 27 June, Lothian stated that although he had not yet discussed the matter with Roosevelt personally, he had reason to believe that the president would agree to a technical exchange; this would result in the full cooperation of the American army, navy, and commercial firms. Inaction on this issue, Lothian warned, would only provide "another argument for the defeatists who say that it is of no use backing a lost cause."[2]

It is uncertain whether Lothian's telegram had any influence on Churchill, for it was not distributed outside the Foreign Office until 1 July, the day after the prime minister finally endorsed the project.[3] Two aspects of the telegram are particularly fascinating: the importance the British ambassador placed on a technical exchange, and just how little information had been imparted to him by the Foreign Office. The only person in the United Kingdom with whom Lothian had contact on this subject was Tizard – via letters received by Hill. Lothian specifically mentioned Tizard's support (which shows his ignorance of Tizard's fall from favour within the government).[4]

All Lothian could do while awaiting word from London was to continue his attempts to secure access to supplies of the Norden bombsight. Accordingly, he raised the question with Roosevelt on 1 July, though to no avail. The president told him that when the British could prove that the Germans themselves had a bombsight "which was more or less equivalent in efficiency to [the] Norden sight," or when the British produced an equivalent sight, he would be able to get Congress to release supplies. The implication was clear: supplying the Norden sight was still politically impossible.[5]

Lothian's pressure on the Foreign Office to reach a decision regarding a technical exchange undoubtedly influenced the speed with which he was finally authorized to approach Roosevelt about one. The Air Ministry rushed through a draft telegram for approval by both the Admiralty and the Foreign Office, and it was dispatched to Washington on 6 July, only seven days after Churchill's decision. The telegram was the basis of Lothian's *aide-mémoire*.[6] While Lothian may have been somewhat out of touch with events in London, he was, as Halifax had suspected when he appointed him, an excellent judge of Americans. Lothian was correct in believing that Roosevelt would endorse the arrival of a British technical mission in the United States; and by going directly to the president, Lothian knew that he would circumvent any opposition to the plan from the State Department, the army, or the navy. The British offer did indeed meet with an enthusiastic response from the Roosevelt administration. It was tentatively approved by the American cabinet on 11 July, and Lothian was apprised of this confidentially by the State Department on 18 July.[7] Four days later, he was officially informed that Roosevelt "would be glad if [the] special mission could come as soon as possible."[8]

Since there is no existing personal correspondence on the subject, Roosevelt's motivation for approving the mission remains unclear. Earlier studies of Anglo-American relations during the period following the German attack on France have claimed that Roosevelt gave his continual support to Great Britain throughout the rest of 1940. However, in a recent study, David Reynolds has argued that Roosevelt's attitude went through three distinct phases. In the first phase, which lasted until the French surrender, Roosevelt did everything possible to assist the Allies; during the second period, from mid-June to the beginning of August, "he trod water," uncertain of Britain's fate and positive that he could offer no support; and in the third and final phase, which began in early August, he decided to do all he could to support the British. This third phase culminated in the destroyers-for-bases deal on 2 September.[9] Roosevelt's decision to support the technical mission falls firmly into the middle period of uncertainty. On the surface, this appears to contradict Reynold's analysis, since we have Roosevelt making a firm decision to assist the British. But the technical mission cost Roosevelt little either politically or militarily. Indeed, politically it cost him nothing; the mission's small size and the need to preserve security meant that it was unlikely to catch the attention of Congress or the press. Militarily, it was seen as causing no immediate reduction in American military capabilities (unlike the many British requests for in-stock equipment that were made in the summer of 1940). Very likely, Roosevelt appreciated that the United States would be the main beneficiary of the exchange, for his country could expect to gain invaluable knowledge on the combat performance of a wide range of military hardware.

Also important in shaping the president's decision was the fact that many of Roosevelt's closest advisers and confidants supported the British proposal. There was general agreement with the British scheme in the American cabinet. Both Henry Stimson, the secretary of war, and Frank Knox, the secretary of the navy, were supporters of closer ties with Great Britain. They endorsed the proposal at the cabinet meeting on 11 July, pending consultations with their military advisers to work out the details.[10]

As we have seen, Justice Felix Frankfurter, a close friend of Roosevelt, had advised A.V. Hill about how to make the offer of a technical exchange acceptable to the American president.[11] Similar assistance had come from Vannevar Bush, who kept Lothian and other embassy staff well briefed on administration discussions on the matter. Bush had joined the administration as head of the National Defense Research Committee (NDRC), the civilian-run defence scientific agency which had been established by presidential order on 27 June 1940. On 8 July, Bush met with George Pirie, who was now an air commodore, and discussed the British mission, offering advice on how to present the proposal to the administration. He had suggested that he hold clandestine meetings on the subject at Pirie's home along with Brigadier Charles Lindemann, the army attaché. In part, Bush made the offer because he wished to be kept informed on the British mission and trusted neither the American army nor the navy to do so. This was the beginning of the NDRC's close relationship with the British Technical Mission; it was to have a pronounced effect on the long-term impact of the mission in the United States.[12]

Despite President Roosevelt's approval, the British proposal triggered some significant objections from the American military. Admiral H.G. Bowen, the director of the Naval Research Laboratory, believed that the information he expected to get from the British on radar and sonar would "possibly prove disappointing." He argued: "For a nation that has been so backward in mechanical and electrical engineering as applied to naval vessels to have established outstanding progress in two other fields of engineering does not seem credible, although it may be possible."[13] Brigadier General George Strong, the assistant chief of staff, War Plans Division, echoed his department's rejection of Kingsley Wood's earlier offer to exchange radar technology; he stated that the army thought that the offer to send the British mission to the United States was "aimed at getting full information in regard to our airplane detector, which apparently is much more efficient than the British have."[14] However, most American officers waited eagerly for the British Technical Mission's arrival, anticipating that they would get a great deal of invaluable information. Although the Americans were still convinced that they had little to learn from the British in terms of technology, it was generally agreed that a great deal would be gleaned about how modern weapon systems performed in combat.

Throughout the spring and summer of 1940, Captain Kirk, the U.S. naval attaché in London, had continued to press for broader Anglo-American technical cooperation, and he had managed to get some support from the Admiralty. American officers, for example, had been allowed to view the damage done to Royal Navy warships by German mines, bombs, and torpedoes. Kirk had also been given samples of captured German magnetic mines, British minesweeping equipment, and degaussing gear. But, as he reported, there was still a great deal of misgiving about furnishing him with any information. He pleaded with his superiors in Washington to show some offical interest in what was being provided and to offer some technical data in return. Although Kirk's pleas went unanswered, the U.S. Navy made at least some provision for a broader technical exchange. In May, Admiral H.R. Stark, the chief of naval operations, ordered the establishment of a committee under the chairmanship of the chief of naval intelligence; its task was to coordinate the interests of the various naval bureaus pending a general Anglo-American technical exchange.[15]

By 22 July the U.S. War and Navy Departments had formally approved a "full and free interchange of technical information." Two conditions were imposed by the military: firstly, that no equipment would be supplied to the British until it was determined that this would not interfere with the American armed forces' own procurement schedules; secondly, that no information would be provided on a few items of a highly sensitive nature. Excluded from the exchange was the still politically sensitive Norden bombsight. Another nine items of marginal military significance were on the list, having been placed there to protect commercial patent holders from British competitors. Both services placed their intelligence chiefs in charge of coordinating their discussions with the British mission. Representing the War Department would be General Sherman Miles, assistant chief of staff, G-2; for the navy, Rear Admiral Walter S. Anderson, chief of naval intelligence.[16] On 29 July the State Department sent Lothian official approval of the mission as outlined in his *aide-mémoire*.[17]

Thus, by 18 July, it appeared that the stage was set for a general Anglo-American technical exchange. Further steps had been taken in Britain to ensure the mission's success. Also, within a week of Churchill's approval, it had been decided to act on one other vital aspect of Hill's recommendations – the appointment of a permanent scientific attaché to the British high commission in Ottawa. By 6 July, Professor R.H. Fowler had been appointed to this post. He had been recommended by Hill while the latter was still in the United States. Hill believed that the person responsible for scientific liaison with North America must be a highly qualified man who was well known to scientists on both sides of the Atlantic. Fowler, he believed, was the most qualified man available.

Fowler had been Plummer professor of mathematical physics at Trinity College, Cambridge. He was Lord Rutherford's son-in-law and had been appointed to head the National Physical Laboratories just before the commencement of hostilities. However, shortly after this appointment he had suffered a stroke, which had forced him to resign his position. When the war began, he informed Hill that he would take on any war assignment he was offered, despite the risk to his fragile health. With all other important scientists involved in vital war work, Hill remembered Fowler's generous offer – and Fowler decided "that it was more important that he should go to Canada than that he should have an additional year of life."[18] By the third week of July, he was on his way across the Atlantic.

One might assume that once the political decisions to launch the mission had been made, the period preceding its departure would be of little interest, involving merely bureaucratic organization. In fact, the opposite was true. We can see in the detailed planning for the mission the intrinsic difficulties of what had been proposed. The British had offered to trade their most closely guarded technical military secrets with a country which, though a friendly neutral, was not an ally. Technical cooperation with a non-allied power of the type proposed goes against the most ingrained instincts of any military officer. Military technical information, particularly new weapon systems not yet in service, are among the most zealously guarded secrets of any nation. There was still a great deal of suspicion on both sides, and the mission could easily have been stymied before it began. In the case of the United States, it was Roosevelt's support, plus the cravings of the Navy and War Departments for battlefield information, that ensured success. In London, it was the realization that Britain's paramount concern was improving Anglo-American relations.

The major points of discussion in Great Britain involved both the composition of the mission and the precise substance of the offer to the Americans. The Air Ministry, as it had done since the autumn of 1939, took the lead in organizing the mission. It had drafted for the Foreign Office the telegram approving the mission which was sent to Lothian on 6 July. The man responsible for developing the ministry's position was Air Marshal Sir Philip Joubert. As the assistant chief of staff (radio), he was responsible for all aspects of radar research and development. Joubert called a meeting at the Air Ministry for 9 July. It was attended by representatives of the War Office, the Admiralty, and the Ministry of Supply, along with Watson-Watt and Hill. Noticeably absent from this list was Tizard, who had been effectively excluded from Air Ministry decision making. Before the meeting, Joubert submitted a brief outlining his proposals for a mission to leave on 17 July for at least three weeks in the United States. He envisioned the mission as representing all three services and expected that all information which "the departments consider [might] be released" would be given to the Americans. Although Joubert stated that this would be a "free" exchange, he hoped that in return the Americans would provide "for [the] manufacture in the USA of the required equipment." He anticipated talks being held with Canadian authorities in order to begin the research, development, and production of advanced-technology equipment in that country.[19] Joubert believed that the mission should focus its attention on providing information on radar and aircraft turrets. He was convinced that it would get information on "ultra-short wave radio, *bombsights*, and other important information which the Americans may be prepared to release."[20]

All the departments at the meeting – with the exception of the Admiralty – agreed to the composition of a team that would primarily concern itself with radar. The Air Ministry had determined that it would send a serving officer and a scientist; the War

Office would send a signals officer; and the Ministry of Supply would send Professor John Cockcroft, one of Britain's leading physicists. It was agreed that a Canadian representative would accompany the mission and that thought should be given to including an Australian. The Admiralty was not yet sure that it would take part, since it was considering sending its own separate technical team.[21] Thus, Joubert's emphasis on radar had skewed the composition of the mission so that it had expertise only in this one technology. There was no major overhaul of composition of the mission, despite the fact that it was asked before it left to discuss a much broader spectrum of technologies.

The Admiralty refused to commit any naval personnel because senior naval officers and officials were engaged in an extensive debate on the value of the mission. This debate began on 4 July when C.S. Wright, the director of scientific research, indicated his continued support for the mission as long as first-rate people were sent.[22] Admiral Sir Sydney Bailey, however, opposed sending a technical mission to the United States and attempted to get the Admiralty to reject the Air Ministry's draft telegram to Lothian. Bailey, a retired former director of the Admiralty's Planning Committee, had been recalled to duty in June to head a committee that was to make preparations for forthcoming staff talks with senior American naval officers. These talks had been approved by Churchill on 30 June, the very day he had agreed to allow the technical mission to be sent to the United States.[23] Bailey argued that the mission would deal strictly with "technical questions of a material nature and of secondary consideration," whereas the naval staff talks would cover all aspects of naval warfare. Because these talks would naturally include technical questions, his argument ran, the technical mission was unnecessary. But if, despite his objections, a joint mission was still to be sent, Bailey believed that a naval officer should head it.[24]

Nevertheless, Vice-Admiral T.S.V. ("Tom") Phillips, the vice-chief of naval staff, rebuffed Bailey's proposal because the "the two things are really quite different and it is probable that those taking part in the technical discussions will not even know that the Naval Staff talks are taking place at all." The technical mission had to take place in the United States, he asserted, because its primary goal was to get American industry to manufacture radar and other equipment for the British armed forces; and a RAF officer should head the mission because radar was supposed to be the main subject of discussion. A.V. Alexander, the first lord of the Admiralty, concurred with Phillips, and both approved the Air Ministry's draft telegram to Lothian.[25]

What Phillips did know and Bailey (who had been absent from the Admiralty since before the beginning of the war) did not was that it had become generally accepted since May that a technical mission with naval representation should be sent to the United States. As early as April, the Admiralty had been compiling a list of technical information it wanted from the Americans and of data it was willing to trade in exchange.[26] In early July, with the mission approved, the director of naval intelligence began consulting all the chiefs of the technical directorates about what they were willing to have discussed with the Americans and what they hoped to get in return.

Some, including C.S. Wright, the director of scientific research, and Captain A.G. Talbot, the director of anti-submarine warfare, enthusiastically endorsed full participation. But Captain M.S. Slattery, the director of air matérial, continued to argue that the exchange should be only on a reciprocal basis. Others were outright opposed to further exchange. As Captain H.C. Phillips, the director of torpedoes and mines, pointed out, the U.S. Navy had already been provided with information on the new German magnetic mine, "with all the measurements taken from them, together with an actual mine complete" with its firing mechanism; data had also been provided on magnetic minesweeping and degaussing gear. Phillips was incensed. Not only had the Americans provided nothing in return, but they had failed to respond when his department required new measurements on the mine that had been given to them. Evincing an angry tone rarely displayed in internal Admiralty memoranda, Phillips reminded his colleagues that the value of the information the Admiralty proposed to give the Americans could not be measured in monetary terms. On the contrary, it represented "knowledge won at a great price" and was "the outcome of intense effort and application." The Americans, he concluded, had nothing to offer his department.[27] So intense was his opposition that Admiral Tom Phillips asked Admiral Bruce Fraser to decide the extent of Admiralty participation in the mission. Fraser was the third sea lord and naval controller and was therefore the man in charge of all the technical departments.[28]

Fraser's initial reaction to Admiralty participation in the mission was less than enthusiastic. Although in May he had supported a free exchange of information with the Americans, by 13 July he was listening to his director of torpedoes and mines. He finally decided that the Admiralty would receive "very little" in any exchange and that consequently no highly qualified scientists should "waste their time" in the United States. Fraser concluded that there would be no immediate practical results from the mission and that the only possible positive effects would be political. Naval representation, he declared, would be confined to members of the British Admiralty Technical Mission, which had just been sent to Canada to supervise naval production.[29]

On 18 July, Fraser modified his position somewhat. This was due no doubt to C.S. Wright's continued lobbying and to the Air Ministry's decision to limit the technical discussions to radar. At this time Fraser authorized Commander Crossman of the Signal School, who was soon to be sent to Canada as part of the British Admiralty Technical Mission, to act on the Admiralty's behalf. Fraser believed that the U.S. Navy should be given access to other information, such as asdic and magnetic mines, but only if specifically asked for. This information would then be given to the American naval attaché in London; it would not be provided as part of the technical mission to Washington. Although Fraser conceded that something might be learned in further conversations with the Americans, he expected little from them in return.[30]

Political developments soon shattered Fraser's hopes that the mission would be limited to radar and that the Admiralty's participation in it would be minimal. This was because of a cabinet decision on the issue. When the proposal for the technical exchange was brought before the War Cabinet in late July, it was by no means as certain to win approval as had been the case in the American cabinet two weeks earlier. This was not because of the differences in the two systems of executive government. It was entirely because of Churchill's erratic behaviour. On 30 June, when he had approved the mission, Churchill had felt confident that Anglo-American relations were progressing well, and he had thus agreed to initiatives such as the mission and the military staff talks in order to bring about further improvements. By mid-July, however, the Roosevelt administration's hesitancy to provide destroyers and other emergency war material had made Churchill rethink the scheduling of the mission. On 17 July – the day before the War Cabinet was scheduled to meet to sanction the mission officially – Churchill was in a very different mood. He sent General Ismay, his liaison with the chiefs of staff, a remarkable memorandum – one in which he tried to scuttle the emerging Anglo-American technical exchange, thus undoing all that had been achieved in this area since early 1940. His timing was little short of outrageous, for it was written six days after the American cabinet had approved the British government's official proposal. The text is worth quoting in full:

> What is the urgency of this matter? Who is making the fuss and what happens if we do not give an immediate decision? Are we going to throw our secrets into the American lap, and see what they give us in exchange? If so, I am against it. It would be very much better to go slow, as we have far more to give than they. If an exchange is to be arranged, I should like to carry it out piece by piece; if we give them our Asdic, they give us their Norden bomb-sight; if we give them our RDF [radar], they give us their highly developed short-wave gadgetry. Generally speaking, I am not in a hurry to give our secrets until the United States is much nearer to the war than she is now. I expect that anything given to the United States services, in which there is necessarily so many Germans, goes pretty quickly to Berlin in times of peace.[31]

The War Cabinet discussions on the technical exchange, which were scheduled for the next day, were cancelled without explanation.[32]

J.V. Perowne of the Foreign Office's American Section saw dangerous if not sinister implications behind the rescheduling of the War Cabinet meeting for one week later. The meeting's agenda had called for the "discussion of policy and the proposal to send a technical mission to the USA." This implied that no policy decision had yet been made. Yet if this policy had not been agreed to, why, he wondered, had the Foreign Office sent its proposal to Lothian on 6 July. He was also concerned that mixing the technical mission with the staff talks would dilute technical discussions. A separate technical mission, on the other hand, would broaden contacts with the American services. Perowne suspected that Lord

Beaverbrook, the minister of aircraft production, was behind the move to remake the policy decisions. He interpeted Beaverbrook's "refusal" to come to the War Cabinet meeting as indicative of his opposition to giving away information to the United States.[33] There is no evidence to support this view, and in fact there is much to suggest that Beaverbrook was in favour of an Anglo-American technical exchange.[34] Perhaps Perowne had heard rumours that someone important in the War Cabinet was having second thoughts about the mission, and it did not occur to him that this someone might be the prime minister himself.

Anxiety increased in the Foreign Office when Lothian informed London on 18 July that the Americans had apparently made a favourable decision. There was again consternation four days later when it was learned that the president had formally approved a British technical mission. From the Foreign Office's perspective, any change in the proposal would undermine the very basis of its American policy. Lord Halifax, the foreign secretary, had informed his Cabinet colleagues on 18 July that the improvement in Anglo-American relations could be achieved only "through the habitual exercise of friendly assistance freely given, together with a general recognition of the other country's needs and feelings."[35]

Perowne was convinced that it would "surely be suicidal" to go back on the offer that Roosevelt had approved.[36] Halifax agreed and wrote to Churchill just before the meeting on the twenty-fifth. He wanted to make things absolutely clear to Churchill: there could be no question of going back on sending the mission, and the War Cabinet should limit its discussion to the "extent and nature of the information to be disclosed to the Americans." In this regrad, Halifax argued that the mission should have the most "liberal" mandate and should be able to provide information in as many areas as possible.[37]

On the evening of 25 July the War Cabinet and senior advisers met at 10 Downing Street to determine the fate of the mission. Churchill opened the meeting by announcing that Roosevelt knew of the British proposal for a technical mission to the United States and "wanted it." Perowne, who represented the Foreign Office, must have been relieved that Halifax's message had worked and that there was to be no discussion about not sending the mission. All the various positions were summarized. Admiral Fraser alone continued to express doubts about the utility of giving the Americans secret information, and he insisted that the technical exchange should take place in London. On the other hand, Alexander, Beaverbrook, Joubert, and Sinclair all spoke in its favour. They were influenced by the technical and production resources of the United States that might become available. H.J. Gough, the director of scientific research at the Ministry of Supply, argued in favour of the technical mission for quite a different reason; it was vital, he said, that British experts should have the opportunity to survey American industrial and scientific facilities. Churchill then decided that the mission would proceed and that it would be broadly based, with all service and supply departments sending participants. Significantly, he decided that it would be headed by "a personality of outstanding eminence in the scientific world," and he proposed as the most suitable man to lead it none other than Sir Henry Tizard. The motion received enthusiastic support.[38]

Historians have always been puzzled why Tizard was chosen. He was, after all, a man on his way out; he was literally packing his files and leaving the Air Ministry. Some have speculated that the appointment was simply to get him safely out of the way. They see it as proof that Churchill regarded the mission as of little consequence. Yet despite his doubts, Churchill now wanted the mission to proceed. Lindemann, the man often associated with plots to get rid of Tizard, also supported it. Although he may have seen Tizard's appointment as a convenient way to rid himself of a still troublesome man, his backing of the mission is unquestionable.

Tizard was still without an official position, yet he continued his fight with Churchill's scientific adviser throughout July. Although he now knew that Lindemann had been right in supporting R.V. Jones about German navigation beams, he still considered the scientific adviser a very dangerous man. On 22 July, Tizard completed a lengthy summary of his opponent's incompetence and obstructionist behaviour, for these were the very qualities that had been hampering the development of air defence since the mid-1930s. Tizard's concluding statement was damning:

> Speaking generally, I cannot think of any original idea of Lindemann's that has been of practical value ... The trouble is that the man with the wrong ideas has had to support him all the drive and enthusiasm of

> Mr. Winston Churchill, whereas my Committee [for the Scientific Survey of Air Defence] has not had the corresponding support. The result has been wasted effort, and dislocation of work. There has been on the other hand, a complete lack of executive drive behind the recommendations of my Committee, with the result that we are now short of weapons and methods that would have been available had we been in the fortunate position of advising Mr. Winston Churchill. I have the documentary evidence for this statement, and am preparing it.[39]

Whether Lindemann had any knowledge of Tizard's continuing campaign against him remains unclear, but in all likelihood he suspected some sort of attack. Certainly, Tizard's appointment to head the mission sidetracked him from his efforts to diminish Lindemann's influence.

Lindemann's desire to remove Tizard from London may explain why he did not object to the latter's appointment. Yet this was not the primary reason why Tizard was offered the post. In fact, he was not the only candidate. Several people had already been offered the leadership – including, Joubert, Air Vice-Marshal Hill, Sir Frank Smith, and even Lindemann himself – and all had declined, citing vital commitments to the war effort. Beaverbrook, who had been made the cabinet minister responsible for the mission, had been despondent about finding the right person. He had told Churchill, "I cannot imagine what to do next."[40]

Other possible candidates had been deemed unsuitable: A.V. Hill, Watson-Watt, Admiral Chatfield the former first sea lord, and Professor John Cockcroft. Although Hill was a brilliant and versatile scientist, he was a physiologist and would be unable to engage in complex technical discussions with American radar experts.[41] Hill's connection with the Royal Society also had made him unsuitable, for the services believed that the Royal Society had been attempting to take the organization of scientific resources away from them in order to create a separate centralized civilian scientific agency. They had resisted this pressure successfully, but they were unlikely to trust Hill with such an important task.[42] Hill had also been one of Lindemann's staunchest opponents. Since Tizard's resignation in June, he had been leading the increasingly bitter battle against Lindemann's apparent monopoly on providing scientific and technical advice to both the prime minister and the War Cabinet. Tizard's memorandum about

Lindemann cited above was used as an appendix to a larger report written by Hill. This report was titled "On the Making of Technical Decisions by H.M. Government."[43] Finally, Hill was now an active member of Parliament and thus a public figure whose arrival in the United States would draw attention to what was intended to be a private affair. As for the other possible candidates for the position, Watson-Watt was highly unpredictable and often tactless, and was therefore unsuitable for a mission that required great diplomatic skill. Chatfield had made an enemy of Churchill in the First World War and had not yet been forgiven. Cockcroft and other government scientists had been considered too heavily involved in war work to be spared for more than a few weeks. Cockcroft's superior at the Ministry of Supply, H.J. Gough, would give him permission to take part in the mission only if his stay lasted no more than three weeks.[44]

By contrast, Tizard was available, was well liked by most in the Air Ministry staff, and was probably the most knowledgeable and capable defence scientist in Great Britain. Many people had been angered by the way he had been treated, and it is very likely that his appointment was seen as a way of making amends. Tizard's appointment was designed not to weaken the mission but to strengthen it. His nomination gave it a much greater chance of success. As Air Marshal A.W. Tedder wrote on 16 July 1940, "It is clear that by far the best leader would be Sir Henry Tizard, who combines the wide scientific knowledge needed with the knowledge of operational requirements, and who has an international standing as a scientist."[45]

Tizard's diary reveals that he first learned of his appointment on 20 July when he went to the Ministry of Aircraft Production to meet Beaverbrook. In a hallway at the ministry he encountered Richard Fairy, who told him, "I'm going to be a member of your staff." When Tizard asked what staff, Fairy mentioned the mission. Since Beaverbrook was said to be busy, Tizard was ushered into the office of Sir Archibald Rowlands, the permanent secretary. Rowlands informed Tizard that the prime minister wanted him to lead a mission to America "for the exchange of technical information," and he handed Tizard a "provisional lists of 'secrets'" that were to be imparted to the Americans and a list of information that was to be asked for in return. These lists were probably confined to the radar technology which the Air Ministry wanted.

Tizard was not impressed. He wrote in his diary: "I said I would not go unless I was given a free hand & that I did not want to go in any case unless the mission was really important for the war. It looked to me at first sight as a rather neat method of getting a rather troublesome person out of the way for a time!" Rowlands then assured Tizard that the mission "was regarded as really important," but Tizard insisted that the service departments be telephoned so that he could find out who was going along. The Air Ministry, it turned out, was contemplating sending only a flight lieutenant, and the War Office did not think it worth including a representative at all. Tizard told Rowlands that this was "absurd" and made it clear that he would not go unless the military sent senior officers. That evening he met with Joubert, who probably told him that the Air Ministry considered the mission to be of supreme importance and that a senior officer would be included.[46]

A War Cabinet meeting five days later dealt with most of Tizard's concerns. The services were instructed to submit lists immediately of what technologies they planned to give to the Americans. It was made clear by all the politicians that cooperation must be complete and wide-ranging. Within the next two days the Admiralty agreed to supply information on asdic and anti-aircraft guns, and the RAF said it would do so on all aspects of radar, particularly microwave equipment. The War Office was still uncertain how to become directly involved, but it was now seriously considering sending a senior officer.[47] Churchill made it clear on 27 July that he was anxious for the mission to proceed forthwith, so Tizard began the final stages of organizing it.[48]

Tizard had by now secured the full cooperation of all the service departments, but he still had two major hurdles to overcome – Beaverbrook and Churchill. Beaverbrook, as minister of aircraft production, had been gradually taking over all the Air Ministry's technical research and development responsibilities, and by 12 July he had become the minister responsible for the Anglo-American technical exchange.[49] Although he had expressed some doubts about the mission in early July, he had soon changed his mind. Joubert had persuaded him to give it his full support when the Ministry of Aircraft Production took over the organization of the mission from the Air Ministry.[50] Tizard's problem was that he did not enjoy a harmonious relationship with Beaverbrook. In fact,

Beaverbrook avoided meeting him throughout the period leading up to Tizard's departure for North America. On 31 July, Tizard confronted Air Marshal Sir Wilfred Freeman, director of development at the Ministry of Aircraft Production, and asked why Beaverbrook had not seen him. Freeman said that Beaverbrook was still upset by the fact that Tizard had refused to meet him in May on the grounds that he was too busy. When Tizard could not recall this incident, Freeman speculated that perhaps Beaverbrook's secretary had forgotten to make the appointment and had then concocted the story. Incensed that Beaverbrook had allowed such a petty matter to affect the mission, Tizard told Freeman that he "would not see Beaverbrook about the mission unless he apologized." Tizard did not relent; nor did he realize that he was being as petty as Beaverbrook. Tizard confided to his diary, "These newspaper barons want teaching manners."[51] The rest of the mission was therefore planned without Beaverbrook's direct input.

While Tizard could avoid Beaverbrook at least for the time being, he could not avoid the seemingly erratic course of Winston Churchill's foreign policy. By the end of July, Tizard must have felt that all was going well with the final planning. He had seen Admiral Fraser, who had been forced to cooperate after the War Cabinet meeting and had agreed to send someone of captain's rank with recent combat and technical experience. The Air Ministry, too, had officially confirmed that it would send a suitably high-ranking and qualified officer.

Late in the afternoon of 1 August, Tizard went to 10 Downing Street to meet Churchill. Although Churchill was ill and being tended by his wife, Tizard was ushered in to see him. Churchill emphasized the mission's importance and reiterated that Tizard was the man to lead it. Then Tizard asked if he was to be given a "free hand" and whether Churchill would rely on his discretion about what to discuss with the Americans. Churchill said "of course" and told Tizard to repair to the lobby to compose a memorandum listing exactly what he required. Tizard's memorandum asked that he be accompanied by an officer of high rank from each service. In addition, he wanted Professor John Cockcroft, a junior radar scientist, and a secretary. He told Churchill that he would interpret his instructions broadly as "to give all assistance I can on behalf of the British Government to enable the armed forces of the USA to reach the highest level of technical efficiency." He said he would try to get information in return from the Americans, "but without making it a bargaining point."[52]

Thus, Tizard left Downing Street well satisfied with Churchill's support. But that evening, when he called Rowlands at the Ministry of Aircraft Production, he was faced with yet another reverse. Rowlands told him that regardless of what Churchill had said that afternoon, he had now temporarily rescinded permission for the mission to go to North America.[53] Churchill had once again grown disenchanted with the pace of discussions concerning the supply of over-age American destroyers, and he resented the Americans' refusal to manufacture British tanks and artillery. When asked to confirm the date of the mission's departure, he had stated, "In view of the holding back on the American side which has manifested itself in the last three days, the question of the departure of the mission should be reviewed."[54]

This continual linking of the mission to what Churchill perceived as the larger picture of Anglo-American relations undoubtedly befuddled and confounded Tizard. Churchill acted as if the mission was a bargaining chip to be offered only if the Americans behaved according to his wishes. The slightest setback – and there were many in the legally and politically complex negotiations with the Americans – was accepted by the Foreign Office as part of normal diplomacy. But Churchill, who bore the burden of the nation's survival, viewed any delay in the negotiations as a personal insult, to be dealt with accordingly. Churchill obviously expected this latest delay to be brief, otherwise he would likely have confided in Tizard. He should have done so anyway, for now serious damage had been done: within a few hours of their meeting, Tizard had come to doubt the prime minister's word.

Remarkably, Tizard did not resign, despite these unfortunate circumstances. Instead, he continued to build the type of technical mission he had envisioned months earlier. Perhaps he stayed on because he realized just how vital it was to Britain's survival to harness the United States' scientific and technical resources. All Tizard could do was write a pleading letter to the prime minister asking him to change his mind once again. Meanwhile, in spite of his "exasperation" with Churchill, he persevered and began to lay the final groundwork for the mission.[55]

While waiting for Churchill to make up his mind, Tizard proceeded to resolve the two most important issues that were still outstanding: who was to be on the mission, and what technical secrets were to be provided to the Americans. The issues were interrelated, because the membership had to be tailored to the technology. To most British officers and scientists, the principal secret they had to offer the Americans involved radar. This is not surprising. In the summer of 1940, Britain's radar detection system was the primary reason why the Royal Air Force was winning its struggle with the Luftwaffe. For a number of years, research into this technology had been given top priority, and several major technical breakthroughs were about to go into service. Dr E.G. Bowen, a young physicist, was leading a team that had built the first airborne radar equipment for use by night fighters and anti-submarine aircraft. Other work had been undertaken to build radar sets to control anti-aircraft gunnery, and the first batteries so equipped had been used in France in May.

Another group of scientists, working at Birmingham University under the leadership of Professor Mark Oliphant, had made an even more significant breakthrough in the area of ultrashort-wave, or microwave, technology. Microwave radar, it was realized, would prove invaluable. It allowed for the development of compact but highly accurate sets that could be mounted in aircraft and small naval vessels. The limiting factor of earlier radar had been that its transmission wavelengths of up to 10 metres required large and cumbersome receiving aerials. The best that Bowen's team could create using conventional radio tube technology was a set that operated at a wavelength of 1.5 metres. The antenna required for this set could only just be carried by larger aircraft and escort vessels. Furthermore, the accuracy of these radar sets was limited, and night fighters using them had to be guided carefully by ground stations to within 3 to 5 miles of their targets.

In February 1940 two members of Oliphant's laboratory, John Randall and Harry Boot, had produced a revolutionary piece of technology. It was the prototype of the first radio valve that could generate sufficient quantities of microwave radiation – the cavity magnetron. Previously, British scientists had been using American-designed klystron valves to produce microwaves. But these had proved inefficient, unable to generate enough power for a useful radar set. At its very first trial, the crude magnetron prototype produced more than double the energy of the best klystron. More advanced models of the magnetron were soon producing one hundred times more power than the original. By the beginning of August 1940, the first dozen production models of this radical new device were completed.[56]

Radar was to be the focus of the mission, though it could not be the only element. The deliberations of the American army and navy dictated the need to broaden the mandate of the mission. Both these departments had produced extensive lists of what could and could not be provided, and what they wanted in return. The navy wanted wide-ranging discussions on radar, radio, sonar, ship machinery and structures, aircraft power turrets, armour, self-sealing fuel tanks, engines, propellers and related aerodynamic technologies, anti-aircraft guns, mines, minesweeping, and camouflage.[57] The army list was similar, with the addition of tanks, armoured cars, artillery, mortars, anti-tank guns, new explosives, aircraft armament, ammunition, balloon barrages, and chemical weapons. Both services wanted as much information as possible; they wanted to known how all this equipment had worked in combat, and to see details of battle damage, German countermeasures, and tactics.[58] Moreover, each naval bureau and army department wanted something from the exchange. Consequently, the Americans were expecting a far more wide-ranging mission than even Tizard had envisioned. London learned of the American services' demands on 2 August.

The Americans wanted few restrictions on the exchange and had excluded a very select list of items. The most important of these, the Norden bombsight, was still zealously guarded from the British. The largest restriction was on "any devices, instruments, or systems under development which have not been manufactured or service tested."[59] They raised some questions about patents and other legal questions, but on the whole downplayed these concerns until face-to-face negotiations with the British could commence.

Tizard intended to please the Americans by providing them with the sort of broadly based mission they desired. The focus was still to be on radar, but other subjects were to be covered either by mission members or by the staff of other British delegations in North America. These included the British Purchasing Mission in New York, the British Admiralty Technical Mission, and R.H. Fowler in Ottawa. In the first two weeks of August, Tizard shaped the composition of his group, assembling a first-class team of scientists and military officers.

Perhaps the best-known scientific representative was forty-three-year-old Professor John Cockcroft of Cambridge's Cavendish Laboratory, one of the country's premier nuclear physicists. A disciple of Lord Rutherford, Cockcroft and his fellow physicist Dr E.T.S. Walton had won international acclaim in 1932 for being the first to disintegrate an atom artificially. This work was to win them a Nobel Prize after the war. Cockcroft was well known in the international scientific community in the later part of the 1930s and had become friends with many leading American physicists, particularly Ernest Lawrence of Berkeley. In March 1939 Cockcroft was appointed to the Jacksonian Professorship of Natural Philosophy. Yet for the next seven years he never lectured. Instead, he became, after Tizard, Britain's most important wartime scientific administrator. At the outset of the war, Cockcroft had been appointed assistant director of scientific research at the Ministry of Supply, and he was soon in charge of the army's radar research program. Since July, he had been heavily involved in planning for the technical mission, and he was to be Tizard's lieutenant in North America.[60]

Rounding out the scientific membership was Dr E.G. Bowen. Bowen was a Welshmen who had just finished his doctorate at King's College, London, when in 1935 he became the first addition to Watson-Watt's team. This was the group that was beginning preliminary research on radar. When Bowen was hired, only the basic theoretical concept of radar existed on paper. In the next five years, he became one of the most experienced British radar research scientists, and he was one of the inventors of small aircraft-mounted sets. Tizard believed that Bowen was a key to the success of the mission, for it was he who was to install and demonstrate the new air-to-surface-vessel (ASV) radar.[61] Tizard considered the ASV to be the most technically advanced and sophisticated piece of completed equipment which Britain had to offer, and he hoped that it would impress the Americans immensely. Tizard was willing to go to great lengths to secure Bowen. When Sir George Lee, the director of communication development (radar) at the Air Ministry, refused to let Bowen go,

Tizard issued an ultimatum: it was either Bowen or no mission. Lee then reluctantly changed his mind.[62]

The military members of the mission also would play a significant role. Tizard wanted relatively senior officers who had recent operational and technical experience. He knew that the Americans craved a first-hand account of the operational performance of new weapons and that the American military was not yet entirely comfortable with talking to civilian scientists about military technology. After much discussion and persuasion, Tizard got the men he wanted. The Royal Air Force sent Group Captain F.L Pearce and Squadron Leader E.W.C. Russell, both experienced pilots who had seen service against the Luftwaffe. Pearce had recently won a Distinguished Flying Cross for his performance in the Norwegian campaign. Representing the Admiralty was Captain H.W. Faulkner, who had just returned from the Mediterranean after serving as first officer of the battleship HMS *Resolution*. Faulkner would later become famous as the captain of the ill-fated HMS *Edinburgh*, which was sunk in 1943 in the Arctic Ocean with a huge cargo of Soviet gold on board. The War Office's member was Lieutenant-Colonel F.C. Wallace, a highly decorated veteran of the First World War who had commanded one of the first anti-aircraft batteries to use the new gun-laying Mark I radar system in combat in France in 1940. Rescued from the beaches of Dunkirk, Wallace represented the ideal mixture that Tizard desired – a seasoned veteran with technical expertise. The final member was A.E. Woodward Nutt, a career civil servant from the Ministry of Aircraft Production. He had been secretary of the Committee for the Scientific Survey of Air Defence (the Tizard Committee) since 1938 and was to fulfil the same role for the mission.

By 8 August everything was just about ready for the mission to proceed to North America. All that prevented its departure was Churchill. Once again, it was the Foreign Office that interceded successfully with the prime minister. The foreign secretary, Lord Halifax, had been informed on 5 August of Churchill's decision to delay the mission further, a decision that had been made without consulting the Foreign Office. So, for the second time in three weeks, Halifax wrote to Churchill to remind him of the importance that Roosevelt placed on the mission's immediate arrival. In order to increase pressure on the prime minister, Halifax told him that the letter was also being sent to the members of the War Cabinet – all of whom were likely to be upset about the further delay.[63] The next day, General Ismay wrote to Churchill expressing a similar concern about the need to send the mission. Ismay warned that a group of senior American officers was scheduled to arrive in London for staff talks in three or four days' time, and he pointed out that after Lothian's meetings with Roosevelt in July, the Americans would expect the talks to include the interchange of technical information. Thus, an "early decision" about the Tizard mission was "required."[64] Reading between the lines of Halifax's and Ismay's memoranda, Churchill was left in no doubt that they considered his decison of 30 June irreversible. If he did not accommodate them, he would risk a major confrontation with the Cabinet. Thus, on 6 August he laconically replied, "I am anxious that they should proceed as soon as possible and under the most favourable auspices. The check of August 1 was only temporary."[65]

With this last obstacle removed, the members of the mission and the directors of scientific research of most of the relevant ministries met at Thames House on 10 August to finalize the arrangements. Only one last-ditch objection was raised to a complete and open exchange. Speaking reluctantly on behalf of Admiral Fraser, C.S. Wright stated that while there should be no limitations to the discussion, the members "should not volunteer information on very new developments." Since the decision to send the magnetron – the newest development – had already been made, Fraser's suggestion was ignored, and there followed a general discussion on the information and equipment that was to be taken. As the Americans had requested, the mission would deal with much more than radar, even though the membership of the group was dominated by experts in that field. Twenty-one different technologies were discussed specifically, including anti-aircraft guns, chemical warfare, gyroscopic predictor gunsights, armour plate, jet propulsion, radio navigation, and self-sealing petrol tanks. There were to be few restrictions on the information that would be provided. Jet engines were to be discussed in only the most general terms, and the navy did not want details of its latest magnetic mines revealed. The Royal Navy coveted this secret, despite the fact that plans and information about these mines had been provided to the French and were more than likely in German hands already. It was agreed to provide as much film, descriptive matter, and samples of the technology as possible. In addition, a list was compiled of technical experts already in the United States who could be consulted on arrival.

The issue of secrecy was also discussed before Tizard's departure. The British and American governments decided that the exchange was to be top secret. Lest there be a risk of stirring isolationist anger in the United States, no publicity would be accorded to the mission members. The mission was to work behind the scenes and not be subject to the scrutiny of either Congress or the press. The British were only too happy to agree to these restrictions, since they would help guarantee the security of the top secret equipment and information that was to be sent to the United States.[66]

On 14 August, Tizard left England aboard the flying boat *Clair*, bound for Montreal via Newfoundland. The rest of the members and all the samples and documentation were to follow by ship two weeks later. The mission had at last begun.

5 The Mission Begins

Well before Tizard's arrival in Washington, the Americans had been preparing the procedures for a wide-reaching technical exchange. Having been well briefed on what type of information the mission was bringing, they were anxious for technical discussions to begin as quickly as possible. In Great Britain, the American army and naval attachés and other officers had been given relatively free access to technical information even before the final decision to approve the mission on 9 August. Their early reports to Washington were very enthusiastic. Brigadier General G.V. Strong had informed General Marshall, the army chief of staff, that "Great Britain is a goldmine of information of a technical nature which should be worked to the limit."[1]

The reports of the American observers in England had spurred both the army and navy to begin laying the groundwork for their handling of the mission well in advance. As we have seen, it was the American services' desire in late July and early August to discuss a multitude of different technologies that had forced the British to expand the scope of the project. By 13 August, both services had decided that few if any obstacles should be placed in the path of an open, frank, and equal exchange. They anticipated that the exchanges would involve "the release of all information necessary to [a] complete understanding of the construction and operation of the devices or systems, including instruction books, operators manuals, schematic wiring diagrams, dimensions of parts, photographs and records of results obtained, or as much of the above material as might be available."[2]

Only a few procedural matters, therefore, were left unresolved before Tizard's arrival. The Americans were still unwilling to talk about ongoing research projects, and the Norden bombsight remained a taboo subject. Patent rights were the most serious problem. In early August the policy was that no information would be provided on technologies that were not under the control of the United States government; this excluded from discussion any "trade secrets and patent rights of American citizens."[3] By 21 August, this was already recognized as an unworkable solution; almost every major weapon systems had at least some components whose patent or trade rights were controlled by private interests. Approval was therefore given to discuss any military technology that was not specifically prohibited. Information on technology that was under the control of private citizens would be given to the British – but only on condition that they would secure licence rights and arrange to pay suitable financial compensation if they wished to manufacture the item. The British were also required to guarantee that American patents would be secured from the filing of similar patents in Great Britain and in the Commonwealth and Empire.[4]

At 12:35 PM on 22 August 1940, Sir Henry Tizard finally arrived in Washington by train from Ottawa. He was accompanied by Group Captain Pearce. Tizard's week in Ottawa had provided him with the opportunity to recover from his long flight, to be briefed by R.H. Fowler and Canadian officials on the current situation in the United States, and to survey the Canadian scientific organization. We shall hear more of his week in the Canadian capital. His arrival in Washington marked the beginning of the main part of his mission. It was now up to him to convince the Americans of the sincerity of the British offer to provide technical information of the most highly classified nature and to do so without requiring any direct *quid pro quo*. Given Tizard's experience in getting his own government to set policy, he may well have expected the negotiations to take a considerable amount of time. During the negotiations, he hoped to instil a sense of trust that would lead to frank and open discussion about technology, tactics, and industrial production, which in turn would encourage further cooperation between the two nations. All this had to be achieved in the two weeks before the other members of the mission arrived. What Tizard was not aware of was that the Americans had already agreed to most of what he wanted, and that the procedural discussion would either take very little time or, if the question on such matters as patents was a hindrance, would simply be deferred to a later date.

Tizard must have found Washington an unusual place. It was a capital still at peace. Reminders that the world was at war could be found only in newspaper headlines or in the ongoing debates about the policies to be adopted towards the belligerent powers and in the state of America's military preparedness. There was neither fanfare nor an official greeting party at the station. Tizard and Pearce were met only by Brigadier Charles Lindemann, the British army attaché and brother of Frederick. This was in keeping with the policy agreed to by both governments that the mission was to be a low-key affair. As previously noted, the secrecy was both to shield the Roosevelt administration from isolationist criticism and to protect technical information from Axis spies.

Lindemann whisked Tizard off to a meeting with British Ambassador Lord Lothian. At the embassy Tizard was "rather annoyed" to learn that there had been no arrangements made for the mission; neither offices nor clerical staff were available. But Lothian was helpful and had made arrangements for Tizard's meetings in the next few days. That evening Tizard went to dinner at the home of Admiral Potts, the naval attaché, where he met Admiral W.S. Anderson, the U.S. Navy's director of naval intelligence, who was responsible for liaison with the Tizard Mission.[5] He began the next day with meetings with Anderson at the Navy Department, followed by an appointment with Frank Knox, the secretary of the navy. And that evening he met with Colonel J.A. Crane, the officer in charge of foreign liaison for the U.S. Army's general staff.[6] Tizard found all the Americans cordial and anxious to receive technical information from him.

On Monday, 26 August, Tizard had his first formal discussions with Admiral Anderson. He and the American admiral analysed the detailed list of technical information desired by the U.S. Navy. Most items, they decided, would be discussed freely. Some would be discussed in general meetings, others by special committees. Tizard saw this as a constructive meeting, for Anderson had made it clear that the Americans planned to open by discussing most of their secrets with the British. The one major exception was the Norden bombsight. Yet Tizard must have found the American enthusiasm worrying. The Americans wanted to begin discussions as soon as possible, but Cockcroft and the mission's other technical experts had not yet left England.

The magnitude of this problem was brought home by an audience that afternoon with President Roosevelt. Tizard was accompanied to the White House by Lothian. They slipped in the back door to avoid newsreel cameras and waited for Roosevelt in the cabinet room. While there, Lothian attempted to explain to Tizard the nature of the American cabinet, which, in contrast to the British system, acted only as an advisory body. Ushered into Roosevelt's office, Tizard found the president to be "very nice" and "a most attractive personality." During most of the meeting, Roosevelt talked about his draft bill on conscription. He believed that he would get it through Congress but that it would probably lose him the November election. But Roosevelt said that it "didn't matter" if he lost, as long as the United States was prepared for war.

They spent some time discussing the mission. Roosevelt explained apologetically that the Norden bombsight was still being withheld – largely for political reasons. If the British could prove the Germans had a similar sight, then it could be released. Tizard replied that he hoped the Americans would have large numbers of the bombsights available when they felt it could be released, and he asked that the dimensions of the device be provided so that British planes could be modified to mount it. He also told Roosevelt that the basic principle of the Norden was well known and that his government was interested only in American production. In fact, Tizard was not particularly concerned about the bombsight. His main interest lay in other technologies. He discussed British radar development in general terms and told Roosevelt that films were being sent to illustrate its usefulness. Roosevelt requested a private showing of the films the following week, but Tizard could not make them available until the other members of the mission had arrived.[7]

The next day was spent at the War Department. After a brief meeting with Brigadier General Sherman Miles, the chief of army intelligence, Tizard was ushered into the office of Henry Stimson, the secretary of war, who briefed him on recent developments in the organization of civilian scientists. Stimson was surprised to discover just how well acquainted Tizard was on recent American technical developments.[8] There followed a meeting with Major General J.O. Mauborgne, chief of the Signal Corps. This was meant to be a brief meeting, but the two men began to discuss each country's radar development and ended up talking for the rest of the morning. It was the first time that an open discussion had taken place on the subject. Mauborgne began by confirming Hill's observation of the previous spring that the Americans had long-wave ground-based aircraft-detection sets. Mauborgne was fascinated by Tizard's description of British radar, particularly the small aircraft-mounted sets, the design of which was just getting underway in the United States. He promised Tizard "full interchange of information."[9]

On 28 August, Tizard held a meeting with officials at the War Department to make final arrangements for the procedures to be used in conducting the exchange. Committees were established to disseminate information once the other members of the mission arrived and methods had been worked out on how other technical information could be obtained. There was already a growing belief within the American services that technical cooperation with Great Britain was vital and should be expanded. Two days later, a meeting of army division chiefs discussed the possibility of sending an American version of the Tizard Mission to Great Britian. Although no decision was made, they clearly considered effective technical cooperation with Great Britain to be a vital part of American defence planning. As far as the War Department was concerned, there was a general agreement on a "full exchange of information" with Great Britain.[10]

Tizard could not help but be pleased. The Americans were already doing exactly what he had hoped – but much more quickly than he had anticipated. If he could only keep the momentum going, the mission would be a success. His enthusiasm must have been dampened, however, by his meeting on the evening of 28 August with Arthur Purvis, the Canadian-born head of the British Purchasing Commission to the United States. Purvis briefed Tizard on the financial implications of the Anglo-American technical exchange. Although details of this meeting do not survive, it is possible to reconstruct what occurred from later developments. One of Tizard's main goals had been to encourage the Americans to manufacture equipment that could be used by the British armed forces. Purvis undoubtedly advised Tizard of the current state of the American neutrality legislation and informed him that no matter what took place, a dramatic increase in industrial purchases from the United States was unlikely. It is unclear whether Tizard had been fully aware before his arrival in Washington that the amendment made to the Neutrality Act in the fall of 1939 involved specific restrictions. For instance, it allowed for the purchase of war material on a cash-and-carry basis only. By the summer of 1940, Britain's hard-currency reserves were critically depleted. Thus, no matter what the consequences of the mission, few if any material advantages would result in the short term. This did not discourage Tizard, but as we shall see, it did change his attitude about what he could accomplish.[11]

That same day, Tizard met with Admiral Furlong, the chief of naval ordnance. Furlong had arranged the meeting in order to tell Tizard that as far as he himself was concerned, no discussions were to take place concerning naval gunnery and anti-aircraft weapons. This display of hostility indicated that there was still a level of mistrust in some circles of the American armed forces. Tizard decided to avoid a direct confrontation and did not challenge Furlong, whose position was a clear violation of Navy Department policy. He decided that if Furlong did not change his mind, he would approach Admiral Stark directly.[12]

Despite these developments, the first five days of the mission were a great success. Tizard realized that in order to maintain this momentum, the work would have to get underway without waiting for the arrival of his technical staff. By 27 August he had established the mission's offices at the Shoreham Hotel. Two secretaries had been seconded from the National Research Council of Canada to serve as the office staff.[13] In addition, Tizard had with him Pearce and Professor Fowler, the scientific attaché in Ottawa. Unfortunately, none of the three had enough technical expertise to end any lingering doubts the Americans might have about the value of technical cooperation, but the growing British bureaucracy in North America provided Tizard with some of the expertise he required. On his arrival in Washington, Tizard had found that there was a bewildering array of ten separate missions, including his own, operating in the United States – all in addition to the embassy's normal staff. Some had overlapping or contradictory responsibilities. American complaints about this confusing bureaucratic muddle reached Churchill in mid-September, and he ordered the matter investigated. However, it was never completely solved.[14]

Most useful to Tizard was the British Admiralty Technical Mission (BATM), headed by Vice-Admiral A.E. Evans, which had been established by the Royal Navy in July, with its headquarters in Ottawa and a liaison office in New York. It was responsible for providing technical assistance and supervision to North American firms undertaking contracts for the Admiralty. Rather than providing its own technical personnel for the Tizard Mission, the navy had ordered Evans to provide Tizard with any technical assistance he required. On 28 August, Evans arrived in Washington. After discussions with Tizard, he agreed to second to the mission three of his technical experts: Commander J.D. Crossman, Mr J.W. Drabble, and Mr A.E.H. Pew. Crossman and Drabble were specialists in radio technology with some knowledge of naval radar, and were in North America to purchase wireless telephones to used as a reserve supply for Royal Navy warships. Pew was a leading authority on asdic production and had been in Canada since early July creating an asdic manufacturing industry.[15]

With the help of the BATM experts, Tizard was able to begin detailed full-scale technical discussions with the War and Navy Departments on 29 July. The results of these first meetings showed just how valuable free technical discussions could be for both sides. At the Navy Department that morning, Fowler and Pew met with representatives of the navy's Bureau of Ordnance and Ships. Pew dominated the meeting, speaking for several hours on asdic, anti-submarine warfare tactics, and operational and maintenance problems. Lieutenant-Commander W.L. Pryor, Jr, from the Bureau of Ships reported: "In this discussion Mr. Pew appeared to completely sincere and unhesitant and discussed all matters freely and, apparently, without reservation." The discussion went on all morning and ended at noon. Furthermore, Pryor and another Bureau of Ships sonar expert continued to converse with Pew all afternoon and evening.

Pryor realized that the U.S. Navy and the Royal Navy had much to learn from each other. When Anglo-American cooperation on sonar had terminated in the early 1920s, one of the most vexing problems with the early sets had yet to be solved – the interference with the reception of reflected sound waves caused by the noise of the ship passing through the water. To this identical problem, American and British researchers had developed completely different solutions. The Royal Navy had perfected techniques to reduce the extraneous noise. It did this by streamlining the dome that housed the asdic receiver and transmitter underneath the ship's hull, by siting the sets below the most turbulent layer of water, and by shielding the equipment from the noise of the ship's propellers. The U.S. Navy had done little to reduce noise levels but had developed transmitters with much higher signal and gain levels than the British equipment. Pryor speculated, "By combining our high output level and our high gain amplifier with the British technique ... we should be able to make considerable progress in increasing range at currently used speeds and in increasing the speeds at which we can obtain currently used effective ranges." Many other recommendations that went well beyond technical issues flowed from the meeting. There had been debate within the U.S. Navy about the need to train specialist operators for sonar equipment. Learning of the Admiralty practice of training ratings to be asdic experts, Pryor argued that this was further evidence that the American navy needed a similar system. Pryor also took copious notes of British anti-submarine warfare tactics.[16]

Pew greatly impressed the Americans, but at first he was not convinced that the Admiralty had anything to learn. He reported to Tizard that he felt that the Americans had not been very forthcoming during the meeting that morning. Their reticence may have been the result of the presence of three members of Admiral Furlong's Bureau of Ordnance, for the discussions later in the day, held without the presence of Furlong's officers, were "full and friendly." Pew noted that while American technology was of good calibre, the Americans had not worked out "the best tactics for using the equipment." This, he believed, was because their scientific personnel had failed to work closely with their operational officers.[17] Pew's chauvinistic attitude was a reminder of the past and was based more on ignorance than on substance. Once he had seen the Americans' submarine-detection equipment firsthand, he would significantly upgrade his opinion of the their technology.[18]

The second meeting at the Navy Department that day involved Fowler, Crossman, and Drabble discussing radio and radar. The two Admiralty experts outlined the Royal Navy's current surface-search sets, which were mounted in cruisers and battleships, but they appeared to be unfamiliar with the latest developments – including the first long-wave small-ship set, the type-286 radar, that was just being deployed operationally on destroyers. Still, the Americans were fascinated by the discussion of the type-71 equipment, and they freely admitted that their radar was at an earlier stage of development.

The British learned for the first time of an important American technical breakthrough, which was destined to improve their radar considerably. Up to this point, British radar had required separate transmitting and receiving antennas. This was because the receiver had to be protected and isolated from the high-power pulses of the transmitter. If this was not done, the receiver would be damaged and unable to separate the reflected radio waves from those being generated by the transmitter. The problem was that there was great difficulty in finding space to mount two different antenna systems on a ship or aircraft.

In 1938 scientists at the U.S. Naval Research Laboratory (NRL) had perfected an electronic switch or spark-gap called the duplexor. By preventing the receiver from obtaining signals from the transmitter by shutting the circuit electronically, this device allowed one antenna to be used. Crossman and Drabble grasped the significance of this development immediately and indicated that it should be fully investigated as soon as Bowen arrived from England.[19] The next day members of the mission had an opportunity to examine a duplexor, which Fowler described as a device "to be of the utmost simplicity and perfectly effective." This viewing took place at a meeting with the leading scientists and administrators at the Naval Research Laboratory. In attendance were Admiral H.G. Bowen, the director; Commander R.P. Briscoe, assistant director; Dr A.H. Taylor, superintendent of radio and radar; and Dr H.C. Hayes, superintendent of sound. This was the first opportunity the British had had to hold discussions with American scientists, and both sides soon found themselves enthralled by the descriptions of each other's research. The NRL scientists were particularly intrigued by descriptions of ASV radar and the magnetron, which were reported for the first time to a non-British audience. Bowen told Fowler that the British mission would now be allowed access to research and production facilities in private companies that were undertaking work for the navy. In return, Bowen asked that arrangements be made to send an NRL scientist to the Admiralty's Signals School.[20]

Meanwhile, Tizard was having similar success at the War Department. Here, too, senior technical officers from the Signal Corps, Coast Artillery, and Air Corps were given a detailed description of British radar, particularly the Chain Home and Chain Home Low Radar defence systems. These radar systems were allowing the Hurricane and Spitfire aircraft of the RAF's Fighter Command to defeat the mighty Luftwaffe over the skies of Great Britain even while Tizard was speaking. Also described was the brand-new "identification of friend or foe" system (IFF), which permitted the automatic verification by radar of the identity of a ship or aircraft.[21]

General Mauborgne, the head of the Signal Corps, was so impressed that he arranged for Tizard, Fowler, and a number British officers to visit the American army's most secret research facilities – the Air Corps laboratories at Wright-Patterson Field in Ohio and the Signal Corps radar and radio research centre at Fort Monmouth, New York. At the latter, Tizard had his first opportunity to watch American radar in action:

> We saw a kind of GL [gun-laying radar] set, the object being to control blind shooting and to direct searchlights. This set looks rather like an EMI sound locator without the trumpets. The aerial's frame was swung completely around. Searching is done that way. One cathode ray tube shows azimuth, the other elevation. They use the split echo method. An aeroplane was made up for demonstration purposes. The readings of the GL were fed into a Sperry predictor. The crew on the predictor was holding the aircraft in the optical sights. A scale showed us how closely the GL operators could follow the optical. Generally speaking the results were good, certainly good enough for searchlight operation but I think it might be difficult to pick up machines quickly enough by this method. Cockcroft will have to look at it in detail.[22]

Although an impressive display, the army radar, a type SCR-268, had not gone into general service use. From a strictly technical standpoint, American radar compared favourably with British equipment, but it had not been tested in combat, nor had it been proven in the hands of inexperienced operators.

The Americans were acutely aware of this gap and were increasingly determined to remove all restrictions from their technical discussions with Tizard's mission. On 4 September the navy formally renounced one of the few major limitations it had placed on information sharing in late August; it was now permissible to discuss research in the radio, radar, and sonar fields even where the devices, instruments, or systems were under development and had not yet been manufactured for service trials. This meant, in effect, that there could be a free exchange not only of hardware but of ideas.[23]

The War Department also wanted to limit the restrictions and expand the scope of the exchanges. On 30 August the chiefs of arms and services decided not to send a full-scale American equivalent of the British Technical Mission to the United Kingdom. They desired first to be briefed about the equipment and technical information being sent from England. By 10 September, however, authorization was given to send individual technical officers to the United Kingdom. General Mauborgne of the Signal Corps had pressed for this change in policy, and on the same day he authorized "without delay the dispatch of Major Paul S. Edwards, Signal Corps, to [the] UK for 3 weeks to observe the operation of the British Air Detection System."[24]

As well as taking action to improve technical cooperation, the Air Corps wanted to incorporate British technology and war experience into its latest aircraft. On 30 August the British Purchasing Mission asked for full details of the design of all American combat aircraft and for permission for British representatives to fly in Air Corps planes. The latter privilege had been suspended in February 1939 after the crash of the Douglas bomber with a French air force officer on board. In order to facilitate technical cooperation, the War Department approved both British requests by 7 September.[25]

The Americans continued to clamour for as much information as possible. They did not have to wait long. On 8 September the rest of the members of the mission – along with their priceless cargo of samples, blueprints, drawings, photographs, and film – arrived in Washington.

6 The Great Exchange

For two weeks after Tizard's departure from England, Cockcroft and Bowen completed the process that Tizard had begun in early August. In assembling the material that was to be provided to the Americans during the course of the exchange, they collected everything they could lay their hands on – manuals, circuit diagrams, blueprints, films, and samples of any item that could be shipped. They placed the most sensitive material in a solicitor's black deed box, which was kept under close guard at Cockcroft's London office at Savoy House, the headquarters of the Department of Supply.

The most important and highly classified item in the box was one of the first twelve production magnetrons. It had been completed in late July. Bowen had been closely briefed in detail about the magnetron's construction, making several trips by underground to the General Electric Company's research laboratory in Wembley, a London suburb. On 11 August he travelled out to Wembley by the underground one last time. After testing each one, he was given the pick of the litter, magnetron no. 12 – a decision that was to have some unexpected consequences. Taking the top secret magnetron, together with blueprints and detailed information on construction methods, Bowen retraced his steps unescorted to Savoy House, still travelling by the underground.

Once safely back, his precious bundle was deposited carefully in the black box.

All told, Cockcroft and Bowen assembled nine crates of material. This included, they believed, a complete ASV Mark II airborne radar set. By the end of August they had gathered all they could. Arrangements were now made for Cockcroft, Bowen, Nutt, Colonel Wallace, and Captain Faulkner to leave Liverpool for Halifax on the evening of 29 August. Bowen was put in charge of getting the black box safely from Savoy House to the railway station in Liverpool. His account of how he spirited it through wartime Britain would seem unbelievable in any mystery novel. With the fate of Great Britain hanging in the balance, he hustled his treasure through public paths in ways that might have daunted His Majesty's Secret Service. It was a task that he took on with a great deal of reluctance, since apparently no security arrangements had been made for the box's safe keeping.

Bowen arrived at Savoy House in the evening of 28 August and took the black box back with him by taxi to his hotel. He had made arrangements with the manager to put the box in the hotel safe, but when the manager saw it he threw up his hands in dismay – it was too big to fit in the safe. There was no alternative but to store it under Bowen's bed. The next morning, Bowen hailed a taxi to take him and his secret cargo to Euston Station for the 8:30 AM boat train to Liverpool. For some inexplicable reason, the taxi driver insisted that the box could not travel inside the vehicle and that it had to be strapped on the roof. With no time to argue, Bowen had to agree, so Britain's most important technical secrets travelled across London on this conspicuous perch. At the station Bowen summoned a porter, who grabbed the box, hustled it onto his shoulder, and headed off at such a pace that Bowen, an old cross-country runner, had difficulty keeping up with him. He could do little more than track the box ahead of him as it weaved its way through the crowded station.

Bowen caught up with the box in the first-class compartment that had been reserved for him. As soon as he entered, the blinds were drawn and large notices were posted on every window announcing that the compartment was reserved. Nevertheless, a minute after he sat down, "an exceptionally trim, well dressed gentleman with a public-school tie came into the compartment." With scarcely a glance in Bowen's direction, he chose a seat diagonally opposite him and busied himself with the *Times*. The train began to move soon afterwards, but there were some late arrivals searching for empty seats. "A couple of bright sparks opened the corridor door and said, 'Here we are chaps, this one is nearly empty' and started to enter." Bowen's companion then spoke for the first and only time. "Out!" he commanded. "Don't you see this is specially reserved?" "It was not what he said," Bowen related, "but how he said it." The interlopers retreated immediately, and there were no other interruptions. For the first time, Bowen surmised that his precious cargo might indeed have had some covert protection.

Once in Liverpool, Bowen was instructed to wait for a security detail from the army to pick up the black box. Still absorbed in the *Times*, his companion stayed behind as well. Soon, a squad of a dozen armed soldiers led by a sergeant arrived. They removed the box and began to march away. As Bowen commented, "I was beginning to feel that things were well looked after. Alternatively, if this was the enemy making off with Britain's secrets, they were making a spectacular job of it." Bowen's silent companion did not moved a muscle until the squad had departed. Then he rolled up his newspaper and "with a barely perceptible nod" in Bowen's direction, departed. Bowen "had no doubt that he was heading for a well deserved drink."[1] Bowen then made his way to the liner *Duchess of Richmond*, where he was met by the other members of the mission. The black box was safely secured and under guard on the bridge. The Captain had instructions to heave it over the side if the ship was attacked and in danger of sinking.

The ship sailed at dusk. But while leaving Liverpool harbour, the city was attacked by one of the first German night bomber raids, which were soon to cause extensive damage to the great British port. Although the bombing was not accurate, it forced the ship to anchor in the roads. Next morning the *Duchess* set off unescorted into the Irish Sea and out into the Atlantic. She was a fast liner and could travel alone. Every twenty or thirty minutes she zig-zagged to prevent submarines from getting into firing position. On board, the mission members continued to brief themselves on the information they would impart to the Americans. The only one with access to the black box was Woodward Nutt, who made occasional visits to the bridge to extract documents from it. He often complained of the difficulty of moving the heavy box from its hiding place on the bridge. At the bar one evening before dinner, these complaints resulted in Cockcroft making a calculation. If the ship was attacked, he concluded, the box would float if thrown overboard. Soon someone drilled large holes in the side of the box in order to guarantee that it could not be recovered by a U-boat.

The mission's fellow passengers included over a thousand officers and men of the Royal Navy, who were on their way to Halifax. Only on arrival did the reason for their presence on board become clear: the *Duchess* entered Halifax Harbour at the very same time as the first of the fifty old American flush-deck destroyers that were being handed over to the Royal Navy as part of the famous destroyer-for-bases deal. The Royal Navy personnel on board were their crew.[2] It is fitting that the members of the mission witnessed this historic moment. After all, the mission's fate had been linked by Churchill to the successful completion of the transference of these destroyers to Great Britain. The destroyers-for-bases agreement along with the mission itself marked a turning-point in Anglo-American relations. From that moment onwards, the United States played an increasingly active role in supporting Great Britain's war effort. The Tizard Mission demonstarted to American army and navy officers the crucial importance of this emerging transatlantic alliance.

Most of the members of the mission went by train from Halifax to Montreal and then on to Washington – this time under the close supervision of an armed guard. They arrived late on 8 September. Bowen, however, headed north from Montreal to the National Research Council in Ottawa. He was accompanied by several crates of equipment. These crates were supposed to contain an ASV radar scheduled to be mounted on a Royal Canadian Air Force Hudson bomber. The bomber was to be flown to Washington and used to demonstrate Britain's technological prowess. But when the crates were opened, they were found to contain unrelated scientific equipment. Several days of desperate telegrams back and forth across the Atlantic ensued as Bowen tried to locate the missing top secret radar set. It was soon learned that someone in England, without informing the mission, had decided not to send the ASV. This was because of a minor technical problem. The ASV was not yet a fully operational piece of equipment. No one seems to have considered the fact that since Bowen had headed the research team that built the first ASV, he would easily be able to maintain it. As it was, the mission had to wait nearly two months before it could demonstrate this vital piece of equipment.[3]

The first meeting of all of the members of the mission since Tizard and Pearce had left Britain took place on the morning of 9 September. Tizard briefed the newcomers on the events of the previous three weeks and outlined the nature of further technical exchanges. He stressed that technical exchanges of any type with American navy and army personnel were to be free and without reservation, but no technical discussions were to be held with anyone outside the services unless he gave authorization. The mission office was to be open daily at the Shoreham Hotel from 9 AM to 6 PM, and at 9 AM every morning the members of the mission who were in Washington were to hold a briefing meeting. Tizard outlined the general role of each member of the mission, placing special emphasis on the representatives of the armed forces. He told them, "I consider it important that Captain Faulkner, Colonel Wallace and Group Captain Pearce should take every opportunity that naturally presents itself to discuss war experience with officers of the U.S. forces."[4] Tizard divided the members of the mission into eight specialty groups:

1 Radar operational methods: Tizard, Cockcroft, Faulkner, Crossman, Wallace
2 Technical details of radar: Tizard, Cockcroft, Bowen
3 Anti-aircraft gunnery, fire control, directors, and searchlights: Cockcroft, Fowler, Wallace, Faulkner
4 Aircraft armament, turrets, tracers: Tizard, Fowler, Air Commodore Baker (British Purchasing Commission), Lindemann
5 Defence against low-flying aircraft: Tizard, Cockcroft, Fowler, Lindemann, Wallace, Nutt
6 Proximity and influence fuses: Fowler, Cockcroft, Bowen
7 Aircraft and aircraft engines: Tizard
8 Means of distinguishing friendly from enemy aircraft and ships: Fowler, Cockcroft[5]

This list does not include the large number of Canadians who participated in the committee discussions. Also excluded were subcommittees that used personnel from outside the mission on special subjects requested by the American armed services.

With his team briefed and ready to start, Tizard was determined to ensure that all would go according to plan. There were still two major obstacles to overcome. The first concerned the broad range of information required by the Americans. Tizard found Canadian technical experts indispensable in solving this problem. The mission's influence on Canada will be discussed in more detail in a later chapter. It should be noted, however, that as early as 29 August, Tizard believed that Canadian help would prove to be essential. This was particularly so in providing technical expertise in fields that were not covered either by the British Technical Mission or by any of the other British representatives in the United States.[6]

The requirement to utilize Canadians in special committees arose because American enthusiasm to benefit from British technical knowledge often exceeded the capabilties of the mission personnel. As we have seen, the early planning had focused on radar, since this was deemed the most crucial technology in modern warfare. Bowen, Cockcroft, Tizard, and Wallace were primarily radar experts. While Tizard also had great knowledge of aviation research, and the others could fill the gaps in various areas, no one had counted on requests for information in such a diversity of topics. Every U.S. naval bureau and army division chief was clamouring for a piece of the British technical pie. Particularly vexing was pressure from the army's Chemical Warfare Service and Medical Corps to discuss their latest technical developments with British experts. This problem was made more acute by the fact that the Americans had provided information in these areas to British military officers who were not directly associated with the mission. Lieutenant-Colonel L.J. Barley of the British chemical warfare directorate had visited the United States in August and had been given full access to American facilties on the assumption that the Tizard Mission would provide similar information on British chemical warfare research.[7]

In order to avert the type of ill will that might have compromised the mission, Tizard proposed to the Americans on 14 September that Canadian "experts" would provide most of the information desired in these two areas. Tizard then requested that C.J. Mackenzie, the acting president of the National Research Council of Canada, arrange to send three experts to Washington. These were Dr Otto Maass and Dr E.A. Flood, National Research

Council chemists who had recently begun Canada's chemical warfare research program, and Sir Frederick Banting, the co-discoverer of insulin, who was a self-proclaimed specialist in aviation medicine. Fortunately for Tizard, the Americans accepted the Canadians and found them adequate substitutes for their British counterparts.[8]

Other Canadians were soon recruited to assist. Dr John Henderson, who headed the National Research Council's radar program, was in Washington through most of September visiting American research facilities.[9] On 23 September two RCAF officers began an extensive investigation of American aerial reconnaissance technology at Wright Field in Ohio and at the Eastman Kodak Laboratories in Rochester.[10] American experts were soon off to Canada to examine British equipment, both that under manufacture and that in service. An American naval team surveyed British sonar at Halifax and Montreal, touring the Vickers shipyard to examine corvettes under construction. Lieutenant-Commander A.R. Pressy of the Royal Canadian Navy arranged for the exchange of sonar equipment and received American assistance with the U.S. Navy's sonar sets on the flush-deck destroyers that were being transferred to the Commonwealth navies under the bases-for-ships deal.[11]

The Canadian option was not always open to Tizard. The U.S. Army Air Corps complained on 24 September that it had received "only generalities in exchange for specific data, except in the limited field of radio and sound developments."[12] With no Canadian experts available, Tizard promptly arranged for several Air Corps officers to go to the United Kingdom for detailed briefings on all matters that were not adequately covered by the mission.

Tizard's other major worry was the continuing lack of cooperation from Admiral Furlong's Bureau of Ordnance. Specifically, Tizard could not understand why this naval bureau had refused to discuss equipment and methods of anti-aircraft gunnery – this despite their not being included in the Americans' rapidly shrinking list of taboo subjects. Although he was to solve this particular problem quickly, its resolution revealed another and much more complex obstacle lying in the path of a permanent system for Anglo-American technical cooperation.

On 10 September, Tizard took the matter directly to Admiral Anderson. Anderson confirmed that Admiral Stark, the chief of naval operations, had sanctioned Anglo-American conversations on anti-aircraft weaponry. With Tizard still in his office, he phoned Furlong and asked him to explain his actions. Tizard recorded in his diary:

> He had quite a long conversation, at the end of which Admiral Anderson explained to me that the real difficulty was connected with the design of the predictor known as the Ford Predictor and, I believe. made by the Sperry Company. It appears that an English firm (?Paul and Isherwood) had sued the U.S. Government for infringements of patents. They have been refused access to the latest U.S. predictors for ship work and had been unable to prove their case. They had shifted their attack on Ford and were suing him. It was felt by Admiral Furlong that if we had full information about the predictor, it might afterwards be said that we handed some of this information to Paul & Isherwood to enable than to fight their case.[13]

Anderson asked Furlong to write to Ford and the Sperry Company to approve discussion with the Tizard Mission as long as the British government agreed not to pass on any information to the British firm. Tizard agreed to provide this assurance. But he also suggested that a better way had to be found to deal with the issue of patents. Since he had no immediate solution to this complex legal problem, he turned the matter over to the embassy legal staff for resolution.

The issue of patent protection had been deferred at the end of August, but clearly it could not be ignored for long. As the incident with Admiral Furlong illustrated, trading any patentable commodity could lead to a legal morass which, if not solved, would imperil all future attempts to exchange technology. As far as both governments were concerned, any patent held outright could be freely traded. The grey area was the problem: what to do with patents held by individuals or private corporations. Patents are, after all, private property and can have enormous economic value. Patent holders would normally be safeguarded by taking out international patents in other countries, but many patents with military applications were classified, and thus their owners had not been able to apply for safety under international law. Both sides were interested in production, and this meant that millions of dollars of licensing rights were at stake. The interim solution to this apparent impasse was to allow general discussions on any device or manufacturing process, but to ensure that each side had to reach agreement with the individual patent holders themselves before discussing detailed specifications. If details had been provided as part of the exchange to government agencies, they should not provide this information to private manufactures without first securing the required licensing rights. [14]

Neither side was happy with this arrangement. It was cumbersome and still did not guarantee legal compensation to holders of secret patents who had not filed for international protection. Also, it was difficult to keep track of what was a commercial or government patent, and it was hard to resist the urge to sidestep the whole process and hasten a vital piece of equipment into production. There were several reported instances of this. For instance, Tizard complained on 23 September that a member of the British Purchasing Commission had discovered that Glen Martin Aircraft had received details of British aircraft turrets and had been invited by the Air Corps to Washington to get complete specifications. Since no specific agreement on the commercial rights had yet been secured, this was a clear violation of procedures. A few incidents such as this could be forgiven, but it was clear that a better solution had to be found or all the good will generated since the arrival of the mission would collapse into commercial and legal chaos.[15]

Ultimately, as Tizard suspected after his meeting with Anderson on 10 September, the matter had to be turned over to lawyers to find a legal solution. It was decided to appoint a committee of four lawyers: Mr John Foster, legal adviser to the British Embassy; Mr Thomas Childs, a lawyer assigned to the British Purchasing Commission; and Lieutenant-Commander Wilbur G. Jones and Major Francis H. Vanderwerker of the U.S. navy's and U.S. Army's Judge Advocate General's office, respectively. Before the committee could meet, Foster outlined the ideal solution to Tizard, though it would require legislative changes that could not be implemented immediately. Foster called for the British government to give American patentees a legal right to establish a claim for reasonable compensation for the reproduction of any device whose details had been communicated to the mission. He argued that legal changes should be made to allow applications to be filled out retroactively – after they had exceeded the normal one-year limit – because of their secret nature in the United States. Finally, he recommended that both sides establish central authorities to act as agents to negotiate suitable compensation for individual patent holders, and he suggested that the British Purchasing Commission act for British patent holders in this regard.[16]

These broad concepts formed the basis of the Anglo-American patent agreements early in 1941. However, when the legal committee met for the first time on 25 September 1940, it had to develop a more workable interim solution that did not require legislative changes. In essence, its solution was very similar to the earlier interim agreement: each government would be required to negotiate patent rights with individual or corporate patent holders, and these patent holders would themselves be responsible for protecting their own commercial rights.

The changes mapped out by the committee at this first meeting involved giving much greater protection to holders of secret patents. The British government promised to allow the holders of American secret patents to file for patents in British or dominion patent offices. In return, the British guaranteed that their patent office would preserve the secrecy of the information and that details would not be released without the permission of the United States. None of the unprotected secret patent information already imparted to representatives of the British government could be used by someone other than the American patent holder to file for a British patent. If British or dominion manufacturing took place before a UK patent application had been filed, then legislation would be passed giving the American patent holder the right to seek fair compensation in the courts. Finally, it was recommended that the time in which holders of a national patent could file for an overseas patent should be extended. This was normally one year under international law. This, too, would require legislative changes. The same procedures would apply for holders of secret British patents.[17]

Tizard did not allow any of these problems to delay the launching of a full and open exchange with the American services. What followed after 9 September was the most far-reaching and comprehensive technical and intellectual exchange of military secrets that had ever taken place. In a series of meetings, the members of the mission imparted to the Americans all the knowledge they had so carefully assembled. It is impossible to describe in detail all that took place, for there were more than one hundred and fifty meetings with American representatives between 9 September and 1 December 1940, when the mission ended officially. It is possible, however, to show the nature and scope of the discussions.[18] In effect, the mission in the United States had two stages. The first lasted from 9 September, with the arrival of Cockcroft and the others, until 5 October, the date of Tizard's return to England. In this phase the members of the mission imparted most of their technical information, along with the samples they had brought. The mission's main function from 5 October onwards, with Cockcroft in charge, was to gather information on American technology, industrial practices, and production. This was not a hard and fast division since some of the most important pieces of British equipment – the ASV radar, the "identification of friend or foe" system (IFF), and the 40mm Bofors anti-aircraft gun – did not arrive in North America until November.

The September meetings all followed much the same pattern. A description of a typical meeting is given in E.G. Bowen's memoirs:

> The usual form of a meeting was for Tizard to make some introductory remark, which he always did in the simplest and clearest possible way. He then called on the appropriate expert to elaborate and produce documentary or filmed evidence, as the case may be. It was immediately obvious from the interest taken and the questions asked that we were faced with experts who either had first-hand experience of what we were talking about or had given serious thought to the same problems. Copies of the British documents and drawings were handed over to Army and Navy Intelligence who were responsible for distributing them within the Services and for the overall security of the material.[19]

Although few American reports have survived of the meetings between the mission members and the American armed forces, and although the British accounts are mostly concerned with information of interest to London, it is possible to arrive at some sense of the importance of these exchanges. Yet the official reports rarely give a sense of the type of friendly and useful debate that resulted from these interchanges of technological ideas. Since no transcripts were kept, we must therefore turn to other sources. Tizard's diary entry for 19 September contains one such example

– an account of a lengthy "conversation and argument" about fighter aircraft design that he had with General Henry ("Hap") Arnold, the commander of the United States Army Air Corps. Tizard was by now used to arguing with any officer, no matter what his rank, and Arnold must have been amazed at the audacity of this mere civilian scientist. Arnold began the meeting by outlining the design of the air corps' latest fighter, the twin-engined single-seat Lockheed Lightning. The general tried to impress on Tizard the great performance expected from this aircraft, whose top speed would be more than 400 miles per hour. Tizard had already been briefed on the Lightning and had been told that its top speed was an impressive 390. Even if Arnold's higher figure was correct, Tizard "told him that judging from our experience I thought he would be disappointed finally with the performance and it was an extremely doubtful policy to construct single seater two engine fighters." RAF experience in the summer of 1940 had shown the vulnerability of this type of aircraft (for example the Messerschmitt 110), to single-engine single-seat aircraft such as the Hawker Hurricane and the Supermarine Spitfire. The next stage, the RAF believed, should be to develop a two-seat twin-engined night and long-range escort fighter, though its performance would not be as good as the single-engined interceptors.

Tizard felt that he had won the debate, believing Arnold "to be argued out of his original standpoint." Arnold concluded the discussion by promising to reconsider his policy. It was a polite way to end a disagreement between friends.[20] In fact, neither of them was swayed and both turned out to be incorrect in part. The Army Air Corps pressed on with the Lightning program, which did prove of great value in the Pacific and, to a lesser extent, in the Mediterranean theatres of war. The answer to the long-range escort dilemma was not solved by a two-engined fighter of any description but by one of the most successful examples of Anglo-American technical cooperation – the single-engined North American P-51 Mustang, an American-designed aircraft powered by a British-designed Rolls-Royce Merlin engine.[21] This type of debate was useful to both sides because they now had mutual respect for each other's technological abilities and were willing to learn. In a little over four weeks the mission imparted to the Americans not only a full year of hard-won wartime experience but also twenty years of peacetime research. Information was provided in a large number of areas, though the Americans soon shared Tizard's belief that the most important discussions involved radar.

A survey of the main subjects of the exchange shows the scope of the knowledge that was imparted. In the field of aircraft armament, the mission provided information on power-driven turrets. The Americans requested more data, and soon full production drawings, two sample turrets, and a mechanic were on their way from Great Britain. Briefings were also provided on trials of small-calibre armaments, incendiary and tracer ammunition, aerial gunnery operational and training methods, bombs, and aircraft armour.

A large number of both conventional and unconventional methods were discussed in the field of anti-aircraft methods. Samples of the British army's most important anti-aircraft guns were provided, including the 3.7-inch and the Swedish-designed 40-millimetre Bofors gun, the first of its kind to be seen in North America. Along with the Bofors came the Kerrison predictor, reputed to be the best mechanical anti-aircraft gunnery control system in the world. Both the Bofors gun and the Kerrison predictor were soon accepted by the army and navy as superior to anything in their inventory and were adopted as their principal medium anti-aircraft gun.[22] Briefings were also given on British research related to proximity fuses, which detonated shells automatically at a lethal distance from the target. This information was invaluable in focusing the American research which eventually perfected the proximity fuse in 1943. Particulars of all naval anti-aircraft guns were supplied, and American naval personnel had a chance to see most of them on visits to Halifax. Also provided were full technical details of all anti-aircraft fire-control methods and searchlights. Cockcroft brought along samples and drawings of barrage balloons and kites. In addition, details of several experimental anti-aircraft methods were provided, though most of these would later prove ineffective. They included aerial mines and anti-aircraft rocket barrages, which were designed to shoot down low-flying aircraft.

A great deal of information was exchanged on the latest developments in aircraft engines, including data on the two-stroke internal combustion engine and internal combustion turbines. Of particular significance was the first description received in the United States of Frank Whittle's new turbojet engine. The Whittle engine technology subsequently became the basis of all American jet engine development. As agreed in England in August, the British summary of this revolutionary new technology was superficial, only the broadest outlines of the Whittle engines being provided. This did not go unnoticed by Vannevar Bush, who later wrote to General Hap Arnold: "The interesting part of the subject, namely the explicit way in which the investigation was carried out, were apparently not known to Tizard, and at least he did not give me any indication that he knew such details."[23] This single case of British reluctance to provide full disclosure of information did not hamper the mission's work in any way. Just as the British ignored their hosts' continued refusal to provide the Norden bombsight, the Americans simply deferred detailed discussions of jet engines to a later date. Gathering details on Whittle's work became a top priority of all U.S. Army Air Corps technical visits to Great Britain in 1941.

Briefings were provided on anti-tank weapons and on German tanks. The latest techniques for controlling field artillery were discussed extensively. Information on new explosives, including RDX, was exchanged. Chemical warfare information was provided by chemists from the National Research Council of Canada.

Already mentioned were the beginnings of the exchange of information on radar and sonar technology. These early discussions were expanded on significantly in later months. By December, American technical personnel had full specifications of all of Britain's latest developments in these two areas and had been able to inspect most operational equipment firsthand. Several samples were delivered for testing, including an ASV Mark II air-to-surface radar, AI (airborne interceptor) Mark IV radar, and an IFF set. Many related areas were also the subject of meetings. In addition to the proximity fuses already mentioned, they included the development of a new generation of anti-submarine weapons, such as an experimental gliding torpedo. In addition, all aspects of radio technology, including radio navigation aids, were covered.[24]

In most meetings the British presentation was balanced by an equal focus on the technical details (which were usually provided by a civilian scientist) and an account by one of the uniformed members of the team of recent combat experience with the devices. Whenever possible, actual combat film or photographs were used to illustrate the discussion. Also, as much information as possible, including documentary evidence and samples, was provided of German equipment and practices. The uniformed members gave separate briefings on British operational experiences to American operational personnel.

These meetings had an electric effect on their American audience. Both the Navy and War Departments reduced the restrictions on technical cooperation still further. There were few who doubted the value of continuing and expanding Anglo-American technical cooperation. In mid-September even Admiral Furlong, at the Bureau of Naval Ordnance, agreed and authorized discussions with mission members.[25] By 28 September virtually every piece of technology, whether in operational use or in the earliest stages of research and development, had been provided. In total, the army restricted access to information on just eight specific items or industrial processes. Most were because of concerns over patent ownership or because their complexity made providing full details at short notice extremely difficult. The majority of these items were made available to the British by the end of October.[26] The navy exclusion list was even shorter, containing just two items – an antenna mine with a two-way firing device and, of course, the Norden bombsight. Just nine days earlier, on 19 September, six items had been withheld from British scrutiny. The Norden bombsight would not be released to the British until 1942. The Americans, Lord Lothian observed, had an obsession about preserving the secrecy of the bombsight. By September 1940, however, it was of such minor importance to the British that this obsession could easily be ignored.[27]

The best example of the impact that the mission's information had on the American services can be found in the dramatic about-face of Admiral H.G. Bowen, the director of the Naval Research Laboratory and the technical aide to the secretary of the navy. In late July 1940, it will be recalled, Bowen had expressed grave doubts about the value of British technology. At the time, he had believed that the information received from the British on radar and sonar would "possibly prove disappointing." "For a nation," he had said, "that has been so backward in mechanical and electrical engineering as applied to naval vessels to have established outstanding progress in two other fields of engineering does not seem credible although it may be possible."[28] However, by the time of the preliminary discussions on Royal Navy radar and sonar equipment, Bowen was beginning to change his mind, and by early October he had become an enthusiastic supporter of continuing and expanding the technical cooperation. On 4 October he submitted to Frank Knox, the secretary of the navy, a detailed report on the information on radar and sonar which the mission had supplied. Bowen now believed that, through the medium of the Tizard Mission, the navy had "received a vast amount of important information from which much benefit can be gained, particularly since the data furnished by the British are based, in great part on the results of actual wartime experience." He added that the mission had been "decidedly liberal" in imparting information on confidential and secret projects and had furnished technical literature with "considerable freedom." In return, the U.S. Navy had provided Tizard's group with data on secret naval equipment and research, though Bowen felt "that the Navy has gained more than the British by the free exchange of information."

Bowen included a detailed examination of British radar and sonar development, which he considered the most "outstanding" examples of the value of continuing Anglo-American technical cooperation. But he felt obliged to defend his own research centre from criticism, since it was impossible to hide the fact that the British were years ahead in this field. Bowen told Knox:

> Because of the urgent requirements of the war, the British have been forced to prosecute the development of their RDF [radar] to a much greater extent than has been reached in this country, and as a result have been able actively to employ the RDF on shore, in aircraft. and in various types of ships. The results obtained by the British have been so encouraging and of such great immediate importance as to warrant the employment in Great Britain of approximately 500 development engineers, with the necessary assistants and laboratory facilities; and to bring about the existence of a complete organization for manufacture, procurement, and installation of RDF equipment. Unavoidable exigencies have thus led the British to forge far ahead of this country in the application of this device.

Bowen took great pains to educate Knox on the history of radar research at the Naval Research Laboratory (NRL), enclosing a three-page appendix summarizing key points in the laboratory's program since 1922. He sometimes took liberties with the truth.

For instance, he claimed that a joint research project of the NRL and the Carnegie Institution, and their 1926 publication of the results of radio-wave reflection, was what had led the British to develop their first radar sets. He failed to mention numerous other published papers on the same phenomena by other scientists. He pointed out that work on radar had begun at the NRL several years before the British program had started. The NRL's development of the duplexor was emphasized, since the British had no equivalent technology. He blamed lack of government and private industrial support for the inferiority of American radar. No mention was made of the lack of support for the early research given by senior NRL administrators or of the interservice rivalries that had hampered crucial work.

Bowen's main message to Knox was of the need to heed the most important lessons learned from the Tizard Mission – that they should greatly expand their radar research and procurement programs and should give them top priority. As Bowen wrote, there were eighteen people working on radar at the NRL – a marked increase since April 1939, when only five had been so employed, but a mere drop in the bucket compared with British research facilities. He concluded that "the U.S. Navy would be unexcusably laggard if it did not immediately take appropriate steps to further the development of radio-ranging-and-bearing apparatus as rapidly as possible."

Bowen's analysis of British asdic was very similar to that in the late-August report of Lieutenant-Commander W.L. Pryor, Jr, which was discussed in detail in the last chapter. Here there was much closer parity in technologies and thus fewer – though still vital – lessons to be learned. Bowen's main recommendation concerned the need to improve the sonar training of both officers and ratings, an area in which the U.S. Navy was clearly inferior to the Royal Navy. Also requiring immediate adoption was the Admiralty's noise-reduction technology, which it was hoped would greatly enhance the performance of American submarine-detection equipment.[29] Bowen's recommendations were acted upon in several stages through October, and on 16 October major purchases of sample British radar equipment was authorized. Then, on 1 November, Admiral Stark approved the wholesale increase in research, development, and production of naval radar.[30]

The Army Signal Corps also desired to expand its radar program by utilizing British technological advances. On 22 October, Major Paul Edwards, the army radar expert who had been sent to Great Britain in September, requested the immediate authorization of funds to purchase ASV, IFF, AI, and other radar equipment. This was necessary because "it will obviate much research and development and to enable service tests to be made without delay." The cost of these acquisitions, he pointed out, "would be infinitely less than covering ground already covered by the British."[31]

One week later, $100,000 was authorized for the purchase of British radar. On 8 November, however, the military attaché in London reported that there were several obstacles for the direct purchase of equipment, primarily British concerns about security. He reported "the necessity for security measures of extraordinary nature to safeguard material which it is possible may be the decisive factor in the aerial conflict." The Royal Air Force proposed that instead of selling the equipment, it would lend the Americans samples from equipment being sent to Canada. This arrangement enabled British officers to check security arrangements before the sets were sent to the United States. The RAF wanted its radar safeguarded with the same zeal that the Norden bombsight was protected.[32] The War Department had no objections to this arrangement; it chose to ignore what might easily have been perceived as an insult, because it wanted technical cooperation to continue and expand. Several other technical experts were sent to England in late September and October including, for the first time, a representative from a private armament manufacturer.

Members of the British Technical Mission had begun to have discussions on technological developments with private corporations when the preliminary agreement on patents had been reached at the end of September. One of many companies involved was Sperry Gyroscope, which Cockcroft, Fowler, E.G. Bowen, and Wallace visited on 8 and 17 October. Sperry was intrigued by British technology and by the possibility of British orders. When the company said it would like to send a technical delegation to Britain, the British Purchasing Commission immediately gave it the credentials to get access to secret facilities and equipment. On 19 October, F.B. Vose of the aeronautical department of Sperry asked the Army Air Corps for permission to send representatives to the United Kingdom so that the company could incorporate British technology and war lessons into its aircraft fire-control equipment. This information would be of "immeasurable value," especially since it could be incorporated when there was "still some degree of flexibility" in its designs. Sperry wanted its scientists to "confer with aircraft armament designers and manufactures, with operating personnel, and with the other officers of the Air Arm, who are directly concerned with the tactical employment of this type of aircraft." The company hoped that its mission would begin long-term cooperation with British firms on the development of this technology.[33] What would have been unthinkable only a few months earlier was approved by the War Department with impressive speed – in just two days: Sperry could send its scientists to Great Britain. They were the first of a flood of industrial experts who crossed the Atlantic in both directions in late 1940 and 1941.[34]

The mission had completed its primary agenda by the time Tizard left for England in early October. At this point, Cockcroft took over the leadership, and the majority of mission members began gathering data about American technology. The acquisition of American technical secrets, although hoped for, had not been expected to be so rapid and open. Thus, the success of the mission caused Cockcroft and the others to stay on far longer than had been anticipated. The value of the information imparted to the British by the Americans was immense, though by their own admission it was nowhere near as important as what they received in return. As we have seen in the case of the duplexor valve, even in the earliest meetings with American technical experts, the exchange was very much a two-way street. The mission members forwarded detailed reports of their findings back to London. The complete set of these reports survive in the Public Record Office and provide a unique insight into American industry and military as the country began to mobilize for war.

In the last half of September, Captain Faulkner, the Royal Navy's representative, toured American naval installations on the west coast and the new American fleet base at Pearl Harbor in Hawaii. While he briefed American naval officers on British operational experiences, he was allowed to observe several fleet exercises. Off the coast of San Diego, he witnessed an impressive night exercise; destroyers successfully engaged targets illuminated by searchlights and starshells from 5,000 to 6,000 yards' range.[35] At Pearl Harbor, he was able to examine several impressive examples of American technological prowess. He was particularly fascinated by one new piece of naval ordnance: "The 5" 38 calibre gun mounted in all destroyers, on HA [high altitude]/long range gun mounts in all modern ships seems to be a splendid weapon and fitted as it is with a triple fuse setter, gives a rate of fire at all elevations superior to any gun of similar type which I have seen in our service." Faulkner also reported favourably on the American damage-control procedures he had observed on the USS *Enterprise,* and on the overall appearance and discipline of the American sailors.

Faulkner was a keen observer, and he did not hesitate to criticize his hosts when he felt it necessary. Ironically, he spotted two weaknesses that were to prove fatal to the Pacific Fleet some fourteen months later. He was shocked to see an absence of short-range anti-aircraft guns, a situation compounded by certain flawed procedures: "I was amazed to see that in this ship [the USS *Maryland*] and all others I visited, no attempt is made to arrange for the accommodation of lookouts and that no 'air defence' position as we know it was arranged for. The operators and control officers were, however, under the prevailing excellent conditions, quite quick at picking up the target."[36] It is impossible to know if Faulkner imparted his criticisms to his hosts, or if he took the diplomatically expedient route and reported his observations only to London. What is certain is that the U.S. Navy's unpreparedness for air attack still existed on 7 December 1941.

Other mission members recorded some of the first British descriptions of many of the weapon systems that soon became standard in the British arsenal. These observations were all the more important because of the subsequent American refusal to manufacture British military equipment. Instead of relying on British-designed, American-manufactured weapon systems, the British would be forced to adopt American-designed equipment if they were to tap into the vast industrial resources of the "arsenal of democracy."

At the U.S. Army's Aberdeen proving ground, Fowler, Wallace, and Colonel H.F.G. Letson, a Canadian representative, inspected the latest in American tank designs. On 3 October they were shown the mock-up of the General Grant, with a 37-millimetre gun in its turret. A 75-millimetre was just being installed, "firing forward on the right side of the driver position about 30 degrees."[37] In late November they returned to Aberdeen and were given a more extensive examination of tank weapon systems. They were particularly enthusiastic about stabilized gun mountings. The mechanism used hydraulic pistons operated through a gyro control to assist in aiming while the tank was on the move. Fowler reported: "[The gyro stabilizer] is trained by shoulder control by the gunner, who grips an arm rest under his arm. The stabilizer contains two gyros. The main gyro gives a vertical with respect to which the mechanism attempts to keep the gun at a constant angular setting, in spite of the pitching of the tank. The whole control system seems to be compact and of sound design." A firing demonstration followed the inspection. The American crew had five hits and four near misses out of twelve rounds as they approached a target from a distance of 900 to 200 yards. Next, Fowler took the place of the machine gunner, and Wallace replaced the gunner. While approaching a target at a medium speed from 600 to 200 yards away, Wallace was able to get off seven rounds, scoring with three and having two very near misses. The stabilization mechanism was then switched off, and on the same course Wallace was able to get off only three rounds, scoring just a single hit. Both Fowler and Wallace were impressed, and they urged the British government to acquire this technology immediately.[38]

A great deal of time was spent examining American industrial techniques. After visiting Aberdeen for the first time, Wallace, Fowler, and Letson were invited to the Watertown Arsenal in New York to examine a secret American process for the centrifugal casting of guns. One indication of how quickly things were changing as a result of the mission is that just two weeks earlier, centrifugal casting had been on the U.S. Army's restricted list. In this plant, gun barrels were made by pouring molten metal through "a small axial orifice" into a round mould. The mould was spun at rates up to 1,200 rotations per minute, depending on the size of the gun. This method of casting, along with the sophisticated machine and cold-working processes that followed, produced artillery barrels that had "higher physical and metallurgical properties" than conventionally forged pieces. They had the additional advantage of being far less costly and less time-consuming to produce. No similar factories existed in the United Kingdom, and Fowler and Wallace arranged for detailed plans to be sent to London as soon as possible.[39]

Numerous other visits were made to American factories, research centres, and military stations throughout October and November. Many of the reports, particularly those dealing with the latest in electronics, were highly technical and will not be examined in detail here. The important point is that by the end of the mission the exchange of ideas, technology, and techniques that had taken place had begun the process of fusing together the combined knowledge of two great industrial and military powers. The question now was whether the mission's work would continue.

This was exactly what Cockcroft asked the War Department at the end of November. He and most of the remaining members had been ordered home, and the mission was about to be terminated. The War Department solicited the opinions of every single technical division about the need to continue the work of the mission. The Engineering and Chemical Corps asked for immediate assistance from further British technical experts. The Ordnance Department did not need aid right away but wanted it made clear "that the British Government [should] be informed that the War Department has found the exchange of technical information to be of great value and that it is desired to maintain this type of liaison." The Army Air Corps was also enthusiastic about continuing the mission's work, though its view was that the British experts in the United States were "top notch" and that no others need be sent. The Signal Corps requested that E.G. Bowen (who had almost finished installing, in a navy Catalina aircraft, the first ASV to reach North America) be retained, and that an expert on proximity fuses be requested from the British.[40]

Bowen was authorized to stay on for an indefinite period – the first sign that the mission was just the beginning of a long-term relationship. He had spent much of October and November arranging for the installation and demonstration of three samples of airborne radar equipment that arrived in North America in November – an IFF Mark II set, an ASV Mark II, and an AI Mark IV. All three systems were successfully demonstrated from mid-November to early December. The British IFF, which allowed for automatic identification of aircraft and ships, was immediately adopted by both American services. This represented a direct superseding of less effective American technology, which was in an early stage of research. Orders for the equipment initially numbered in the thousands, eventually growing to the tens (if not hundreds) of thousands. The ASV set was installed by Bowen and two Canadian assistants in a PBY Catalina aircraft based at the Anacostia Naval Air Station. It flew for the first time on 30 November and was demonstrated on 2 December. American observers were impressed when the set picked up a large ship 60 miles away. By early 1941, navy and army orders for ASV had been placed for several thousand of the North American version, which was produced by the Philco Corporation and Canada's Research Enterprises Limited. Ultimately, 17,000 sets were built in North America, the vast majority being used by the U.S. armed forces. Here, too, far more primitive U.S. naval and army research programs were terminated in favour of the British technology. The AI set, a type not yet even under consideration by the U.S. armed forces, was mounted on a Douglas A20 aircraft at Wright Field. It performed well enough in demonstrations to be ordered into service by the Army Air Corps. Early in 1941 Western Electric was given a small contract to build the sets, called in U.S. service the SCR 540.[41]

The technological transfer of aircraft-mounted radar was one of the most significant results of the mission. Used throughout the war in every theatre of operation, IFF became indispensable in separating friendly aircraft and ships from the enemy's. The North American version of the ASV played a vital role in defending against the first great U-boat offensives in the western Atlantic and Caribbean in 1942. Neither would have been in U.S. service until 1943, at the earliest, if it had not been for the bold initiative to provide this top secret technology while the United States was still a neutral power. By itself, this particular aspect of the transfer guaranteed that the mission was viewed as a success, but it was by no means the most significant immediate consequence. Much more momentous developments, involving an even more closely guarded radar secret, had begun even before the first airborne systems were tested. This involved the mission members in much more than the mere shifting of technology, for they became crucial players in the transformation that was then underway in the relationship between American civilian scientists and the military establishment.

7 The Transformation of American Science

As one of the official historians of the American scientific war claimed, it was "the most valuable cargo ever brought to our shores." Yet throughout most of September, the magnetron lay in a suitcase stored under a bed in one of the secretary's rooms at the Shoreham Hotel.[1] Although the principles of this device, which allowed for the generation of high-powered microwave radar, had been described to the U.S. Navy and the War Department in late August, the magnetron brought by Bowen remained hidden from view. It remained concealed because an internal struggle was taking place within the American government concerning who would control wartime scientific research and development. The revelation that microwave radar was now much more than just theory quite unintentionally thrust the Tizard Mission directly into this bureaucratic donnybrook.

At the centre of the battle for the control of scientific resources was a brand-new civilian agency whose creation had been orchestrated by its first chairman, Vannevar Bush. This was the National Defense Research Committee. Bush was the son of a Boston Universalist Church minister. He had excelled in mathematics at Tufts University before completing a doctorate in 1916 in electrical engineering at the Massachusetts Institute of Technology (MIT) and Harvard. After working on anti-submarine technology during the First World War, Bush was appointed an associate professor in the Department of Electrical Engineering at MIT. Here he was expected to supplement his income by outside consulting, which he did with great success. He helped his college roommate turn inventions – some of which were his own – into profitable commodities. This led to the founding of the new vacuum tube company – Raytheon. Bush showed a remarkable knack for combining his skills as a mathematician and inventor. He developed complex equations for the analysis of power circuits, and when these equations were found to be too intricate to be solved by normal means, he developed the differential analyser, a sophisticated mechanical predecessor of the electronic analogue computer. It was soon found to have a wide range of scientific and industrial uses.

A popular teacher at MIT, Bush was also an excellent administrator, and he was appointed dean of engineering and vice-president of MIT in the early 1930s. In 1939 he moved to Washington to assume the presidency of the Carnegie Institution, and in that same year he was made chairman of the National Advisory Committee for Aeronautics (NACA). The NACA, it will be remembered, was the one institution that had brought together academic, industrial, and military researchers in the interwar period. It was an official agency funded by the government, and it reported directly to the president. Much of its research was funded by a revolutionary contract system in which academic and industrial scientists conducted their projects in their own research facilities.

It was through his post at the NACA that Bush became acquainted with the slow pace of American defence research programs. As early as 1937, he frequently discussed the state of military technological research and development with a group of leading academic and industrial scientific administrators. They included Frank Jewett, the president of the National Academy of Sciences and vice-president in charge of research at AT&T; Karl Compton, president of MIT; James B. Conant, president of Harvard; and Richard Tolman, a dean at the California Institute of Technology. All were pro-Allied and all were convinced of the need to defeat Hitler and of the key role that science would play in the victory. Each one, Bush in particular, believed that America's vast scientific potential would be poorly utilized if left to the army, navy, and scientific institutions that had been around since the First World War.[2]

In 1916 the National Academy of Sciences had created the National Research Council (NRC) to manage the war research of academic scientists. However, the NRC was not a government agency and did not have direct access to government funds or executive authority. The services had established competing organizations, particularly the Naval Consulting Board under the leadership of Thomas Edison. As we have seen, it took the NRC considerable time to win any recognition; indeed, not until mid-1917 did it begin to receive a reasonable level of support from the military services. Even then, it did not have the power to coordinate scientific research, much of which continued in a haphazard manner, often with duplication of effort.

Bush was just out of graduate school in 1916, and he wanted to develop a system that would detect submarines. He aimed to do so by creating a magnetic field around a wooden-hulled submarine chaser which would be disturbed when it passed over a submerged metal object. This disturbance of the magnetic field would trigger a receptor to give off an audible tone in a headphone. The closer the submarine, the louder the signal. When Bush approached Robert Millikan, chairman of the NRC's anti-submarine committee, he was denied the chance to present his idea to the navy for funds. So he turned for money to a private corporation owned by the financier J.P. Morgan. There followed a disillusioning year and a half for the young engineer. His program was hampered by lack of liaison with other researchers. Bush discovered by accident that there were at least two other groups working on similar devices. Moreover, he received contradictory and technically impossible demands from the navy which greatly delayed the project. In one case he was ordered to mount the sets onto steel-hulled destroyers, despite the fact that the magnetic detection system would not work on such vessels. Ultimately, Bush was able to develop his submarine detector, and one hundred of them were ordered. But only three sets actually made it into an operational area before the war ended.

This experience left Bush convinced that a radical departure was needed in the way science was organized for war. He recalled in his memoirs: "The [First World] war ended, and no set had ever found a single German submarine. But I learned quite a bit about how not to fight a war. That experience forced into my mind pretty solidly the complete lack of proper liaison between the military and the civilian in the development of weapons in time of war, and what that lack meant."[3] Bush had developed a strong belief that the army and navy could not be trusted with establishing proper liaison with and coordination of the civilian research effort. Although he had a great deal of respect for the military research teams working at such places as the Naval Research Laboratory, he believed that the defence establishment still tended to stifle the type of independent creative thinking that was required for rapid technical progress. Also, he had evidence that some of the most senior technical officers in the services did not really understand the value of large-scale research programs during wartime. At a meeting with General Mauborgne, the head of the Signal Corps, Bush and Frank Jewett were astounded to hear him proclaim, "When a nation goes to war it is necessary to freeze all new developments – developments should stop because production problems of the present day are so vast. You have to fight a war with what you have."[4]

In May 1940, Bush used his extensive political connections to arrange for a meeting with Harry Hopkins, President Roosevelt's secretary of commerce and his most trusted adviser. Bush outlined his proposal for a radically new type of scientific organization for the wartime emergency. Although Bush was known to have opposed the New Deal, which Hopkins had done so much to establish during the Depression, the two men saw eye to eye on this issue. They agreed on the need for the effective mobilization of all the nation's resources in preparation for a conflict which both men viewed as inevitable. Hopkins agreed with Bush's outline for the new scientific agency, the National Defense Research Committee (NDRC). It would be part of the executive branch and thus would have direct access to government funds without reference to the military.

In early June, Bush was ushered into a meeting with Roosevelt carrying a four-paragraph proposal. After ten minutes, the president said, "That's okay. Put 'OK, FDR' on it."[5] On 27 June 1940, the official order establishing the NDRC was proclaimed. Bush was appointed chairman of its executive committee. Also on the executive were Conant, Compton, Jewett, Tolman, Conway P. Coe, the commissioner of patents, and one representative each from the army and navy. Bush envisioned that the new organization would not establish its own research facilities but would act as a contracting and coordinating agency. It would be the existing universities and corporations that would receive the research contracts.

Despite Roosevelt's support for it, the army and navy both opposed the imposition of this civilian-dominated agency. In order to prevent an open revolt, the president instructed Bush that work undertaken by the NDRC should not "replace any of the excellent work which these services are now carrying on, either in their own laboratories or by contract with industry."[6] Thus, although Bush had a powerful agency on paper, its mandate was limited to conducting research in fields that the service laboratories were not pursuing. This usually meant unpromising or highly experimental areas. Radar research, for instance, was already being given high priority at both the Naval Research Laboratory and the Signal Corps facilities at Fort Monmouth. However, the few avenues of research open to the NDRC in the radar field included two subjects on which the services had done limited work: microwaves and proximity fuses. The military had left out these areas because they appeared unlikely to have short-term results.

In the spring of 1940 no one in the United States – not even A.V. Hill, the British scientific attaché – knew of the recent discovery of the cavity magnetron at the University of Birmingham. Any competent physicist or electrical engineer versed in the radar secret could understand the theoretical advantages of microwave radar. Its much smaller wavelength (10 centimetres or less, compared with 1.5 metres or more for long-wave equipment) allowed for a highly accurate set, which could detect very small targets or make extremely accurate range calculations using a much smaller antenna system. Microwave radar would therefore be ideal for mounting on aircraft and small ships; it would allow for radar control of all types of gunnery, from the main armament of a battleship to a small anti-aircraft gun; and it would enable the detection of targets such as partially surfaced submarines, which long-wave sets could not find. But there was a problem. The klystron radio tubes, the most powerful microwave generators known in the United States before the arrival of the mission, could not produce enough power to make the theory practicable.

In June 1940, Alfred L. Loomis approached Bush about his research on microwave radar. A first cousin of Henry Stimson, the secretary of war, Loomis was a retired investment banker, who conducted research in physics at the private laboratory he had established at his home in Tuxedo Park, New York. The army and navy had terminated their own experimental work on microwave radar in 1937 in favour of the more promising long-wave equipment, so they raised no objections to others pursuing it.[7] Thus, by accident, Bush's new agency was made responsible for developing the magnetron; literally overnight, this ingenious device made practical microwave radar possible. The magnetron would make Bush's dream a reality by transforming the experimental microwave research program into one of the most important fields of investigation in the entire rearmament program. Not only that, but it gave the NDRC a central role. With the magnetron, Bush later recalled, "we ran away with the ball."[8]

Bush had been an active though quiet supporter of Anglo-American technical cooperation since A.V. Hill's mission to the United States; he had advised Hill on the sensitive state of American public opinion and had supported the idea of establishing a permanent scientific liaison office in Ottawa. During July 1940, he had met with British officials in Washington in search of the best way to approach the Roosevelt administration in order to gain approval for the proposed British Technical Mission; and when Tizard arrived in Washington, Bush had been briefed about the mission, not by his own army or navy (which had excluded the NDRC from their meeting with the mission) but by the British Embassy. It was understood, stated Bush, that the NDRC and members of the Tizard Mission could only "get together behind the barn."[9]

On 28 August 1940, Bush and Tolman had dinner with Tizard and R.H. Fowler at the Cosmos Club in Washington. Here they discovered that they were very much kindred spirits. Both Tizard and Bush believed that civilian scientists had an important role to play in determining military research priorities. This meant that they had to have access to the most senior levels of the military planning process. Tizard was no doubt sympathetic to Bush's goal of making the NDRC the central coordinating agency for the scientific war effort. Although no such agency existed in the United Kingdom, many scientists wanted to see one created under the auspices of the Royal Society. This idea had been thwarted by the strenuous objections of the Admiralty, the Air Ministry, and the Ministry of Supply. Determined not to let their desire to exchange technical information hurt the NDRC's struggle to assert itself, Bush and Tizard agreed that the British would initially confine their discussions to the War and Navy Departments. Bush, meanwhile, would work from inside the administration to gain permission to begin technical interchange with the Tizard Mission.[10]

While Bush worked behind the scenes, the mission members worked more openly for authority to begin formal discussions with the NDRC. A large part of one of the early meetings at the Naval Research Laboratory was spent discussing with Admiral Bowen the proper procedures for opening discussions with the NDRC. If they made a formal request to him, Bowen told them, he would do "everything in his power to facilitate such discussions." Fowler and Pearce represented the mission at this meeting. They reported that while they were certain Bowen would make the arrangements, it was "also clear that the Navy Dept. and Research Laboratory were jealous or in danger of feeling jealous of Dr. Bush and his committee." This was despite the fact that Bowen had been appointed the navy's representative on the NDRC.[11]

On 31 August, Tizard made a formal request to Admiral Bowen to allow mission members to meet with the NDRC, but no immediate action was forthcoming.[12] Bush, however, continued to press for permission to meet with the British formally, and on 12 September the War Department authorized "a free interchange of views" between the British Technical Mission and the NDRC. Four days later the Navy Department also acquiesced, but it did so with more stringent restrictions. Bush was reminded that no discussions could take place on items on the navy's exclusion list, and he was requested to include a naval officer in all discussions in which the department had an interest.[13]

The first meeting on microwave radar took place on 19 September in Alfred Loomis's room at the Wardman Park Hotel. Loomis had invited Cockcroft, E.G. Bowen, and Dr John Henderson, a Canadian radar expert, to meet with himself, Karl Compton, Admiral Bowen, and Carol Wilson, Bush's executive assistant who was soon to be placed in charge of all international liaison for the NDRC. The British members were fully briefed on American research and development work. It soon became clear that the

Americans had made excellent progress in receivers, waveguides, and horns, but they had nothing to compare with the magnetron for transmitting power. The magnetron was then quietly brought forth, and the Americans were astounded to learn that this small device could produce more than one hundred times the power of the best klystron tube then available.[14]

A follow-up meeting was promptly arranged for the weekend of 28 and 29 September at Loomis's laboratory at Tuxedo Park. This meeting was to be one of the most important in the history of the mission and of the NDRC. Cockcroft and Bowen arrived at La Guardia airport on the morning of 28 September. They were picked up by one of Loomis's cars and driven the fifty miles north through the beautiful fall colours of the Catskill Mountains to his colonial-style mansion at Tuxedo Park. Next door was an older house in which the laboratory was located.

The British were impressed by Loomis, a man some have called the Benjamin Franklin of the twentieth century. As well as being a wealthy investment banker, he had served as an artillery officer in the First World War and had then become chief of research and development at the U.S. Army's Aberdeen proving ground. In the 1920s he was a part-time scientist making important discoveries in the field of ultrasonics. He also played an important role in the development of the electroencephalograph, used for the measurement of brain waves. His crucial work placed the new technology on a sound instrumental basis. In the 1930s, he had served as a quiet philanthropist, assisting Ernest Lawrence in his quest for funds and material to construct his famous cyclotrons for use in subatomic research. If all this was not enough, Loomis was also a successful amateur sailor who had once built a contender for the America's Cup. He was modest man, more than willing to go unrecognized for his efforts. But he was the father of American microwave radar technology and should not be forgotten.

Cockcroft and Bowen met with Loomis, Carol Wilson, and Professor Edward Bowles, an electrical engineer from MIT. The next day they were joined by three others: Hugh Willis, another member of the NDRC microwave committee and director of research for Sperry; Dr Charles Lauritsen of the California Institute of Technology; and J.W. Bell of the National Research Council of Canada. The meeting involved a complete exchange of detailed technical data on both countries' microwave radar research and on the benefits of this type of system over existing army and navy equipment. The climax of the meeting took place on Sunday evening. Once again the magnetron was revealed, along with all the detailed specifications and plans. "The atmosphere," reported E.G. Bowen, "was electric – they found it hard to believe that such a small device could produce so much power and that what lay on the table in front of us might prove to be the salvation of the Allied cause." All were agreed that if the device worked as the British claimed, the NDRC's Microwave Committee would immediately contract Bell Telephone Laboratories to begin construction.[15]

The best gauge of the American scientists' reaction to the British technology can be found in Henry Stimson's diary, where he described a meeting he had with Loomis on the Wednesday after this weekend session. Loomis came in "full of excitement" about the benefits of technical cooperation with the British mission: "He said we were getting the chance to start now two years ahead of where we were and we were getting infinitely more from the British than we could give them." This fascinated Stimson, since his cousin's great scientific knowledge and practical business sense made him unlikely to exaggerate. Stimson called in General George Marshall, the chief of staff, to be briefed. Loomis diplomatically praised the army's role in encouraging openness with the British and stated that the navy had initially been far less cooperative. However, the fruits of the mission had now, according to Loomis, swept away any doubts about the great value of free and frank Anglo-American technical exchanges.[16]

For the members of the Tizard Mission, the meeting at Tuxedo Park was one of the critical moments of their work in America. Tizard certainly felt that he had achieved all the principal goals that he had set for the mission before its departure. By allowing his group to talk directly to the NDRC, the Americans had removed the last important bureaucratic barrier to the exchange of technical information. The magnetron and all accompanying documentation had been turned over to the Bell Laboratories, and, in short order, a preproduction batch of twenty would be built. Tizard had little doubt that mass production on a scale that was impossible in Great Britain would soon follow. This meant that his main job was done. It was now up to the technical experts – Cockcroft, Bowen, Pew, and others – to carry on while he ensured that in London the mission's good work was continued and reinforced. He was particularly concerned about the repeated failure to ship sample radar equipment to the United States. He arranged to return to London via the Pan Am clipper, leaving New York on 5 October.

Tizard asked E.G. Bowen to accompany him on the flight from Washington to New York, for there were several issues he wished to discuss with the youngest member of the mission. Of specific importance was the need to continue to encourage the NDRC to begin full-scale research, development, and production of both the magnetron and the radar systems based on it. Of all the British experts then in the United States, Bowen was the most conversant in the technical details of radar. He was now thrust into a central role in assisting the Americans to adopt British radar technology. As we have already seen, Bowen was instrumental in installing the long-wave aircraft and IFF sets that finally arrived in November. But, in many ways, his accomplishments in the microwave field in October were far more significant. Ably assisted by Fowler and Cockcroft, and occasionally by F.C. Wallace, Bowen played an important part in beginning the new and greatly expanded American microwave radar program.[17]

Bowen's work commenced in New York on the very day he arrived there with Tizard. He met with representatives of the Bell Telephone Laboratories at the company's headquarters. After a brief session with senior executives, including the director Mervin Kelly and his deputy Ralph Bown, Bowen was introduced to the leading members of Bell's radio tube research group, including, J.G. Wilson and A.L. Samuel. These men were among the most important industrial research scientists in the United States, well known to Bowen through their numerous scholarly publications. Here the magnetron was given its first detailed examination. The Americans found that its individual parts were nothing new, and therefore there would be no difficulty in producing copies in the United States. However, they were sceptical about the ability of these relatively simple devices to generate high-power microwaves, and they asked Bowen to supervise a demonstration. Bowen informed them that he required a powerful magnetic field of 1,500 gauss and a pulse anode capable of producing 10,000 volts to power the device. It was therefore agreed to reconvene at the company's Whippany Laboratory in

New Jersey as soon as possible. Bowen left the magnetron in the care of Bell's staff.

Bowen was busy with other meetings until Sunday, 6 October, but as the Bell scientists were too anxious to wait for Monday, he was driven across the river from Manhattan to the Whippany Laboratory that morning. Bowen and the Bell scientists first attached the magnetron to a powerful modulator, which produced a short burst of electricity at 10,000 volts. The requisite magnetic field was provided by a large electromagnet. All present realized that the magnetron had not been tested for two months and that it had travelled over 3,000 miles since then. Perhaps it would not work. The magnetic field was put in place and the modulator connected to the magnetron. Next, they "very gingerly" switched on the anode potential and "were immediately rewarded with a glow discharge about an inch long coming from the output terminal."

The Bell staff were amazed at the power generated by the device. Bowen believed that it produced nearly 15 kilowatts, almost 50 per cent more than he had anticipated. When asked at what wavelength the magnetron was generating signals, Bowen estimated 10 centimetres. This was confirmed when a wavemeter showed that the wavelength was exactly 9.8 centimetres. Suddenly, all doubts were cast aside. Mervin Kelly revealed to Bowen that he had already received instructions from Loomis to proceed with the manufacture of thirty copies if the British claims were verified. Bowen left well satisfied, convinced that the American production would proceed smoothly.[18]

It did proceed smoothly, but not before a rather comical incident occurred, one which showed that the British had not yet completely won the trust of the American technical experts. The next day Bowen received a "rather rude shock" – an urgent telephone call from an agitated Mervin Kelly. Kelly could not give details on an open line, but he said that a problem had developed which required Bowen's immediate return to the New Jersey laboratory. It was clearly something drastic, and Bowen first thought that the magnetron had blown up.

Catching the first morning flight from Washington to New York, he went straight to the Whippany Laboratory. There he was ushered into the conference room, where he was confronted by a grim Mervin Kelly and several equally serious members of the laboratory's staff. Kelly began by outlining the events of the last few weeks leading up to the magnetron being turned over to Bell. J.G. Wilson then produced the magnetron and laid it in the middle of the table. Kelly asked Bowen, "Is that the magnetron that you brought here last week?" Bowen agreed that it was. Wilson then produced the plans of the internal arrangements of the magnetron that had been handed over at the same time. Kelly asked Bowen if these were the plans he had provided. Bowen agreed again. Next Kelly produced a photograph. "'It may interest you to know,' he said, pointing dramatically to the magnetron laying on the table, 'that this is an x-ray picture of the magnetron.'" Bowen looked at the photograph and could not believe what he saw. The photograph showed that the magnetron he had brought with him was entirely different from all the drawings, specifications, and samples of the device he had ever seen. The plans he had brought from England had shown that the resonant cavity of the magnetron contained six rings emanating from its central core, whereas the x-ray clearly showed eight holes.

Bowen asked to telephone the General Electric Company in Wembley to discover the reason for the discrepancy. He talked to Dr E.C.S. Megaw, who had supervised the production of the first batch of magnetrons. At first Megaw could not understand the discrepancy, but after a few moments he suddenly remembered its cause. He had placed the order for the magnetrons late one afternoon at the end of July, and later that evening he had gone back to the laboratory on a whim in order to carry out an experiment. He had instructed the foreman to build ten of the magnetrons with the normal six rings, one with seven, and one with eight. Under the stress of the time, Megaw had forgotten about his improvised experiment. Thus, when Bowen arrived at Wembley, he had accidentally selected the experimental eight-holed unit, assuming it to be a standard six-holed model. With this mystery solved, the Bell staff agreed to proceed with production. They decided to ignore all the technical specifications and blueprints brought by Bowen, and instead took detailed measurements from the eight-holed sample. Within a few weeks the first American-built magnetron was ready, and within a month the first thirty preproduction units had been completed.[19]

Arranging for the production of the magnetron was a relatively simple matter compared with the creation of an NDRC radar research program that could utilize the full potential of the magnetron. If the NDRC was to research and develop microwave radar, it had to create an entire organizational structure to manage and coordinate the program, along with new central research facilities to undertake the work. Also, the NDRC needed to be able to establish which types of radar would be developed. According to the official historian of the NDRC radar program, the British scientists (and Bowen in particular) played "an active and influential part in these discussions, by describing the British Air Ministry's radar research organization, and by helping to lay down the specific objectives for the microwave program."[20]

The microwave radar research projects already being undertaken by Loomis and other researchers under contract with the microwave committee were small-scale efforts, small enough for much of the work to be conducted at Loomis's private laboratory at Tuxedo Park. Other research teams at the Massachusetts Institute of Technology and Stanford University also contributed. At the first Tuxedo Park meeting on 28–29 September, those present realized that the magnetron had created a new situation: microwave radar was no longer just an experimental project; it had an immediate practical military potential and thus demanded a much larger organization.

It is indicative of the spirit of international cooperation that existed among scientists in 1940 that the members of the British mission were immediately asked to assist in planning the expanded microwave radar research and development program. There were no hints of nationalistic jealousies among these men. The American scientists regarded their British counterparts as equals in every way. They shared a common belief that the war against fascism and totalitarianism could be won only by making the most effective use of technological and scientific developments. They believed that rapid progress in the power and capabilities of weapon systems was inevitable, and that their enemies – whose scientific skills they greatly respected – could easily win this war of science. If science was to be fully utilized, it had to be carefully managed and organized. Although the American scientists were equal to the British in scientific knowledge, they recognized that Cockcroft and Bowen had infinitely more experience in managing the development of military hardware and in the techniques for successfully cooperating with the military services.

Thus, the British scientists played a crucial role in the establishment of the United States' most important wartime research centre – the Radiation Laboratory.

Planning for the expanded microwave radar research program began in the first two weeks of October in a series of meetings held at Cambridge, Washington, New York City, and Tuxedo Park. At first it was thought that a research facility should be established in the Washington area, and arrangements were begun to secure the use of part of the Army Air Corps' facilities at Bolling Field. Meanwhile, the details of the proposed organization were fleshed out at meetings held from 11 to 14 October at the Carnegie Institution, at Tuxedo Park, and in Loomis's apartment in New York City.[21]

At the first of these meetings, at the Carnegie Institution on Friday the eleventh, Cockcroft and Bowen joined with Bush, Compton, and Bowles. A new member of the American planning team was also present – Professor Ernest Lawrence of the University of California at Berkeley, the famous nuclear physicist. Loomis had recruited Lawrence to assist the NDRC's microwave committee at this crucial juncture by adding his tremendous talents and influence to an already impressive team. At this meeting Bowen outlined in detail the British radar organization, particularly that of the Air Ministry Research Establishment (AMRE, later renamed Telecommunications Research Establishment). In this unique organization, academic scientists and their techniques had been closely integrated with the requirements of military research. Although it was a top secret facility, there was within the AMRE a free and open atmosphere similar to that in a peacetime university laboratory. A.P. Rowe, its superintendent, had encouraged the development of close cooperation between scientists, engineers, and servicemen, whatever their rank or qualifications. They were encouraged to exchange ideas on current research and future requirements. This free and open exchange of views was a vital part of Britain's success in developing radar. It was successful because it was accepted that the researchers, the development engineer, and the user all needed to have input. Bowen placed particular emphasis on the need to have service aircraft close at hand for testing, and on having the closest of working relationships with the services. He suggested that initially the Americans might wish to "establish a nucleus of about twelve scientists, recruited from universities, and to expand as rapidly as possible." The meeting concluded with a promise to provide all available details on British microwave radar development.[22]

So important were these discussions that it was agreed to continue them over the weekend in the less formal setting of Tuxedo Park. There, Bowles, Lawrence, Cockcroft, and Bowen were joined by Loomis and Carol Wilson, representing Bush. There was a series of animated meetings throughout the day, interspersed with leisure activities. They did not work "too hard," Bowen recalled, because, "after all, it was a Saturday." They adjourned for tennis and later in the day were joined for pre-dinner drinks by Loomis's neighbour, Averell Harriman.[23]

Despite – or perhaps because of – the relaxed atmosphere, at least one crucial decision was made. It was agreed that the NDRC would concentrate on the research and development of three types of microwave radar systems. These were, in order of priority, airborne interceptor radar (AI), long-range navigation equipment, and gun-laying radar for ground and air applications. This priority list was primarily determined by the requirements of the British, since it was anticipated that they would be the first to deploy American-produced radar operationally. The American services may not have been completely in sympathy with this logic. Bowen then outlined the type of equipment that a research group would need in order to assemble prototype sets. A discussion followed about the specifications for each item, particularly with regard to performance, space, and weight, and which manufacturers might be approached to supply it.[24]

The next day's meeting was even more fruitful. The first discussions centred on the organization of the American microwave research centre. Loomis quickly agreed that its structure should follow the British examples; the new laboratory would be run by civilian scientists and would maintain close links with both the military and industry. It would be located near or on an airfield, though no firm decision was taken on its exact location. The equally difficult problem of how to staff the new facility was discussed at great length. Cockcroft and Bowen described how university people had taken to military research programs in Great Britain "like ducks to water." Ernest Lawrence was "particularly enthusiastic" about the British idea of recruiting engineers and scientists from the universities. Since industrial and military scientists already had their own crucial role to play in the growing rearmament program, academe offered the only untapped source of technically trained talent available.

They then turned to technical discussions on the radar and radio navigation sets which the laboratory would build. Cockcroft sketched out the specifications of gun-laying radar, while Bowen provided similar information on AI. A more general set of specifications was outlined for a radio navigation system whose range would be 1,000 miles or more with an accuracy of plus or minus five miles. Bowen described the basic technical requirements of a radio navigation aide – later to be known by its code name GEE – which was being developed in Britain. GEE used three spaced transmitters whose synchronized signals were picked up by a special receiver mounted on an aircraft. The receiver would indicate a grid or "gee" reference. The grid reference was then checked against a special map overlay to give a location with an accuracy of five miles. Because the transmitters were located only a few miles apart, its range was limited to targets over the Ruhr.[25] No decision was reached, however, on the specifications for American-designed equipment.

Next, Loomis proposed that the primary task of the laboratory would be to construct the first American prototype of a microwave radar using the magnetron. With such a set one could test the characteristics of high-powered short-wave radar on ground targets such as buildings. This would provide the experience necessary to construct sets for military use. This was agreed. Bowen described the rest of the meeting: "We listed desirable figures for things like pulse width, receiver sensitivity, cathode-ray tube displays and so on. On scratch pads and the back of envelopes, we sketched the block diagram of a typical system right there, with a modulator, a transmitter incorporating the magnetron, a receiver and indicator and appropriate power supplies."[26]

The next day Loomis, Bowles, Lawrence, and Bowen reconvened at the former's apartment on East 79th Street in New York City. Cockcroft was absent, having previously scheduled a meeting at the Navy Department, and Wilson also had returned to Washington. The men where joined by Mervin Kelly of Bell Telephone Laboratories, Ralph Beal from RCA, and Hugh Willis representing the Sperry Corporation. Representatives from General Electric and Westinghouse had been invited but were unable to attend at such short notice. Loomis asked the industrial scientists which components of a microwave radar they could deliver within thirty days. Accustomed to the lethargic pace of peacetime and unaware that Loomis considered this to be a wartime emergency program, they replied that tender proposals could certainly be ready in thirty days. "No, you misunderstand me," said Loomis. "I want you to submit your tender next week and to deliver thirty days after that." The three industrial experts were "stunned." They would agree only to draft a tentative list of contractors for the components needed to assemble the first microwave radar. Once this was accomplished, all concerned agreed to end this remarkable series of meetings. It was decided to reconvene in Washington on Friday, 18 October, with senior officials of the NDRC, the armed forces, and the various companies concerned.[27]

After everyone else had departed, Loomis held further discussions with Bowen and Lawrence, which demonstrated the results that could be produced by the Anglo-American exchange of technological ideas. Loomis traced out a scheme which he had thought up the evening before for solving the radio navigation problem. Having heard Bowen's description of the GEE radio navigation device, he said he was struck by the fact that its range was limited to less than a thousand miles, and he had thought up a solution incorporating some of the British technology with a concept of his own. GEE's range, he explained, was limited to a few hundred miles because it used three transmitters only a short distance apart. Why not, he suggested, use two transmitters a thousand miles apart sending out signals simultaneously? The signals from the two stations could be coordinated using highly accurate quartz clocks. They could bounce signals off the ionosphere for ranges of up to two thousand miles. This was the basic outline of the long-range navigation system that would soon be known to the world as LORAN. (The LORAN design was developed by the Radiation Laboratory's radar scientists during 1941.)[28]

For the rest of the week, Cockcroft, Bowen, and Fowler toured the plants of various electronic companies to ascertain whether they would be able to manufacture radar components. Discussions were meanwhile underway among the members of the NDRC Microwave Committee concerning the location of the proposed laboratory. In a last-minute change of plan, it was agreed on 16 October that the Massachusetts Institute of Technology would be preferable to the Washington area. There was a variety of reasons for this decision, including delays at securing space at Bolling Field, but the most important factor was that the NDRC was not empowered to have laboratories of its own. It was supposed to contract work out to existing institutions. MIT was already engaged in microwave research, in collaboration with Loomis's research team, and it had facilities immediately available. Also, it was close to several airports.[29]

There then followed one of the most important meetings in the history of the United States' scientific moblization effort. On 18 October at the Carnegie Institution in Washington most of the important decisions were made; only the final form of the proposal still had to be worked out. In attendance were E.G. Bowen, Bush, Loomis, Compton, Bowles, and Lawrence, along with two representatives from the Navy and War Departments and from General Electric, RCA, Sperry, and Westinghouse. It was decided to allocate $455,000 for the establishment of what was to become known as the Radiation Laboratory, and it was agreed that, with a few minor exceptions, all the components necessary for the first prototype microwave radar would be ready within the thirty days proposed by Loomis. Recruitment of technical staff, as proposed by the British, would be from university departments. The final scheme was approved with minor alterations by the NDRC on 25 October. Most of the promised delivery dates for equipment were met; as a result, a fully functioning microwave radar research centre was ready to start operations by late November. By the end of December, the first prototype 10-centimetre-wavelength radar was ready to begin trials. It would be the first of many successes for the staff of the Radiation Laboratory.

Starting with a staff of only 50 people housed in 14,550 square feet of MIT buildings, the Radiation Laboratory would expand until by 1945 it employed 3,724 people and occupied a total of 408,080 square feet.[30] It became the largest single scientific research laboratory in the Western Alliance. More importantly, it was the centre of wartime microwave radar research and development. The vital role played by the Tizard Mission in bringing the magnetron to the United States and in helping to plan the Radiation Laboratory was the single most important result of this unprecedented international cooperation. As a direct consequence, microwave radars were in large-scale production in American factories by the time of the attack on Pearl Harbor – at least a year and a half sooner than would otherwise have been the case. Indirectly, it ensured that Bush's NDRC (later made part of the Office of Scientific Research and Development) would become the most important scientific agency in the United States. No one, of course, can predict what would have happened to the NDRC if microwave radar research had not been given such a dramatic boost by the magnetron. But it would certainly have taken longer for Bush to establish the primacy of his agency and to secure this transformation in American scientific-military relations.

Bush and other NDRC scientists realized the significance of the British gifts and were determined to guarantee that the cooperation continued. In late October, Bush proposed establishing permanent procedures for wide-ranging technical information exchanges. Soon afterwards, methods were agreed on for transferring data, for establishing direct communication links between research teams working on similar projects, and for continuing a regular series of visits between American, British, and Canadian scientists. Most of the communications were to be handled by the permanent British scientific liaison office in Ottawa, headed by Fowler. Carol Wilson was appointed as the NDRC official in charge of liaison. A firm link in the future Atlantic alliance had been forged. By ensuring, with some minor exceptions, that the technological war would be waged with a minimum amount of competition and duplication of effort, this agreement continued to have a profound impact on the Allied war effort until the end of hostilities.[31]

The impressive influence of the Tizard Mission on the formation of the Radiation Laboratory was not mirrored in the establishment of the other great wartime program that transformed American science – the building of the atomic bomb. Apart from commencing Anglo-American discussions on the subject, the Tizard Mission's direct involvement in developments that led to the building of the bomb were minimal. It is ironical that it was in the field of atomic research, in which the members of the mission had more expertise than any other, that it accomplished so little. Cockcroft and Fowler were leading research physicists, and Tizard had been involved in determining nuclear policy since the beginning of the British government's investigations into an atomic explosive in 1939. All three men were very well briefed on the experimental and theoretical developments that had taken place by August 1940, and at least some of these pointed to the practicality of a powerful nuclear bomb using a small amount of uranium-235.

To understand just why the mission had little direct impact on the development of the atomic bomb one must appreciate the state of knowledge of nuclear fission in the summer of 1940. Just nine months before the beginning of the war in Europe, the discovery of nuclear fission had launched a series of rapid developments in what until then had been the esoteric world of atomic physics. Several early scientific papers on fission had concluded that one of its products was the release of further neutrons. This proved most disturbing, for if these neutrons caused further fission reactions, these in turn would release more neutrons than the rate of neutron loss; such an occurrence would result in a sustained chain fission reaction. Most physicists, however, discounted the possibility of an explosive nuclear energy release. But something unsettling could not be denied: there was a remote possibility of developing an immensely powerful nuclear bomb.

By the spring of 1939, these discoveries had convinced scientists in the United States and Great Britain that government action was required if there was even the slightest possibility of a military application for fission. Professor G.P. Thompson of Imperial College and Professor W.L. Bragg of the Cavendish Laboratory decided in April to approach the British government about securing stocks of uranium that were believed to exist in Belgium. Tizard was asked by the government to investigate. He had already been briefed by Thompson, and he doubted that a fission bomb could be developed; he had calculated the odds against it as 100,000 to one. Although Tizard made inquiries about purchasing the Belgian uranium, no action was taken.

Several of Britain's leading physicists – including Thompson and Professor James Chadwick, the discoverer of the neutron – studied the question further throughout the rest of 1939 and the winter of 1940. It was still highly unlikely, they concluded, that an atomic bomb could be built. Even if it could be constructed according to existing knowledge, Chadwick surmised, it would require up to 30 or even 40 tons of uranium to reach critical mass; this was the mass required for a sustained fission reaction. By February 1940, Thompson had almost decided that atomic energy was not worth pursuing as a wartime project.[32]

At the end of February, however, two refugee scientists, Otto Frisch and Rudolf Peierls, who had been working at the University of Birmingham on nuclear fission since the beginning of the war, completed a three-page report in which they drew a startling conclusion: "A moderate amount of U-235 would indeed constitute an extremely efficient explosive." Earlier investigations into a nuclear bomb had missed two critical points – that the uranium isotope U-235 was extremely fissionable, and that the critical mass of a nearly pure sample of the isotope might be as little as one kilogram. The effects of such a bomb would be devastating. A five-kilogram bomb would have the same explosive power as "several thousand tons of dynamite, while that of a 1 kg bomb, though about 500 times less, would still be formidable." Nor did they ignore the effect of radiation, which "would be fatal to living beings even [a] long time after the explosion."[33]

Peierls and Frisch's report was the first scientific paper anywhere to conclude that a nuclear bomb was not only possible but was almost a certainty. The paper was based solely on mathematical theories that were in direct contradiction to the one attempt that had been made to measure experimentally the cross section of fissionable properties of U-235. Yet this paper so brilliantly explained a number of anomalies in the then current understanding of nuclear fission that it could not be ignored. In April the subcommittee of the Committee for the Scientific Survey of Air Defence on the U bomb (soon to be renamed the MAUD committee) was formed to deal with atomic research. Among its original member was John Cockcroft. One of its first actions was to request that A.V. Hill expand his scientific intelligence-gathering mission to include American uranium research.[34]

By the spring of 1940, the American government's atomic research program had reached about the same stage of indifference as that of the British project prior to the Frisch-Peierls report. Official American interest in nuclear fission had begun somewhat earlier than in Great Britain. In January 1939, just days after the appearance of the first published report of nuclear fission, scientists at the Naval Research Laboratory had contacted physicists at the Carnegie Institution about the possibility of developing nuclear-powered engines. In mid-March Enrico Fermi, the refugee Italian physicist then working at Columbia University, had briefed the Navy Department about the still very remote possibility of an atomic bomb. The navy was sufficiently impressed to provide $1,500 for further research, but no more came of this initiative.[35]

It was in October 1939 that Alexander Sachs, the Russian-born economist who was a confidant of Roosevelt, personally delivered to the American president the famous letter signed by Albert Einstein which outlined the possibility of constructing an atomic bomb. In large part, this letter had been written during the preceding summer by the Hungarian refugee physicists Leo Szilard and Eugene Wigner. Even though they believed that there was only a remote possiblity of an explosive fission reaction, they were deeply worried that the Germans might construct such a device first. Einstein was asked to sign the letter because of his prestige as the world's most famous scientist. The letter asked Roosevelt to appoint someone in government to maintain contact with the physicists and to safeguard the world's supply of uranium. Roosevelt concurred and authorized the establishment of an advisory committee on uranium headed by Lyman Briggs, the director of the National Bureau of Standards.[36] Although Briggs's committee had managed to provide some modest funding by the spring of 1940 when Hill began his investigation into American nuclear research, few scientists were greatly concerned about the development of an atomic bomb.

In contrast to the American secrecy surrounding radar research, Hill found American scientists more than willing to talk freely about their atomic research. They told him that there was "no possibility within practical range" of using uranium either as a power source or as an explosive. In their view, nuclear research was "for present practical needs probably a *wild goose chase*." Some friendly physicists suggested that Hill should advise his government that diverting British scientists from projects with an immediate military application would be "a sheer waste of time." Instead, it should be the American physicists – with their superior facilities and without the pressing need to undertake emergency war work – who should pursue matters as peripheral to war research as atomic energy. Still naive about military security, the American scientists confidently promised Hill that they would immediately inform the British government if they discovered anything conclusive about the military application of nuclear fission.[37]

By the time Hill's report arrived in London in June, the MAUD committee had taken steps to find conclusive evidence either for or against Peierls and Frisch's theory that a super bomb could be built. In the weeks leading up to the departure of the mission for North America, however, no significant discoveries concerning nuclear fission had been made – at least, none that altered the generally held scepticism about a nuclear bomb. Before his departure for Canada in July to establish the scientific liaison office in Ottawa, Fowler was carefully briefed by Thompson on all aspects of the nuclear research program, though no one anticipated that he would have to spend a great deal of time dealing with this issue. Only one nuclear-related task was asked of him. He was to discover whether Canada had suitable facilities for two refugee physicists, Hans von Halban and Lew Kowarski, to continue their research program on heavy water.[38]

While planning for the mission, Tizard and Cockcroft did not envision nuclear research as being a major component of their work. Cockcroft certainly did not foresee any possibility of a bomb being developed during the war, if ever. Perhaps the most remarkable example of his scepticism can be found in his unrehearsed performance while crossing the Atlantic aboard the *Duchess of Richmond*. After it was learned that there was a famous scientist on board, he was asked to give a lecture to the British sailors who were in transit to crew the American flush-deck destroyers that were being transferred to the Royal Navy. Not feeling free to talk on any classified matters, Cockcroft decided to lecture on atomic energy. As Bowen recalled, he gave "a marvellous lecture" on radiation and on the potential energy stored in the nucleus. With an eye to his lay audience, Cockcroft invented a new unit of measurement, "the battleship foot," for the energy required to lift a 50,000-ton battleship one foot into the air. He then calculated that there was enough energy in one cup of water to lift a battleship high enough out of the sea to break its back. As he told his audience, "It was a very safe subject to talk about because there was no hope at all that such a thing would be achieved during the present war!"[39]

In view of such doubts, it not surprising that nuclear energy was very much a secondary concern of the mission. The Americans were equally disinterested in fission. While there were numerous meetings on radar, sonar, explosives, aeronautical engineering, and other technologies with a direct military application, there were in total only three meetings on nuclear research. One of these took place in Canada. The first and most important was held in Washington on 7 October between Fowler, Cockcroft, and the Briggs committee. The meeting focused on current efforts to develop techniques for separating U-235 from uranium. The safety of international uranium stocks was also discussed. Cockcroft outlined for the Americans the British research program, but his report of the meeting mentions no discussion of Peierls and Frisch's remarkable theory. It simply concludes rather laconically: "In general the Committee considers this to be a long term programme."[40] According to the American official history of the development of the atomic bomb, a copy of the Peierls and Frisch report was not received in the United States until April 1941.[41]

Why was this most important paper on the military application of nuclear fission apparently withheld from the Americans when Britain's most closely guarded technical secrets were freely available? Given the attitude of Cockcroft and others on nuclear research, the British silence was not for security reasons. Nor was it in their interest to hamper the American research program in any way. There are two possible solutions to this mystery: either such great reservations still prevailed about Peierls and Frisch's theory that it was not considered wise to alarm the Americans unduly, or else Cockcroft simply did not believe their conclusions. This disbelief is perfectly understandable – even for a highly skilled physicist such as Cockcroft. There was as yet no experimental evidence supporting this radical theory. Indeed, much wishful thinking was current that such awesome power would never be under the control of humanity.

American-based researchers had the same doubts about the practicality of a fission bomb as their British colleagues. When Cockcroft, Fowler, and the Canadian physicist A.G. Shenstone met with Enrico Fermi at Columbia in November, Fermi "was convinced that no uranium mixture could ever be any use as an explosive owing to the long relaxation time of the fundamental process concerned, the slow part of which is the slowing up of fast neutrons. Before anything devastating can pile up the mixture is bound to blow itself apart."[42] With such sceptisim on both sides of the Atlantic, it is not surprising that the mission's direct influence on the atomic program was minimal. There was far more important work for it to do, both in the Unites States and in Canada.

8 The Mission and Canada

On 19 October 1940, the day after the final meeting at the Carnegie Institution authorizing the creation of the Radiation Laboratory, Cockcroft, Fowler, Wallace, and Nutt headed north to Canada. Their destination was Ottawa; their goal, the completion of the one remaining task of the mission – the full mobilization, for the British war effort, of Canada's scientific and high-technology resources. In a matter of a few days they managed to alter the nature of Canada's wartime advanced-technology mobilization.[1] Their advice swayed the Canadian government to approve the creation of a huge program of radar research, development, and production, a project radically different from others undertaken by Canada during the war. Unlike the other major industrial projects, which mainly dealt with the mass production of equipment using well-established techniques and materials, the radar program involved the utilization of Canada's meagre high-technology research, development, and electronic manufacturing facilities to produce the most sophisticated military hardware.[2]

The role of the mission in shaping the nature of Canada's war effort has usually been lost in the far greater story of its impact on the United States' scientific mobilization and on Anglo-American relations. As we have seen, the scientists, soldiers, diplomats, and politicans who were involved in planning the mission all believed that its primary tasks were in the United States. But it was always considered to have an important secondary responsibilty north of the border. Here, too, the mission had a dramatic impact not just for Canada but for the entire Allied war effort.

The important role of the British Technical Mission in shaping Canadian wartime scientific and advanced-technological mobilization has long been ignored. This is primarily because the nature and extent of Canada's participation in this type of industrial endeavour has until recently not been subject to critical examination. While it is true that the Canadian effort was dwarfed by the far larger American and British programs, recent writing has revealed the extensive contribution made by Canada to the scientific and technological war between 1939 and 1945. Canada made a major contribution in the research, development, and production of the atomic bomb, radar, proximity fuses, sonar, explosives, aeronautics, chemistry, and underwater acoustics.[3] However, the research has also revealed that there were severe problems within many of these programs, ranging from outright system failures to lengthy delays, which often left Canadian production lagging far behind the British and American. These difficulties were principally caused by the lack of a prewar scientific-industrial infrastructure. This made it difficult, if not impossible, to mobilize Canadian resources effectively in wartime. The research, however, leaves unanswered the question of why Canada decided in the last half of 1940 to mobilize its technological and scientific resources. The most remarkable aspect of Canada's involvement with high technology in the Second World War is not that the nation had great difficulty in the timely production of equipment of suitable quality and adequate quantity, but that it attempted to manufacture sophisticated military equipment at all.

Prior to 1939 many sectors of the economy, such as the electronics industry, lacked an independent research and development capability. In part this was the result of high industrial tariffs, which encouraged the development of a branch-plant economy. Branch plants were satellite factories of foreign, mainly American, companies, and they usually had little or no independent research and engineering expertise. Another contributing factor was the absence of Canadian defence expenditures that would have led to the development of a military industrial complex. Despite some small Anglo-Canadian educational orders for aircraft, machine guns, and artillery pieces placed just before the war, most Canadian plants were manufacturers only and were dependent on their American parents for engineering and design expertise.[4] Although Canada had several indigenous world-class scientific institutions, such as its National Research Council, which could partially compensate for the lack of industrial research and development capability, it had little experience in military design and development. Until the summer of 1940, the British government was reluctant to invest in long-term advanced-technology industrial projects, for the war was expected to last no more than two years. British industrial experts cited an acute shortage of machine tools and a lack of dollars as the main stumbling blocks, though they were aware of the absence of development expertise.[5] On 23 January 1940, at a meeting of leading British radar scientists, including Sir Henry Tizard and Robert Watson-Watt, it was decided not to pursue close cooperation with Canada. Despite the fact that no detailed studies of Canadian capabilities had been undertaken, those in attendance concluded that Canada had only a "nucleus organization" for military scientific research.[6]

Without British leadership, the Canadians were both unable and unwilling to begin the mobilization of their scientific and technological resources. Although Canadian scientists were eager to be involved in the war effort, they were too far removed from the fighting and too unfamiliar with the technology of war to be able to judge accurately what work needed to be done. Even when the National Research Council proposed war projects such as radar research, the Canadian government refused to provide funding. This was because, for the first nine months of the war, the government was still operating under peacetime fiscal restrictions. For this reason, no project could proceed without the guarantee of British orders.

The fall of France in the spring of 1940 has often been regarded as the starting point of Canada's scientific mobilization. While it is true that the collapse of Britain's most important ally crystallized Canada's political will to mobilize for total war, the event did not of itself lead directly to the decision to commit the nation's scientific and industrial resources to the war effort. Ottawa had no way of knowing what equipment was needed. Indeed, in the tumultuous summer of 1940, the British had little time to consider how best to provide the necessary technical guidance or the information on production priorities that would have enabled the

Canadians to begin to mobilize science and industry. Instead, specific Canadian initiatives triggered a few projects, particularly the preliminary work on asdic production, which began in July 1940. Other projects, including the Canadian radar program – which was destined to be by far the largest scientific and advanced-industrial program of the war – suffered because of an inability to determine the scope and direction required. What was needed was on-the-spot British assistance in planning the direction of Canada's advanced-technology war effort.

The Canadian connection with the British Technical Mission can be traced back to A.V. Hill's investigations in North America. Hill had been briefed to examine Canadian scientific resources, and he made at least two trips to Canada while he was in North America. Aware that Britain had already mobilized most of its skilled personnel, Hill was appalled to discover that in Canada highly trained scientists, engineers, and technicians were being used hardly at all, even though the Canadians were more than willing to undertake any project the British assigned them. The reports that Hill circulated in London in June not only pressed for the quick dispatch of a technical mission to North America, but they also argued that improving technical contacts with Canada should be given almost the same emphasis as establishing cooperation with the United States. Hill wrote: "Everything I saw and heard convinced me that there had been a grave lack of imagination and foresight on our part in failing to make full use of the excellent facilities and personnel available in Canada."[7] In another report he said "that Canada may have to exercise a fundamental role in Imperial Defence, and that we should do everything possible to get things going there to improve their resources. The very friendly relations between Canada and the USA allow these recommendations [concerning liaison with the United States and Canada] to be dovetailed into one another."[8]

Perhaps the most interesting aspect of Hill's reports on Canada is what he did not observe, for he did not take into account the inherent weaknesses in Canadian advanced-technology manufacturing. As a physiologist, Hill did not have the training to observe the absence of expertise in industrial development, and he seems merely to have noted the number of people with a PH D, the amount of laboratory space, and the enthusiasm of Canadians in general to undertake useful war work. He did not even consider the background of the scientific leaders he met in Canada. For instance, C.J. Mackenzie, head of the National Research Council (NRC), was a civil engineer by training and had been dean of engineering at the University of Saskatchewan, a small prairie university, before becoming NRC president in the fall of 1939. He had limited experience in managing large scientific programs and had no knowledge of military industrial production. Hill did, however, stress the need to maintain ongoing technical contact with the Canadians in order to provide guidance to their effort. Unfortunately, the effect of Hill's oversight was compounded by the subsequent failure of the mission's scientists to investigate more thoroughly the state of Canada's military scientific industrial capabilities or to establish adequate permanent technical liaison.

In the discussions that followed Hill's return to England, his colleagues generally accepted that Canada would be an important albeit secondary concern of any technical mission that was sent to North America. Tizard was ordered to "establish relations with Canadian authorities with the object of commencing research and manufacture of required equipment in that country."[9]

It was therefore a deliberate part of Tizard's planning that his work in North America began in Canada. On 15 August 1940, when Tizard and Group Captain Pearce arrived in Montreal after a gruelling flight via Northern Ireland and Newfoundland, they were met by Dr Otto Maass, head of the National Research Council's chemistry division. After a leisurely lunch at the University Club, Maass drove Tizard and Pearce to Ottawa. Tizard had firm reasons for beginning the mission in Canada: he wished to rest up on friendly ground after his long flight, to be briefed by Professor Fowler on the developments in the United States since Hill's visit, and then to get a first-hand view of the Canadian situation. Tizard had been instructed to approach the Canadians about the possible production of radar for the British government so that there would be a safe reserve for the vital industry. By the time Tizard headed south to Washington, he had decided to invite leading Canadians to join the mission.[10]

The mission formally began on 16 August, when Tizard visited the National Research Council in Ottawa to meet with Mackenzie and Fowler. If Tizard hoped to discuss his work in North America, he must have been disappointed. His diary records that he found the two men busy interviewing an inventor by the name of "Cross who had a new 'bullet proof material' – the stuffing being a kind of aluminum silicate." Tizard was dubious of the inventor's claims but spent the rest of the morning witnessing repeated tests of the material. His doubts were confirmed when it failed to stop a bullet at a range of fifty yards.

However, Tizard was able to meet leading Canadian politicians, soldiers, and scientists during the rest of the day, which culminated in a dinner at Prime Minister Mackenzie King's estate at Kingsmere. Understandably, Tizard did not know what to make of the eccentric Canadian prime minister. King, we now know from his private diary, spent much time gazing into a crystal ball to communicate with his dead mother and dog, and manifested many other signs of bizarre behaviour. While Tizard did not know the secret aspects of King's private life, he certainly considered him rather unusual. He recorded in his diary: "He is a quaint character. He has two houses there, quite close to each other, in about 400 acres of land. Moves from one house to the other, according to inclination. Picks up bits of old houses, including the Houses of Parliament, London and erects 'ruins.' Dummy animals are stuck about the garden here and there. He was a delightful host, however, and we had a most pleasant dinner." They had a long talk after dinner, during which King told Tizard that he was scheduled to meet President Roosevelt the next day. He promised to speak to the president about the mission but made no other commitment to greater Canadian involvement with the scientific war.[11]

Tizard spent the next three days assessing the Canadian research establishment and gaining information on the situation in the United States. He also had lengthy briefings from Fowler, who had become closely involved with the Canadian scientific war. Fowler told Tizard that Mackenzie spent his time interviewing inventors such as Cross because the NRC had nothing more important to do. The Canadians, while anxious to get involved in useful war work, were hampered by an acute shortage of funds and by a lack of information on British requirements, equipment policy, and technical specifications.[12] Tizard was given an in-depth briefing on the sorry state of the Canadian scientific war, including its radar program.

Tizard knew that the NRC had been briefed by the British on radar technology in the spring of 1939, and he must have been disappointed with what little had been achieved since then. Indeed, he learned that active work on radar research and development had only begun in September 1939, financed by a small grant of $18,600 from the army and air force. An additional request for $57,740 had been rejected by the fiscally conservative cabinet in November, ostensibly because the British had shown no enthusiasm for the Canadian work.[13] No more funds were available until May 1940, when $40,000 was approved. This money was, of course, insufficient for a major program. It might have been marginally adequate if Canadians had been working at the cutting edge of technology, but the NRC scientists were still trying to reinvent the wheel, so to speak, for they were duplicating British research that had been done several years earlier. An independent attempt by the NRC to design an airborne interceptor radar had collapsed in disarray when the prototype failed to function during tests in June. By July, the NRC had been able to show only one concrete result: the design and the installation that month of a single primitive coastal-defence radar set for the navy at Halifax.

In July the government had approved the establishment of a small crown-owned plant to manufacture radar. It was to employ 130 to 140 people, and to provide sufficient equipment for the Canadian services. This was estimated to be about 117 sets.[14] But by Tizard's arrival, no funds had been provided. Nor were there suitable designs available to begin production. The first British radar sets sent to Canada, two already obsolete gun-laying Mark I's, had arrived in Ottawa just three weeks earlier. They were being meticulously examined by the NRC staff, who soon abandoned their own technology in favour of what they readily recognized as far superior British equipment. Before any British electrical apparatus could be manufactured, however, it had to be redesigned to match the American electrical standards that were used in Canada.

Tizard found other military scientific projects underway in Ottawa, but few had yielded any better results than the radar program. A.E.H. Pew had arrived the previous month and had begun to set up asdic manufacturing in cooperation with the Royal Canadian Navy. But even though he found the "resources for A/S [sonar] production in Canada most promising," he did not expect results from his work for at least a year.[15]

Tizard confirmed the observations of both Hill and Fowler that the facilities at the NRC were excellent. And he agreed with them that Canadians were now both willing and able to undertake even more important tasks. But when judging Canadian capabilities for industrial development, Tizard – like Hill before him – failed to look beyond the scientific facilities. Instead of studying the Canadian situation carefully, he immediately attempted to provide direction to the Canadian research program. On 19 August he met J.S. Duncan, deputy minister for the air force, and Air Vice-Marshal A.V. Stedman, who was in charge of research for the RCAF, and he convinced them to authorize the establishment of a flight of aircraft for scientific work. Tizard insisted that it would greatly assist Sir Frederick Banting's work on aviation medicine and the NRC's research on radio aids to navigation. Tizard also heartily endorsed Canadian proposals to design and build high-performance wooden aircraft; when writing to the Ministry of Aircraft Production in London, he requested that aviation specialists be sent to assist in this project.[16]

Two days later, Tizard left Canada for the United States, having arranged for three Canadians – Mackenzie, Stedman, and Colonel H.E. Tabor, the master general of the ordnance office – to join the mission in Washington as soon as possible. Tizard received permission to take with him two NRC secretaries to provide clerical staff, and he also obtained authorization for Canadians to provide technical assistance as soon as the mission had begun the exchange of information in the United States.

On 9 September, when the other members of the mission had arrived in Washington, Tizard and Fowler briefed them on the Canadian situation. Tizard expressed his convicton that the Canadians should concentrate their research on the development of "radio navigation aids," an early wartime cryptic phrase for radar, and asked them to consider "what organization should be started to ensure that the exchange of technical information between the USA, Canada," and Great Britain would proceed unhindered.[17]

Stedman and Mackenzie arrived in Washington on 13 September 1940 and began Canadian participation in the daily morning meetings of the members of the mission. At dinner the next evening Tizard told Mackenzie that having consulted with his colleagues, he was convinced that Canada should immediately begin work on the production of air-to-surface-vessel (ASV) radar.

Mackenzie endorsed the idea and proposed that production be handled by Research Enterprises Limited, a crown corporation established in August to manufacture secret optical equipment. He told Tizard that on his return to Ottawa he would arrange meetings with representatives of the company.[18]

The arrival of the Canadian technical experts in the United States soon made it clear that the mission marked not only the beginning of Anglo-American cooperation but of Canadian-American cooperation as well. In Washington in September 1940, C.J. Mackenzie met Vannevar Bush for the first time. The two men agreed to establish full and open cooperation. During negotiations in October, which ultimatley led to the signing of the formal Anglo-American documents on scientific and technical liaison, Bush ensured that Canada was included in the agreement. Bush also invited Canada to continue its participation in American scientific mobilization by sending permanent liaison officers to such facilities as the Radiation Laboratory.[19]

The opening of wartime scientific cooperation with the Americans probably had a more immediately beneficial effect on Canada than on Great Britain. When Canada had declared war in September 1939, the enforcement of the Neutrality Act had partially cut the vital link with American facilities for research and development. In order to adapt British radar designs to North American standards, Canada needed the latest in American vacuum-tube technology and machine tools. Suddenly this barrier was partially lifted. However, certain constraints, especially fiscal ones, continued to hinder American-Canadian technical relations until the signing of the Hyde Park Agreement in 1941.[20]

The importance of this opening of American-Canadian technical cooperation should not be underestimated. Before the Second World War, the Canadian military had relied on British technology, despite the fact that most Canadian industry used American standards and components. As well, Canadian scientists had a much closer relationship with their American counterparts than with their colleagues in Great Britain. The Canadian military's reliance on British technology was an anomaly caused by tradition and by political considerations. By opening military technical cooperation between Canada and the United States, the Tizard Mission initiated the Americanization of the technology used by the Canadian armed forces. This process continued until the late

1950s, when American technology and standards were the norm. There were other advantages as well. Canadian scientists benefited greatly from attending the technical briefings on the latest technological advances which were given to the Americans by members of the mission. At these briefings, NRC scientists viewed the cavity magnetron for the first time. They were soon discussing with the British the feasibility of producing both the magnetron and short-wave radar in Canada.[21]

After a month in the United States, it was becoming apparent to the members of the mission that immediate American material assistance was out of the question. Although the Americans had provided valuable information on a variety of equipment, political and financial barriers still prevented the immediate large-scale utilization of American resources. Tizard realized that until these barriers were removed, the short-term practical results of his mission lay in Canada. Thus, at the end of September, he returned to Ottawa to try to confirm the understanding reached with Mackenzie about radar production. On 25 September he met with Colonel J.L. Ralston, the minister of national defence, Angus Macdonald, the minister of defence for naval services, and General H.D.G. Crerar, the army chief of staff. He briefed them on the results of the mission and on the need for Canada's agreeing to radar production. Ralston then ushered Tizard into the office of G.K. Sheils, the deputy minister of munitions and supply. In Tizard's words, "Mr. Sheils told me that he thought Research Enterprises could undertake the manufacture of some secret equipment."[22] Sheils then arranged for Tizard to have breakfast on the twenty-seventh in Washington with C.D. Howe, the minister of munitions and supply, in order to confirm the decision. Before leaving Ottawa, Tizard had one more meeting with Mackenzie, at which they agreed that if radar production got underway, it would be mutually beneficial that an entire British radar project team – likely those already working on 50-centimetre gun-laying radar – should be transferred to Canada. In return, Canada would send a group of its younger, more gifted physicists and electrical engineers to assist the British and to gather technical knowledge, which they could later take back to the National Research Council.[23]

Tizard's breakfast meeting with C.D. Howe confirmed all the arrangements made with Mackenzie. Tizard found the head of

Canada's wartime economy characteristically enthusiastic about undertaking radar and the related vacuum-tube production – provided, of course, that the British placed firm orders. All that now had to be decided was the type of sets to be built in Canada, and the size of the Research Enterprises facilities needed to produce them.[24] Eight days after meeting with Howe, Tizard turned over the leadership of the mission to Cockcroft and headed for home.

The need to finalize the preliminary agreements made with Howe brought Cockcroft and most of the other members of the mission to Canada for the last twelve days of October. On 24 October the mission members briefed the Canadian War Cabinet on their dealings with the Americans.[25] Cockcroft, Fowler, and Wallace – joined briefly by E.G. Bowen – held a series of meetings with officials from the Department of Munitions and Supply, the National Research Council, and the armed forces. The British were pleased to learn that the mission had already had a profound impact in Canada. It had created a willingness, in the highest reaches of Canada's political, military, scientific, and industrial leadership, to make major commitments to advanced-technology production. However, Cockcroft was disturbed to learn that the Canadians had still not authorized the beginning of work on the Research Enterprises facilities. It was explained to him that as yet no official word had been received from London about production priorities, and it was suggested that the British scientists propose them.

Cockcroft could not understand London's silence. Here was a unique opportunity to guide the Canadian industrial and scientific mobilization. Had Tizard been unsuccessful in securing authorization for the Canadian production of radar? Or had there been some sort of bureaucratic bungle, and no one had seen fit to cable the decision to Ottawa? Cockcroft was sure that Canadian production had already been authorized or certainly would be, and he decided to proceed accordingly. He submitted to the army's assistant chief of staff a memorandum, which formed the basis of Canadian radar development and production for the next three years. In it, Cockcroft recommended that work begin on nine projects. He suggested that top priority in radar work be given to the manufacturing of ASV sets, followed by short-wave gun-laying and airborne-interception equipment. He advised that plants be established to manufacture special tubes such as the magnetron and that research commence on radio proximity fuses for anti-aircraft shells. Cockcroft and Fowler also suggested that the Research Enterprises facilities should be large enough to accommodate orders from the United States as well as from Great Britain.[26]

In early November, Cockcroft's advice led directly to the final approval of some much more extensive plans for Research Enterprises' radar plant. The value of orders for machine tools, originally placed in September, rose from $124,000 to $700,000. This not only meant that the radar assembly plant had to be larger, but it meant that certain key components, which were to have been purchased in small numbers from the United States, would have to be manufactured in Canada. On November 25, Howe authorized $750,000 to build a 50,000-square-foot building to manufacture cathode ray tubes. The plant was to be part of Research Enterprises Limited, though it was to be managed by Canadian General Electric Limited.[27] Research Enterprises subsidized at least a dozen private manufacturers in establishing new production lines for components. Northern Electric Limited was placed in charge of producing high-power micropup long-wave tubes and cavity magnetron tubes. The Canada Wire and Cable Company built a new plant near Research Enterprises Limited to manufacture British ultrahigh-frequency cables.[28]

In convincing the Canadian government to establish a large indigenous radar-production program, the Tizard Mission had as important an impact on Canada's scientific war as it had already had on that of the United States. While Research Enterprises Limited was certainly not as important to the overall war effort as the Radiation Laboratory, it nevertheless had a significant effect on both Canada and the Allies.

Cockcroft returned to Canada once more in late November. He arrived to work out the final details of the Research Enterprises plant. He also spent time meeting Canadian researchers who were working on atomic fission. On 22 November in Ottawa he met with National Research Council physicists G.C. Laurence and E.W. Stedman. The two men outlined details of their research for Cockcroft and Fowler. Laurence was investigating the possibility of a slow neutron chain reaction in a 10-to-1 mixture of uranium and carbon oxide. At that point, Laurence had already assembled a 1-ton pile. Cockcroft suggested that according to recent theoretical work in the United States, a pile ten times larger would be required. He recommended that Laurence coordinate his research with research teams south of the border. Stedman discussed with Cockcroft the use of a "molecular pump" to separate the U-235 isotope. Here, too, Cockcroft recommended American researchers whom they might contact.[29]

Cockcroft was impressed with the Canadian work and with the resources available to pursue further research. In 1942, when the idea of moving the British atomic energy program to North America was under discussion, he would recall his observation about Canada. Meanwhile, he encouraged the Canadian scientists to continue their work and to develop close ties with their American counterparts, and he asked the Canadian government to provide them with funds to carry on their work. Laurence quickly followed up Cockcroft's suggestion and held meetings in New York in early December with Dean Pegram, Harold Urey, Lymann Briggs, and Enrico Fermi. Laurence was more interested in the details of their work than Cockcroft had been, and he submitted to London the most extensive report on the state of American research available up to that time. He also began the close and friendly cooperation on nuclear research between Canada and the United States which was to prove so important to the Manhattan Project.[30]

9 Aftermath of the Mission

When John Cockcroft boarded an aircraft for England on 1 December 1940, the British Technical Mission officially came to an end. With some very minor exceptions, it had been a triumphant success, exceeding all expectations in furthering Anglo-American cooperation. Almost all the barriers that had so hindered military technical and scientific exchanges before August 1940 had been breached. The only glaring exception was the Norden bombsight, which the U.S. Navy still kept hidden from view. But even here, ways had been found around the problem. The Americans had offered the Royal Air Force supplies of the similar Sperry bombsight, which had been developed for the Army Air Corps and was just then coming into service. The National Defense Research Committee, the U.S. Navy and War Departments, and the Government of Canada had begun to establish a permanent technical liaison system with the British. This system was designed to ensure an uninterrupted flow of information long after the mission had ceased operation. In late November, the U.S. military requested that the British liaison office be permanently moved from Ottawa to Washington.[1]

Americans and Canadians were very eager to continue the open exchange of information. They had no hesitation in continuing the mission's work. Of course, the niggling problem of settling a permanent patent protection mechanism remained, but this matter was the subject of ongoing legal discussions and was settled in the winter of 1941.[2] Back in London, however, there was somewhat less excitement for the mission's accomplishments. Tizard's early departure for the United Kingdom at the end of September had been partly because he was aware that there was a threat that the work already well underway in North America would not be allowed to continue. He knew that the open and complete exchange of technical and scientific information had been approved only for the duration of the mission; no one had guaranteed that it would become permanent policy. Tizard had seen some disturbing evidence that even the work of the mission was under threat, particularly with regard to the ASV radar set, which had not yet been delivered to North America. Soon after his return home, Tizard had his suspicions confirmed.

In order to understand why, in Great Britain, certain powerful people questioned the desirability of continuing open technical cooperation with the United States, it is necessary to understand the peculiar realities of Anglo-American relations before the passage of the Lend-Lease Act in March 1941. In the last four months of 1940, three key issues still limited British acquisitions of war material from the United States: first, the failure to establish supply priorities between the American and British services; second, the shortage of hard currency reserves either in dollars or gold to pay for American purchases; and third, doubts about the technical suitability of American equipment for British military requirements.

The settling of production supply priorities was already being decided. One of the immediate consequences of the mission was the commencement in mid-September of conversations between members of the British Purchasing Commission and the American services to work out their differences about production priorities. The problem was how to distribute the limited industrial manufacturing resources in view of the fact that they were required by both the British and the American armed forces. A dispute, one month later, concerning the allocation of machine tools made it clear that a formal apparatus was required to administer supply priorities. On 15 October the War and Navy Departments established the Army and Navy British Supply Committee. Its members included the chief of naval operations, the army chief of staff, the chief of the production division of the

National Defense Advisory Commission, senior officials in the Department of State and the Treasury, and members of the British Purchasing Commission. Several subcommittees were also created to implement general policy on specific types of technology, such as those relating to aviation and electronics.[3]

The growing shortfall in currency reserves created a much more serious obstacle. Arthur Purvis, the head of the British supply organization in North America, had briefed Tizard about this critical shortage in late August. With one exception, therefore, the mission did not immediately lead to any major new manufacturing contracts going to American firms. The growing British frustration with the Roosevelt administration's failure to solve the fiscal crisis would soon affect the discussions about continuing the work of the mission. The Americans were perceived as trying to suck the British Empire dry of all its convertible assets and gold reserves. On 28 December 1940, Churchill composed a letter to Roosevelt in which he complained that the Americans were behaving like "a sheriff collecting the last assets of a helpless debtor." This draft of the letter was never sent to Washington, but it reveals the depth of British concern as the country waited for Roosevelt to initiate the lend-lease policy; for it was this policy that would open America's huge industrial resources to a cash-starved Britain.[4] The introduction of the act in Congress in January 1941 dissipated British anger. This, too, had a direct effect on the British policy about continuing technical cooperation.

The fiscal crisis was not the only factor that hampered Tizard's efforts to guarantee continuation of the mission's work. He found it difficult to point to any immediate tangible advantage to Britain's war effort that had resulted from his work in America. Certainly, he had accomplished all of the more indirect goals of the mission. These included establishing better relations and ensuring that, in future, American industry would produce equipment that was useful to the British armed forces. But since the immediate concern of most Britons at the time was the very survival of the nation, it was difficult to persuade people to continue the open Anglo-American technical cooperation when it seemed to have no direct benefit to the war effort. In the official report of the mission that he wrote for Churchill, Tizard freely admitted that "broadly speaking, the Americans are far behind us at present in technical equipment for war." In sum, he could point to only four specific pieces of equipment that were of immediate use to the British armed forces: the Sperry bombsight, the Ford director for naval gunnery, a naval radio warning buoy, and a blind-landing system for aircraft.[5]

Before leaving North America, Tizard had written a list of seven important policy decisions that had to be reached on his arrival in England. Three of these involved Canada, including securing authorization for radar production at Research Enterprises Limited, and the transfer of radar research groups to make use of the abundant resources of the National Research Council of Canada. Of the four policy decisions involving the United States, only one concerned production contracts: ordering from the General Electric Company four types of radio tubes for use in radar – including the first contract for American-built magnetrons. The other immediate issues relating to the United States all concerned the transfer of certain items of British equipment that had not been brought by the mission. These included a complete power-driven Bofors anti-aircraft gun with its Kerrison predictor. In only one of these cases did the British receive something in return. In a direct trade, the Americans agreed to supply two stereoscopic height finders in exchange for an equal number of British coincidence height finders.[6]

At the time, Tizard faced the difficulty of not having an official position within the government. Although he was still chairman of the Aeronautical Research Committee, its main work of promoting research and education about aviation matters had largely been suspended or superseded during war. He no longer held any official position at either the Air Ministry or the Ministry of Aircraft Production; his last official act as head of the British Technical Mission was his report to Churchill written on 19 October. Fortunately, a remarkable change of attitude on the part of Lord Beaverbrook prevented Tizard from being lost to government service. In November, Air Chief Marshal Sir Wilfrid Freeman, the air force's member for production and development, was leaving the Ministry of Aircraft Production to become the vice-chief of the air staff, and Beaverbrook requested that Tizard temporarily take over his responsibilities. Beaverbrook, it will be remembered, had barely been on speaking terms with Tizard in July. His change of heart came about because of his growing mistrust of Lindemann and his belief that he required an impartial scientific adviser. From this new position, Tizard continued to influence scientific and technical policy towards the Americans during the crucial months before the passage of the Lend-Lease Act.[7]

But even before Tizard could report to Churchill, the future of the mission had come under fire from an unlikely source. Back in July, H.J. Gough, the director of scientific research at the Ministry of Supply, had given Cockcroft permission to join the mission – but with great reluctance. Gough had insisted that Cockcroft's stay in North America be limited to no more than three weeks. Gough, of course, had generally supported the dispatch of the mission, and in early 1941 he was to play an important role in guaranteeing that its work would continue uninterrupted. But he was furious that his most valued scientific administrator had not returned with Tizard. As Gough wrote that autumn, he was "very strongly of the opinion" that Cockcroft, who was slated to take over the directorship of the Air Defence Experimental Establishment, would be better employed in the United Kingdom than as an adviser in North America. Gough was far more interested in developing gun-laying radar and proximity fuses than in the long-term benefits of continuing Anglo-American technical cooperation.[8]

Tizard held his first briefing meeting on 14 October. In it he reported the results of the mission to senior technical and scientific administrators from all the service and supply ministries, including Gough. Tizard told them that he was generally pleased with the American response to Britain's gift of its most secret military technologies, but in doing so he linked the American reluctance to part with the Norden bombsight with the British failure to deliver an ASV radar set. The set had, of course, not been sent, and he needed to discover where it had gone. Some discussion followed about the continuation of the mission's work, with Tizard suggesting that a central scientific agency be established in North America to coordinate all British requests for information. He asked that Cockcroft be allowed to remain and continue the work in North America until a permanent mission could be established. This at least would guarantee its continuance in the short term. But Gough was not swayed; he demanded Cockcroft's immediate recall.

A rather heated discussion on the subject followed. Tizard was shocked when the majority supported Gough's right not only to recall Cockcroft but to recall the entire mission. The minutes of the meeting were subsequently edited and do not reflect this development. They simply note that a discussion on the subject took place, with no decision being reached.[9] This misrepresentation of the meeting enraged Gough even further and caused him to write to several other participants about their recollections of the discussion. Both D.R. Pye of the Ministry of Aircraft Production and Robert Watson-Watt of the Air Ministry confirmed Gough's version of events. Watson-Watt pointed out to Gough:

No one questioned your obvious right to decide [about Cockcroft], nor the rightness of your views. It was agreed without dissent that the mission, now led by Cockcroft, should be recalled by cable, and that you should do the cabling to cover Cockcroft and the others, without the need for separate action on each member. I have the impression that it was Tizard who suggested that you should cable the agreed recall … The sense of the meeting being in no doubt Tizard did not press or re-express any continuing disagreement with that sense, whatever his internal reservations, in any other way other than by a mild sotto voce "I think he would be of great use to the Purchasing Commission." I had not the slightest doubt that he had accepted the majority views.[10]

By the time Gough was able to rally support, however, Tizard had already approached higher authority and had received permission to delay the recall of Cockcroft until after he had reported to the prime minister.

Tizard's report to Churchill of 19 October was a masterly upbeat summary of the mission's success and of the need to continue its work on a permanent basis. He told Churchill: "Before we left information was being freely given, and, indeed, offered to us. I have no doubt that, provided we have suitable representatives in North America, whose efforts are suitably co-ordinated we can get the U.S. War and Navy Departments, selected manufacturing firms, and American scientists co-operating fully with us and the Canadians in the development and production of war equipment which both nations want increasing quantity and quality." Tizard freely admitted that the mission could be of advantage to Britain only in the long term, and that this would be possible only if Britain was determined to continue the mission's work. However, the long-term rewards would be great. By acting "quietly and not ostentatiously," British technical advisers could substantially influence the American rearmament program and could ensure that the equipment being manufactured would be of use to the armed forces of both nations. This window of opportunity was fast closing, he said. Any hesitation might result in the Americans producing equipment that had already proven obsolete in combat or that would not meet the requirements of the British services. In the short term, Tizard argued, Cockcroft, Wallace, and Bowen simply had to remain in North America. Although he acknowledged how difficult it was to spare Cockcroft from the Ministry of Supply, he believed that Cockcroft could do "far more towards winning the war by staying another two or three months in the USA than he would by coming home."

An effective permanent technical liaison structure would require a major restructuring of the British supply missions in North America. Such a restructuring, of course, went far beyond Tizard's mandate. His forthrightness demonstrates just how far Tizard the scientist had come from the sheltered hallways of academia. In his report to Churchill, Tizard was very critical of the organization of the British missions in North America. The only department with an adequate permanent technical presence there was the Admiralty, he stated. Its technical mission in Ottawa had an excellent staff of experts and only required strengthening with the addition of radar experts, especially with officers who had recent operational experience. The Americans were particularly interested in learning how modern weapon systems were actually performing in combat. Tizard advised that it was also necessary to restructure the North American organizations of the Ministry of Aircraft Production and the Ministry of Supply. Among the various British supply and technical representatives in North America there was a general lack of coordination and a confusing duplication of permanent and temporary missions. For example, the British supply and technical organizations in Canada and the United States were operating independently of each other. Tizard cited the case of an American officer who had complained of being asked "for the same information from six different British sources." It was a complete "muddle," and the Americans were under the impression that the British suffered from a general lack of efficiency. "Are they far wrong?" Tizard asked. To curb this chaos, he advocated establishing air and army technical missions in Ottawa similar to the British Admiralty Technical Mission. Each would be headed by a senior officer who would have the authority to coordinate all technical inquiries and missions. The three technical bodies would themselves be controlled and coordinated by "a man of prominence and experience, and of Ministerial Status."[11]

Tizard's recommendations were of such scope and magnitude that it was decided that a subcommittee of the North American Supply Committee should develop an interim policy. This subcommittee was headed by Sir Arthur Salter, and it included prominent representatives from all the service and supply ministries. Tizard was appointed as a special adviser. At its first meeting on 29 October, it was agreed that Cockcroft, Wallace, and Bowen could remain in North America for the time being, while the matter was investigated at the most senior levels of government. No action would be taken on a permanent technical organization in North America before Purvis and Sir Walter Layton had made a scheduled visit to London in early November. Despite continuing protests by Gough and others at the Ministry of Supply, Tizard had ensured that the work of the mission would continue for at least seven weeks after the demand for its recall had been aired. This was a vital strategic success. For if Gough had been allowed to recall the mission in early October, Bowen and Cockcroft would never have been able to make such an impact by directing the American and Canadian scientific industrial mobilization. Given the importance placed on the mission's work by senior politicians, scientists, and officers in both of the North American countries, it is difficult to imagine the effect an early recall would have had on Anglo-American and Anglo-Canadian relations.[12]

Several other steps were taken by Salter's committee to continue the work of the mission. The committee agreed to authorize that measures should be taken by British legal representatives in the United States to establish a permanent agreement on patent rights. This allowed for a long-term continuation of technical cooperation. The mystery of the missing ASV radar set was solved when it was revealed that the ship carrying it had been sunk. Another set was dispatched, together with an airborne interception set.

Since there was no official policy on a permanent free and frank exchange of information, all the services provided briefs about current policy and procedures. But, in fact, in the previous few months, all three services had shown the Americans almost all of their technical secrets; they had given American attachés and other officers detailed samples of British equipment as well as tours of bases, ships, and aircraft. However, there was some disquieting evidence to suggest that this openness might not last. In early November, Colonel J.J. Llewellin, representing the Ministry of Aircraft Production, reported to Tizard that Lord Beaverbrook had ordered a review to see whether at least some information should be withheld from the Americans. According to Sir Harold Brown of the Ministry of Supply, an American request for a copy of the British green book on chemical warfare, which had already caused Tizard some difficulty, was a violation of the instructions he had received from "higher authorities." Tizard countered by pointing out that the War Office had sent Colonel Barley in August to gather information on American chemical warfare technology, and Barley had been given a full briefing. All that the Americans wanted, Tizard retorted, was to be treated with the same courtesy. No decision was reached on this contentious issue, and it continued to be a major problem in the following months.

Tizard was aware of the long struggle that lay ahead to preserve the mission's work, and he was determined to find allies. On 4 November he briefed the new Scientific Advisory Committee of the Cabinet. This committee had been established in October after a lengthy campaign by members of the Royal Society for a formal structure to be established to allow scientists to advise the government on scientific and technical policy. Its original chairman was Lord Hankey, and its members were the two secretaries of the Royal Society and the secretaries of the Department of Scientific and Industrial Research, the Medical Research Council, and the Agricultural Research Council. Even at this early date, however, the committee had no real power. Its advice tended to be either ignored by Churchill or thwarted by Lindemann. As a result, it could lend Tizard nothing but moral support.[13]

Meanwhile, Sir Arthur Salter was carrying out further inquiries about technical cooperation. His memorandum of 13 November to the War Cabinet concluded that "the disclosure of secret information (both operational and technical) has become essential to the success of our supply arrangements in the United States of America." The major difficulty was that there was no consistency between departments on what type of material they would make available to the Americans and how it would be transferred. Some departments were providing all available information, while others were beginning to hold back what they considered to be highly sensitive material. Data on a given subject might readily be provided on one occasion, only to be followed by a reluctance to keep it up to date. There was a reason for this tightening of restrictions on cooperation: some senior officials in Britain were once again fearful that American security arrangements were not adequate to safeguard British secrets. Particularly worrisome was the information now required by private American companies who wanted to manufacture many of the devices brought by the Tizard Mission.

This confusing inconsistency, Salter confessed, was deeply unsettling. It was giving the Americans the impression "that we give information when it suits our immediate purpose and present it in a form that suits our immediate purpose but are unwilling 'to put all our cards on the table.'" Salter had discussed the issue with Lord Lothian, and they had agreed that it was essential that all restrictions should be removed; anything less would constitute a serious breach in Anglo-American relations. At stake was the "partnership in defence preparation" that Britain needed if it was to survive. Lothian could discuss security concerns frankly with President Roosevelt. One possible solution, suggested Salter, might be cooperation between the British and American security services.[14]

The War Cabinet met on 21 November to discuss whether to continue to disclose secret operational and technical information. Salter opened the meeting with a summary of the main point of his memorandum. It might be possible, he added, to protect secret information further; they could ask the Americans to restrict access to certain highly sensitive material to a select group of senior political and military leaders. Churchill, however, once again displayed his rigid stance on the old policy of *quid pro quo*. He was against Britain providing information unless they could realize a direct tangible benefit in return. With no sign of any easing of the American restrictions on supplying war material on credit, he linked technical cooperation with this vital issue. This is precisely what he had done in the summer when he had connected the dispatch of the mission to the successful completion of the destroyers-for-bases deal. However, the exchange of technical information was a special case. Churchill argued that there should be a distinction between the devices that would be manufactured in the United States for the British services and those that the Americans wished to produce for their own requirements. Information on the former should be made freely available, but for information on the latter they should demand an adequate *quid pro quo*. Churchill wanted similar restrictions on providing details on operations. In both cases, he cited concerns about lax American security.

During the meeting, Tizard's report was only briefly discussed, and none of his recommendations was considered. Astonishingly, Churchill used the report to support his desire to limit future contacts with the Americans, telling his Cabinet colleagues, "Sir Henry had reported that on the whole the United States had much less to tell us than we had to tell them." Lord Halifax was astounded by these conclusions and warned that there would be "disastrous" consequences if the Americans learned of this remarkable lack of confidence in their security arrangements. He reminded his colleagues of Salter's suggestion that Lothian discuss these concerns with Roosevelt. But Churchill would not be swayed. In a typically Churchillian burst of illogic, he said that the Americans should of course be told that they were trusted, but they must understand that Britain was fighting for her life and that some secret information could not possibly be divulged. At the end of the meeting it was agreed that Lothian would communicate the Cabinet's decision to Roosevelt. It was also decided that the three supply ministers would form a new committee to work out the details of the more restrictive new policy. Churchill, however, reserved for himself the right to communicate directly with the president on a personal basis any information he deemed necessary – on the understanding that its disclosure would be restricted to Roosevelt's "immediate associates."[15]

This meeting of the War Cabinet came at a time of heightening tension about American policy. It threatened to revert technical cooperation back to the disastrous times of *quid pro quo*. On 3 December the secretaries of the War Cabinet's new Committee on the Disclosure of Secret Information to the United States composed a memorandum outlining what had already been provided and how further information could be traded. They were hard pressed to find one area in which at least some information had not already been provided without preconditions. Despite this, they suggested that all future exchanges should require a specific counteroffer from the Americans. The major portion of this lengthy memorandum consisted of a detailed list of what Britain might offer in trade – along with the specific American technology that would be demanded in return. Some of the demands were for a direct exchange of information (for instance, on microwave radar), but others were rather arbitrary demands, similar to the disastrous *quid pro quo* exchanges prior to the mission's departure. They required, for example, that if the Americans wanted data on gyropredictor gunsights, they would have to provide information on their productive capacity for communications equipment.[16]

The Foreign Office and the British Embassy in Washington did all they could to modify and delay the transmission of the War Cabinet's decision. They wanted at least to wait until the Roosevelt administration's scheme for assisting Britain had been made public. Lothian cabled London on 3 December expressing his dismay at the "friction and misunderstanding" that would result if he informed Roosevelt of the new British policy. He dismissed British concerns about the reputedly lax American security precautions. Even if there were doubts about the Americans' ability to safeguard secret information, he said, cutting them off was the wrong approach. Lothian reiterated his earlier argument that it would be far better to bring British apprehensions to Roosevelt's personal attention. This, he said, would result in a cooperative approach to solving any American weaknesses in security arrangements.[17]

This telegram was Lothian's last significant contribution to the issue of Anglo-American technical cooperation. Just nine days later, on 12 December, he died suddenly from uraemic poisoning. A Christian Scientist, he refused medical treatment. Churchill paid him a great tribute, calling him "our greatest ambassador to the United States." At least in the furtherance of full and frank technical cooperation, his influence was perhaps (with the possible exception of Tizard's) the greatest of all. By defying the War Cabinet's explicit instructions, he had helped secure a delay that prevented Churchill's hard bargaining tactics from undoing all the work of the Tizard Mission.[18]

Nevertheless, Great Britain implemented restrictions on information exchanges, though it did so without officially informing the Americans. By the first week in December, Brigadier General Martin Scanlon, the American air attaché, was aware that the situation had become "a bit sticky." "For some reason or other," he informed Washington, "most of the information on British and enemy activities has been either cut off completely or very greatly curtailed, so that what is received is not much more informative than the morning papers." Writing to the Air Ministry, he warned, "If they expect our help, it is a hell of a poor time to become secretive." Scanlon was somewhat consoled by the fact that his contacts in the Air Ministry were trying to "get the matter straightened out." But in attempting to explain their government's action, the British revealed Churchill's concern about lax American security, though they did not mention his anger about the fiscal crisis. Scanlon asked Herschel Johnson, the American chargé d'affairs, to make an official protest to the Foreign Office about the new policy.[19] On 5 December, Johnson met with Lord Halifax and expressed his concern about the restrictions on operational information. He warned of a "most unfortunate impression in the United States" if the situation continued. Halifax promptly relayed this friendly admonition to Churchill and other cabinet members.[20]

These warnings about the immense diplomatic consequences of overtly limiting the flow of information to the United States appeared, to the Americans, to have had the desired effect. By 18 December, Halifax was able to tell Johnson that there would be no further curtailment; indeed, any restrictions imposed would be rescinded.[21] In truth, however, Churchill's desire to link the extent of information transfers to the availability of American credit had not altered. What Johnson was not told was that his warnings had resulted in new procedures to make restrictions on information exchanges appear less obvious to the Americans. The War Cabinet subcommittee that had been established in November to investigate secret disclosures to the United States agreed on 21 December that "if we did not desire production for our own accounts, our attitude should depend on the attitude the United States Authorities were at the time adopting towards us on supply matters."[22] This clandestine policy proved to be both unworkable and short-lived. By the end of December, Roosevelt had made his announcement of lend-lease, using his famous garden-hose analogy. This public pronouncement was enough for Churchill, and for the time being there was no more pressure from him to undo the work of the mission. What made the policy unworkable was the fact that a system already existed whereby it was virtually impossible to withhold information without the knowledge of the Americans.

On 4 January 1941 the Chemical Warfare Board decided to terminate the exchange of information with the Americans. As we have already seen, ever since Tizard's return to Britain in October there had been a reluctance to provide data in this area. This was the case despite the fact that Colonel Barley, a British officer unattached to the mission, had visited the United States to survey the U.S. Army's Chemical Warfare Service facilities. Being unfamiliar with the lack of coordination that characterized British missions to North America, the Americans had expected the Tizard Mission to provide them with equivalent details on their chemical warfare research. It will be recalled that Tizard had improvised by calling in chemists from the National Research Council of Canada, who were able to provide at least some of what the Americans wanted. This and other Canadian involvement in the mission had established intimate collaboration between Canada and the United States on military research.

As the director of scientific research, H.J. Gough was asked to investigate the practicality of cutting the Americans off from information on chemical warfare. He submitted his report on 7 January 1941, after having talked with Tizard and Cockcroft. It was a damning indictment of the Chemical Warfare Board's decision. Gough had come to the conclusion that severing connections with the Americans would not only be politically disastrous but would probably be impossible. All chemical warfare liaison, he pointed out, had until now been carried out by two Canadians – Dr Otto Maass and Dr E.A. Flood. As a result, it would "be necessary to inform Canada explicitly of the restriction." But Canada now had "intimate co-operation" with the United States. "It is no longer practical," he argued, "to interfere with this co-operation and it is likely to be impolitic to require Canada to compromise it by accepting relevant information from us which may not be passed onto the Americans." Only two options, therefore, remained: either to cut the Canadians off as well as the Americans, or else to do nothing to interfere with full open technical exchange with North America. Gough strongly advised the latter. He pointed to the absurdity of cutting off Canada, Britain's most important ally. This advice, he asserted, applied to all information, not just to chemical warfare.[23] His logic was irrefutable, and it was generally agreed that open and frank technical cooperation would continue.

Deliberate policy decisions, both political and bureaucratic, were just a few of the obstacles that had to be overcome if the mission's work was to flourish. Political and bureaucratic obstinacy defied policy as well. One of the most ambitious undertakings of the mission had been the attempt by Tizard and Cockcroft to convince the Canadians to develop a far more extensive program in radar research and production than they had originally envisioned. There should have been no objections to this program; Canada was going to finance it, and all that was required from Britain was technical guidance and support. As Canada was an ally and a Commonwealth partner, no one anticipated any difficulty in implementing the proposals. Yet even before Cockcroft met with the Canadian War Cabinet in order to urge it to approve the plan, Tizard's idea of sending a radar research team to Canada had been rejected by Lord Beaverbrook. Beaverbrook, the Canadian-born head of the Ministry of Aircraft Production, informed Tizard of this decision on 29 October 1940:

> I am of the opinion that it would be a mistake for us to embark on a project of the kind you outline. The stimulus of war conditions and war necessities is something we are bound to take into account.
>
> The continuous interplay of theory and experience as between scientists and fighting officers is of immense value. And the problems imposed on us by war change very rapidly.
>
> For these reasons I feel bound to resist a proposal to send skilled research workers across the ocean.[24]

When Cockcroft returned to Great Britain in early December, he discovered that the entire Canadian radar production scheme was under threat. Not only had Beaverbrook refused permission to dispatch a research team, but officials in the Ministry of Aircraft Production had begun to doubt that Canada had the industrial skill and the necessary machine tools to undertake radar production. Without informing either Tizard or Cockcroft, they had been refusing to issue contracts for Canadian-produced radar since early September. Studies conducted by industrial experts in 1939 had convinced them of structural weaknesses in the Canadian economy. Despite strong lobbying by representatives of the Canadian Department of Munitions and Supply and by the National Research Council, the Ministry of Aircraft Production refused either to place orders or to send further specifications and prototypes. This caused grave concern, for the Canadians required one or two ASV radars to examine so that they could design a similar set using North American circuitry. The one ASV set that had been dispatched had been in Ottawa only briefly, while E.G. Bowen installed it in an aircraft for demonstration to the Americans. Some measurements of the device had been made at this time, but not enough to allow for a finished design. Cockcroft strongly supported the Canadians' demands and lobbied on their behalf at the Ministry of Aircraft Production; and by the end of December, the Canadians and Cockcroft had finally managed to persuade everyone except Lord Beaverbrook to support Research Enterprises' production scheme. They could only do so by giving assurances that adequate machine tools were being purchased from the Americans for Research Enterprises. By a happy stroke of fortune, C.D. Howe, the Canadian minister of munitions and supply, arrived in London at the beginning of January 1941 and successfully intervened with Beaverbrook.[25] Thus, by mid-January, two more ASV prototypes had arrived in Canada, and design work was soon completed for a North American version of the set. Production began in late 1941. By the time production finally wound down, more than six thousand sets had been manufactured for the American, British, and Canadian air forces.

Thus, by mid-January 1941 it was generally agreed in Britain that the policy initiated by the Tizard Mission of full and frank technical disclosures without demanding reciprocity would become permanent. The only restrictions were in supplying information on new equipment vital for operations planned to occur in the near future, or if the technical device had not yet reached a sufficient stage of development or trial. If any request for information could not be honoured, the Americans were to be provided with a "proper explanation."[26]

On 15 January a new War Cabinet subcommittee on releasing secret information to the United States met to discuss the formation of a permanent scientific liaison organization. Discussion on the structure of the scientific organization that would be required had started with Tizard's memorandum to the prime minister in October. Tizard's plan for a radical restructuring of the technical organization with a person of ministerial rank in charge was never seriously pursued. Instead, while the Cabinet decided general policy, the Ministry of Supply's Directorate of Scientific Research took the lead in establishing a less radical and therefore more acceptable solution to the organizational logistics of cooperation.

Despite his objections to Cockcroft remaining in North America, H.J. Gough carefully followed the reports sent by his most trusted scientific administrator. By mid-November he had received details of the proposals that Vannevar Bush had made to Cockcroft in late October about a permanent system for scientific and technical exchanges. Bush had suggested that after the British Technical Mission returned home, liaison between Great Britain, Canada, and the United States should be handled by an organization headed by R.H. Fowler in Ottawa and the chairman of the National Defense Research Committee's (NDRC's) office in Washington. They would act as "the channel of communication" by sorting requests, checking for duplication, and controlling all visitors, who would require accreditation from the liaison offices. Bush offered "full disclosure" of all research work under NDRC control. Soon he was able to extend this to include work under the jurisdiction of the army and navy, though the services would continue to manage their own liaison network through their attachés.[27]

Cockcroft's endorsement of Bush's plan was enough for Gough to propose that it be adopted without significant alteration. The fact that Fowler worked under the auspices of his own Ministry of Supply made the plan all the more acceptable. He advocated "as direct a link as possible" between his directorate and the NDRC. By the end of November, Gough had received authority for his directorate to continue to control the scientific liaison office in North America. No steps were taken to establish a more permanent organization until after Cockcroft's return on 12 December.[28]

On his arrival in London, Cockcroft provided a more extensive outline of the proposed central technical office. In response to

American requests, it was now to be based in Washington. This office continued to exert influence on the direction of America's scientific mobilization. It also functioned as a central clearing house and library for all information requests both to and from Great Britain. Thus, any request for information was supplied from the library if available, and otherwise the office directed the inquiry to an appropriate British expert in North America. If the request could not be dealt with in North America, the office forwarded it to the appropriate directorate of scientific research. As much as possible, Cockcroft felt that the office should act as an independent body in close contact with both the embassy and the purchasing mission. However, it was to report to the North American Supply Committee of the Ministry of Supply. The organization was to be led by a permanent director, who would replace the ad hoc triumvirate of Fowler, Wallace, and Bowen.[29]

Cockcroft's proposal was supported by Arthur Purvis and Sir Andrew Duncan, the minister of supply. It was approved by the War Cabinet subcommittee at its meeting on 15 January.[30] This led to the establishment in March of the British Central (later Commonwealth) Scientific Office in Washington. The subcommittee's approval meant that the British government had now formalized the permanent policy of free and full military scientific and technical cooperation with the United States and Canada. But one more obstacle remained.

Since September, British and American legal experts had been trying to work out the intricate details of how commercial patent rights could be protected without compromising either secrecy or the rapid dissemination of information on current research. To the layman, the long delay associated with working out all the legal minutia required for the protection of patent rights was frustrating. As we have seen, it had been agreed at the end of September that the United States and Great Britain would in the interim have to negotiate with individual patent holders before starting to produce any device. This was a cumbersome procedure, and by the end of October the U.S. Navy was looking for a better solution. Frank Knox, writing to the British Purchasing Mission on 30 October, asked for permission to use information received from the British. He wanted to do so "without regard to present patent rights, leaving for later negotiation the settlement of rights that may be involved." The purchasing mission sought legal advice, and more than six weeks passed before it replied, on 13 December, stating that the navy had permission to go ahead as planned – but with one important proviso. The Americans could manufacture any British device without the patent holder's prior approval only if the "manufacture and use in the United States will not prejudice any application for a patent that might subsequently be filed in the United States." Unfortunately, Knox could not provide such assurance. The patent laws specifically stated that public use of an unpatented device would invalidate any patent filed more than one year after its first manufacture in the United States. Knox suggested that the British could inform any potential patent holder in sufficient time for a patent application to be filed within the one-year grace period, but the British did not consider this sufficient protection. As a result, it was impossible to go beyond what had been tentatively agreed in September without a change in the patent laws.[31]

It was realized by the Navy Department that the power to change the patent laws lay with Congress and that other departments, including Commerce, State, and War, had to be involved in the drafting of any new legislation. On 6 February a meeting was held at the State Department with representatives of all the departments concerned. Conway P. Coe, the commissioner of patents and the representative of the Commerce Department, outlined a new piece of legislation designed to protect the British patent rights of devices that were deemed vital for national defence. It covered three basic points of law: patent rights would be protected; the time limit for filing patents would be extended; and any dispute would be arbitrated by a Joint Defence Claims Commission. Those attending the meeting agreed that, for the course of the present national emergency, further legislation would be proposed to suspend injunctions and other legal hindrances that might cause manufacturers producing vital war material to become involved in a patent dispute.[32] By mid-February the procedures outlined by Commissioner Coe had formed the basis of an Anglo-American accord on patents. Although legislation still had to be enacted in both countries, the agreement was considered sufficient to end any concern that there would be legal obstacles to continuing technical cooperation at all levels.[33]

This last obstacle cleared, it was now time for the final act in the history of the technical mission. Soon after the members of the mission had begun discussions with representatives of the National Defense Research Committee (NDRC), it had become apparent that the mission could be only the beginning of a continuing story of technical cooperation. The establishment of the British Central Scientific Office in Washington was only one-half of the necessary infrastructure required. As early as October 1940, the NDRC had requested that it be allowed to send a reciprocal group to Great Britain and set up a permanent NDRC liaison office in London. Permission for this reciprocal visit was delayed while the various obstacles to continuing the work of the mission were worked out. It was therefore not until late January 1941 that both sides agreed to the mission's dispatch.

Dr James Conant, Bush's deputy at the NDRC, was chosen to head the mission. He was an appropriate choice. Not only was he second in command of the NDRC, but he was one of the United States' most important chemists and was president of Harvard University. As a member of the pro-British White Committee, Conant was one of the leading advocates of expanding American support for the Allied cause. His scientific accomplishments and interventionist statements were well known by a wide cross section of the British academic, intellectual, and political community. Among those accompanying him were Carol Wilson, the NDRC's chief liaison officer; Frederick L. Hovde, assistant to the president of Purdue University; and Kenneth Bainbridge, an atomic physicist at Harvard. As well as being an excellent administrator and a chemical engineer by training, Hovde was a former Rhodes Scholar. Bush had selected him to head the NDRC's London office.

Conant's mission was a very different affair from Tizard's, for it was more of a diplomatic than a scientific affair. When Conant's team arrived in London in March 1941, most military technical and scientific secrets had already been exchanged. Rather than being involved in a secret exchange of classified information, Conant's mission was a public affirmation of the growing ties between Great Britain and the United States. Nevertheless, it was not without its unhappy moments. The Americans arrived in London just as Winston Churchill was going through another of his periodic bouts of anger over American procrastination. This time he was peeved about the lend-lease legislation's agonizingly slow passage through Congress. On 6 March 1941, Conant was asked to lunch with Churchill, his wife Clementine, and Frederick Lindemann in the bombproof basement dining room beneath 10 Downing Street. There he found the prime minister in a foul mood, not willing to talk to his American guest. Instead, Mrs Churchill led the conversation. At the first opening in an otherwise icy luncheon, Conant described his very supportive testimony to the Senate on the lend-lease bill. Sensing an ally in Conant, Churchill began to talk about his deep worries. "This bill has to pass," he said. "What a state it would leave the President in; what a failure he would appear before history if this bill is not passed. What would happen in the United States if the bill was rejected? Would the president resign; if so, who would then become President, the Vice President?" Conant was "amazed" that Churchill could display such a remarkable ignorance of the American constitution. He politely explained the difference between a prime minister and a president, and suggested that even if the bill was defeated, Britain would require much more help than America's industrial production. Churchill disagreed and said that all he wanted were the "tools" to finish the job – not American manpower. This, Conant suspected, was a more diplomatic Churchill, a Churchill fearful of any indication reaching the United States that the British government desired the Americans to have any further involvement in the war beyond lend-lease.

In the following weeks, Conant was invited to a number of public functions. His hospitable reception illustrated the remarkable change of attitude taking place in Great Britain as a result of the United States' growing involvement in the war. On 14 March, Conant received an honorary doctor of science degree from Cambridge University. That evening, at dinner, Professor A.V. Hill handed him a slip of paper with the following written on it:

> J.B. Conant
> Cambridge and Harvard
> As arrows are in the hand of the mighty man,
> As are the children of his youth.
> Happy is the man that hath his quiver full of them;
> He shall not be ashamed
> When he speaks with enemies in the gate.
> Psalm 127

It was a fitting passage from the man who had done so much to launch open and frank technical cooperation. It symbolized not just the link between the two universities but the growing relationship between the two greatest unvanquished democracies left in the world in early 1941.

A further sign of this growing bond occurred several days later at the annual Trinity College festival at which Conant was an honoured guest. The sole speaker at dinner that evening was the new master of Trinity – the famous historian Professor Macaulay Trevelyan. The audience responded with thunderous stamping in approval when Trevelyan stated that Conant was "more welcome here than any other man in the world." Other social engagements followed, including an audience with the king and a second lunch with Churchill – this time at Chequers, his country retreat. By then, the lend-lease bill had finally been passed, so instead of being moody and angry, Churchill was a charming and intelligent host who led an entertaining conversation on the battles of the American Civil War.

Conant and the other members of his mission also had many official duties to attend to. These included visits to military research centres and radar stations, and the establishment of the NDRC's office in London. The Americans continued to learn much from the British.[34] Most significant was a discovery made by Kenneth Bainbridge. As a result of the Anglo-American technical and scientific information exchange agreements signed in Washington in October 1940, Bainbridge was allowed to sit in on the top secret meetings of the MAUD committee,[35] and he found that by March 1941 a remarkable transformation had occurred in British opinion about the feasibility of the atomic bomb. The MAUD committee had accepted the conclusions of the Frisch-Peierls memorandum, and further experimental and theoretical studies had swung opinion to the horrifying conclusion that a bomb could indeed be built if suitable means for separating plutonium or enriched uranium could be developed. Of pivotal importance among this new information were measurements of the cross section of uranium undertaken by Dr M.A. Tuve of the Carnegie Institution in Washington – an early example of the fruit of Anglo-American nuclear cooperation which the Tizard Mission had made possible. "The first test of this theory," wrote Peierls in March 1941, "has given a completely positive answer and there is no doubt that the whole scheme is feasible (provided the technical problems of isotope separation are satisfactorily solved) and that the critical size for a U sphere is manageable."[36]

Bainbridge's report of the remarkable transformation in British attitudes towards nuclear research persuaded Vannevar Bush back in Washington that an atomic bomb was not only feasible but might actually be built during the war. Further information, suggesting that the Germans were undertaking similar research, galvanized Bush to push for a dramatic expansion of the American atomic program.[37] Later that summer the final report of the MAUD committee confirmed the theoretical feasibility of building an atomic bomb. This stimulated further efforts on the part of Bush and other American scientists for a massive American atomic bomb program.

By 12 April, Conant's work in Great Britain was finished and he boarded a plane to Lisbon to begin his trip home. He was happy with the results of his mission, though not content. During his journey he had witnessed many aspects of wartime life in Britain, including several bombing raids on London. It was the height of the Blitz on the British capital, and he saw little to be optimistic about if the United States did not soon enter the war.

This pessimistic view was confirmed by Churchill. Two days before Conant left, he had a meeting with the British prime minister to say goodbye. Conant was ushered into the Cabinet Room at 10 Downing Street just as a group of high-ranking officers were leaving. Churchill was sitting amidst a multitude of maps that had just been used to discuss the hopeless situation in Greece. "The Prime Minister was sombre," Conant recalled. "'Here we are,' he said, 'standing alone. What is going to happen.' What I replied I cannot now recall. I do remember the intensity of my feelings as I left London ... I was prepared to give the isolationists some frank talk." As far as most American scientists were concerned, the Tizard Mission had already drawn them into the war. It would be only a matter of time, Conant believed, before the entire country accepted its growing commitment to the Allies and joined the scientists at war.[38]

Epilogue

"The Tizard Mission," wrote a British scientist in June 1942, "sowed remarkable seeds." The seeds from this unprecedented scientific and technical exchange had already produced extraordinary fruit.[1] In 1945 an American scientist agreed that the Tizard Mission had provided knowledge and experience that was of "inestimable value" for the subsequent U.S. war effort.[2] His point is well taken, for the long-term consequences of the mission make it one of the most important events in the history of the Second World War.

Had the mission involved nothing more than the transfer of technology, its significance would still have been very great indeed. Britain's gift of the cavity magnetron provided the United States with the single most important piece of electronic equipment developed during the course of the war. The microwave radars, which the magnetron made possible, proved crucial. They helped to defeat the U-boat menace in the Battle of the Atlantic and to deprive the Japanese navy of its superiority in night fighting in the Pacific. They made possible the development of more effective night fighters, and they assured the precise control of all forms of gunnery and of highly accurate all-weather bomb-aiming devices. The magnetron's importance was enhanced because, unlike their involvement in other radar technology, the Axis powers neither emulated microwave radar nor developed effective countermeasures against it.

The exploitation of this British technological breakthrough by American researchers and industry was crucial in another sense as well. It enabled the development of new types of magnetrons that were vital to the later war effort. In October 1941 it was decided in Great Britain to concentrate research on improving existing models of radar equipment rather than developing new types of sets.[3] There was a dual reason for this: the shortage of scientific and technical expertise, and a corresponding shortfall in industrial development resources. It was thus the American researchers at the Radiation Laboratory who had the task of developing new types of magnetrons; these functioned with even shorter wavelengths than the approximately 10 centimetres of the first-generation microwave radars. Within just a few weeks of the first detailed examination of the magnetron brought by the mission, discussions took place about developing a version with a shorter wavelength. By the early spring of 1941, Ratheon Corporation's model shop had built the first prototype of a 3-centimetre magnetron, and in the spring of 1943 the first 3-centimetre radar, an airborne interceptor set called the AIA, entered production. By early 1944, other types of the new radar equipment were being produced. The most important of these new sets was the SU, the first 3-centimetre set built for naval use. Mounted on American-supplied destroyer escorts (called, in the British service, captain-class frigates), this set was invaluable in defeating the last wave of the German attacks on shipping by snorkel-equipped U-boats. By the end of the war, a whole new generation of radar sets using even shorter wavelengths was under development at the Radiation Laboratory. These entered service in the postwar period.[4]

Many other radar technical secrets were provided by the Tizard Mission. For example, the long-wave ASV and AI radar sets provided the basic model for all subsequent American wartime airborne-radar equipment and small-ship sets. Until microwave radar became available, the longer-wave aircraft-mounted sets played a vital role in throwing back the German submarine offensive in North American waters in the summer of 1942.

Although radar technology dominated the Tizard Mission, it was not the only important part of the exchange. The mission was directly responsible for the American adaptation of the 40-millimetre Bofors gun as the standard medium anti-aircraft weapon of the Second World War. Britain provided guidance to the embryonic American proximity-fuse program, which was invaluable in the successful development of these weapons. The first description of the Whittle turbojet engine was provided by the mission, and it ultimately led to the development of an entire new industry in the United States. Every American-designed jet engine can trace its heritage back to the Whittle engine. The origins of this technological transfer was the Tizard Mission.[5]

It is an irony of history that the much-coveted Norden bombsight – the one piece of technology withheld from the exchange – ultimately proved unimportant to future Anglo-American technical cooperation. The American reluctance to give up the bombsight secret had caused much turmoil in Anglo-American technical relations prior to the summer of 1940. Yet by early 1942, when the Americans finally provided the British with the bombsight, it failed to impress the first Royal Air Force officer to see it. Wing Commander C.D. Dann, described in American documents as "the foremost British authority on bombsights," stated that "it was his opinion that the Royal Air Force had no need for the M-series [Norden] Bombsights except for a limited number of specially trained squadrons as he believes that the bombsight, like all of the synchronous bombsights, is not satisfactory for attacking targets as heavily defended by anti-aircraft [defences] as are the targets in Germany and in France."[6] In Dann's view, the bombsight's fatal flaw was the amount of time it required the bomber to fly in a straight line on approaching the target. The RAF considered it suicidal to fly planes in the way demanded by the bombsight. The RAF had long since abandoned prewar concepts of daylight precision bombing in favour of safer nighttime area attacks. Although the Norden saw widespread service in the U.S. Army Air Forces and the U.S. Navy, it never lived up to its reputation as a war-winning weapon. Even the U.S. Navy, which had so zealously guarded the Norden secret, had to admit at the end of the war that the bombsight had at best been marginally effective against maritime targets. By the end of the war, the U.S. Navy had removed the sight from service and had transferred all existing stocks to the Army Air Forces. The latter had made more extensive use of the sight, but by 1945 were replacing it with microwave radar-bombing systems. The radar sets were far superior to the optical sights because of radar's accuracy in all weather and light conditions.[7]

The Tizard Mission was of course much more than a means for transferring hardware; it also involved the exchange of intellectual property of all types. Britain passed to the American armed forces much critical information on the performance of modern equipment in combat. This allowed the Americans to integrate much hard-won British experience into their weapon systems prior to their entry into the war. It is impossible to say exactly how much effect the mission had on improving the combat preparedness of the American armed forces, but it cannot be doubted that receiving full technical details of British combat experiences with modern weapon systems more than a year before the United States entered the conflict, made it possible for them to improve doctrines, tactics, and weaponry. Moreover, it is possible to assess the consequence of one failure to learn from British combat experience. A.E.H. Pew noted in August 1940 that while American anti-submarine warfare technology was good, the Americans had not worked out "the best tactics for using the equipment." This, Pew believed, was because their scientific personnel had failed to work closely with their operational officers.[8] While the U.S. Navy was willing to absorb technical lessons from the British, it ignored advice on ASW tactical doctrine. As one recent study has pointed out, this "failure to learn" was the major cause of the near-catastrophic losses inflicted by U-boats on Allied merchant vessels off the American coast during the first six months of 1942.[9]

American and British scientists found much commonality in their ideas of how to organize their profession for war work. Scientists on both sides of the Atlantic believed it necessary for them to have input into the basic planning of research programs, and an equal say in all stages of the design, development, and utilization of new weapon systems. Even before the war, Tizard had shown the effectiveness of treating scientists as equal partners in the development of the British radar defence system. Vannevar Bush already understood this, and he used the tools provided by the mission to win for the NDRC a central role in the making of defence policy. Here, too, the magnetron was a crucial ingredient, because of the fortuitous circumstances that had given Bush's organization control over microwave radar research. What would have happened to the NDRC if the magnetron had not arrived when it did is a matter for speculation. It is certain, however, that the magnetron guaranteed the success of Bush's vision over that of rather strenuous military detractors.

The British scientists imparted to their American colleagues their hard-won experience in establishing smooth-running defence research facilities. The key was to develop a laboratory in which scientists could work effectively with one another and in conjunction with the requirements and experiences of the military. The Radiation Laboratory was closely modelled on British research centres, and it in turn served as the archetype for many of the other laboratories established during the war, including the Los Alamos nuclear facility.

Historians who have examined the early history of the NDRC have failed to evaluate properly the important role played by the Tizard Mission. In large measure, this omission has been caused by the lack of appreciation of the scope of the opposition from the army and navy to the NDRC in the summer of 1940.[10] The image of Bush, despite his presidential authority, skulking into secret meetings with Tizard and Fowler, and earlier with members of the British Embassy staff, illustrates the precarious nature of the NDRC's position. No doubt the downplaying of the mission's significance to America's scientific mobilization has also been caused by a certain amount of misplaced nationalism. The mere thought that ideas from Great Britain could have influenced twentieth-century American scientific history seems to be anathema to a powerful minority of historians of science and technology.[11]

The British influence on American scientific mobilization extended far beyond the mission's involvement with planning the NDRC's microwave radar program. As we have seen, Anglo-American exchanges of information on anti-submarine equipment had been one of the first accomplishments of the mission. However, the U.S. Navy's refusal to learn tactical lessons from the Royal Navy made it among the least successful. Part of the reason for this failure was that the U.S. Navy maintained control of all anti-2submarine warfare (ASW) research and zealously guarded its domain against civilian upstarts. Remembering his First World War experience, Bush had resolved that he would surmount naval opposition to the creation of an ASW-research division at the NDRC. He began his assault on the navy by commissioning a report from the National Academy of Sciences on the present state of ASW research. The report criticized the navy's failure to utilize scientific fundamentals, and Bush used it to convince Secretary Knox to order the Bureau of Ships to support an NDRC study of anti-submarine devices.[12]

The result was that the NDRC established Section C-4 under the leadership of University of Minnesota scientist John T. Tate. The Bureau of Ships wanted Tate's section simply to develop gadgets, but the scientists insisted "on applying scientific methods on the whole problem of detection and the destruction of submarines, and the environment in which the submarines operated."[13] The navy would not support such a wide-ranging research program, so Tate turned to the British connection to learn the technical details of ASW. In June 1941 he went to England, where he received full cooperation from the Royal Navy, including information on tactics, the capabilities of German U-boats, the idiosyncrasies of asdic and depth charges, and a full briefing on current and future research programs. The British stressed "the tendency of researchmen [*sic*] to continually improve and delay production" and the necessity of having one person who would decide when a device was ready for service.[14]

The British provided Tate with enough information to allow the American scientist to put forward a plan for an extensive NDRC research program on ASW problems. During the summer of 1941, Bush provided more than $1.5 million of funding to establish two new ASW laboratories. Faced with this *fait accompli*, on 5 September 1941 the Bureau of Ships reluctantly incorporated Tate's section into its research and development program. The British had once again proven vital in pushing Bush's agenda. Close cooperation on ASW research between the NDRC and the British lasted for the rest of the war.

British influence on the United States' scientific structure should not be exaggerated, however. As it developed during the war, the American research organization in many ways proved to be more effective than its British counterpart. Bush's vision of a powerful, centrally controlled, civilian research coordination agency was achieved with the formation of the Office of Scientific Research and Development in May 1941. This agency, with Bush as its director, coordinated the work of the NDRC and the Medical Research Council. Ultimately, Bush had a great deal of influence, if not control, over all aspects of defence research. Numerous attempts by British scientists to create a similar central agency both before and after the mission were thwarted not merely by the combined opposition of the service and supply departments, but by Lindemann. Although he wielded tremendous power as Churchill's chief scientific adviser, Lindemann never commanded the respect of his scientific colleagues, nor was he given the power to control the scientific war. In order to manage their scientific mobilization, the British relied instead on informal contact between researchers and on a series of ad hoc committees.

The Tizard Mission was but the beginning of the much longer story of Anglo-American scientific and technical cooperation. However, the British Central (later Commonwealth) Scientific Office (BSCO), which had been established by both countries to administer the smooth exchange of information after the mission, never functioned as intended. Although it continued to be the primary clearing house for information, it never received authority to act as a coordination agency for all British ministries. Denied the executive powers proposed by Tizard in October 1940, the BCSO was unable to prevent needless duplication and competition by the supply and service ministries. As a result, Americans and Canadians became accustomed to various British ministries competing for data, as well as for the allocation of manufacturing and research resources. This frustrated the scientists of both countries considerably, for they had become accustomed to their own more centralized control of technical liaison. In 1942 Dr W.L. Webster, the secretary of the BCSO, resigned over the growing impotence of his office. He insisted that the BCSO was filling no useful purpose and should therefore be closed. Webster's proposal was rejected, and the BCSO continued to function until the end of the war as the central clearing-house for scientific information.[15]

Far more successful was the NDRC's organization in Great Britain that was established during the Conant Mission. The liaison office in Britain was greatly expanded during the course of the war. In 1943 a British branch of the Radiation Laboratory was created to provide assistance to the armed forces in operating and maintaining new types of equipment. It was also responsible for sustaining the close contacts with operational personnel that members of the Tizard Mission had considered so important. As

American scientists had learned from Tizard, getting criticisms of current equipment and the requirements for the future directly from those engaged in combat was crucial to the success of the Radiation Laboratory's research and development program. E.G. Bowen played a key role in establishing the British branch of the Radiation Laboratory. In the fall of 1942, Bowen "for the first time fully and vigorously expounded" before the Radiation Laboratory's steering committee the requirement to create a field service organization. The British branch served as the model for similar organizations that were established throughout the world by the Radiation Laboratory and other divisions of the NDRC during the course of the war.[16]

The long-term interaction between the United States and Great Britain in all areas of military technology and scientific research and development had a major impact on the course of the war and continued to influence the organization of science in the postwar period. The atomic bomb program is just one example of this continuing influence. Stanley Goldberg, in a recent article, has shown the crucial role of Bush in pushing for an active American atomic research program as early as April 1941. The title of Goldberg's paper is "Inventing a Climate of Opinion: Vannevar Bush and the Decision to Build the Bomb"; he would have been more accurate if he had called it "Transferring a Climate of Opinion." As we have seen, Bush did not invent anything, but he was in a position that made him one of the first to learn of the new British attitude towards building the bomb. His acceptance of the British view that a bomb could be built during the war led him to transfer this "climate of opinion" to the United States' scientific, military and political élite.

The Tizard Mission had a very minor direct role in the Manhattan Project, because it took place just before the awful truth of the Frisch-Peierls memorandum was accepted by the MAUD committee. Yet its indirect influence is so important that the mission can be said to have been as crucial to the atomic bomb program as the all too famous 1939 letter by Albert Einstein to President Roosevelt. Neither the mission nor this letter started the Manhattan Project, but both profoundly shaped opinion towards building the ultimate weapon.

There are many examples of how this international scientific and technical collaboration materially affected the outcome of the war:

the transfer to the United States of the basic concept of the new science of operational research; the American development of LORAN long-range radio navigation; the British discovery of penicillin and the development in the United States of ways to mass-produce this vital medicine. These striking innovations are just a few of the products of Anglo-American technical cooperation.

Nor was this all. The cooperation allowed for the far easier integration of the armed forces of both countries when the United States at last joined the war. Although universal standardization of equipment did not take place, the mission led directly to some of the more important successes in this area, too. The American adaptation of British IFF sets, for instance, created a universal identification system for aircraft and ships. As a direct result of the mission, joint discussions were begun to coordinate the allocation of all radio frequencies; this was a necessary precursor to the development of a universal IFF system.

An even more significant long-term consequence of the mission came from the Americans receiving British technical and tactical information before they had even entered the war. Some data and material had been provided in the months leading up to the arrival of Tizard in Washington, but the mission turned this trickle into a flood. The Americans were able to incorporate much of this knowledge into a wide variety of their weapon systems, and they were able do so without large-scale industrial disruption. The impact on both countries was tremendous, since after the passage of the Lend-Lease Act, Britain increasingly relied on American industrial production.

The mission created both the atmosphere and the organization to allow for the most extensive collaboration of military research resources in history. This collaboration was not always perfect. In 1943, for instance, there was a complete breakdown in cooperation on atomic research. This occurred after the British had made their most significant contributions to the atomic research effort and when the American program had far surpassed the British one in size and in results. This was a particularly painful incident for the British, who were thus deprived of information that had been available from the American program. The rupture of relations was caused by security concerns, by the desire to secure postwar commercial rights, and by a simple lack of communication. It took a full eight months to repair the damage done to Anglo-American scientific relations. Only after a formal agreement on nuclear cooperation was signed by Roosevelt and Churchill at the Quebec Conference in August 1943 did information exchanges recommence. But this incident appears to have been the exception to the rule. It was caused by the unique nature of the atomic bomb program. On the whole, the spirit of cooperation which was begun by the Tizard Mission continued for the rest of the war.[17]

The Tizard Mission's marked success in instigating Anglo-American technical cooperation makes it much more difficult to evaluate its impact on other aspects of the emerging alliance. After the summer of 1940, for instance, there was no need to continue the discussions about broad policy on technical cooperation at the political or diplomatic level. This was necessary only in the field of nuclear research. The brief relapse into *quid pro quo* on the part of the British government in late 1940 was, as we have seen, only a temporary check. Legal discussions concerning patent rights created an effective system for dealing with this contentious issue; the system worked with little change until the cessation of hostilities.

The effect of the mission on changing the attitudes of the American and British services towards each other is difficult to measure, and it is impossible to say what effect it had on the opinions of such American officers as General George Marshall, General Hap Arnold, and Admiral Harold Stark. But by educating senior American military officers on the importance of maintaining close contact with the British armed forces, the mission played an important role in sweeping away the chauvinism of the prewar era. It similarly influenced the thinking of high-ranking British officers. After December 1940, British officers no longer believed unsubstantiated rumours about the security risk of providing the Americans with classified information. Certainly, the mission fostered mutual respect for both sides' technical and scientific abilities.

The mission was, of course, just one part of the gradual evolution towards the alliance of the United States and Great Britain. Other contemporary events were equally important ingredients in this transformation. These included the first Anglo-American staff talks (which began in London in August 1940, just before Tizard's arrival in Washington) and the destroyer-for-bases deal. Of all these events, however, the Tizard Mission stands out as being the most unselfish of all. It therefore had a profound psychological impact. It stripped away any pretence of petty nationalistic security concerns which would otherwise have impeded the free and open exchange of information. It is no coincidence that Anglo-American intelligence cooperation really began to develop at the very same time that the mission was taking place. Exchanges of information on radio interception networks and on cryptographic equipment, for example, first took place while the mission was in the United States.[18]

The Tizard Mission's impact on Canada was very different from that on the United States. When the British Central Scientific Office was opened in Washington in March 1941, the British decided to shut down Fowler's Ottawa office, for the BCSO was given the power to administer all scientific liaison between the United States and the entire British Empire. This unilateral decision came as no surprise to C.J. Mackenzie, the president of the National Research Council of Canada. Fowler had informed him of the British intentions in January, and Mackenzie had objected strongly. As he noted in his diary, "I told Fowler that we would not waive our right to negotiate or exchange information directly with the Americans, as we had built up contacts over many years which we did not propose to drop, and that we would not accept the position that our dealings with the Americans had to be through any British organization!"[19] When the BCSO was established in March, Mackenzie simply refused to cooperate with it; he continued as if the British office did not even exist. The BCSO complained to Carol Wilson, the senior American liaison officer, who refused to be drawn into the argument between the Commonwealth partners. In the end, the BCSO had to acquiesce with Mackenzie's insistence on maintaining the National Research Council's special relationship with the Americans.[20]

When the BCSO transferred its offices to Washington in March 1941, the British sent no immediate replacement to Ottawa. This was a startling omission, since Hill, Tizard, and Cockcroft had all viewed maintaining close technical contact with the Canadians as vital to the success of projects such as the radar production program.[21] Because of their limited experience with advanced-technology manufacturing, the Canadians were not immediately aware of the difficulties involved in producing sophisticated military equipment without adequate British assistance. C.J.

Mackenzie at first did not believe that a permanent Canadian technical liaison office was necessary. Not until August 1941 – long after the other dominions and the United States had established a permanent liaison presence in London – was a small Canadian scientific liaison office opened. This office was initially staffed by a single National Research Council scientist, though this did not rectify the problem of inadequate technical expertise. It soon became apparent that the failure of the British to follow up on the policies implemented by the mission was crippling the Canadian effort. W.E. Phillips, the president of Research Enterprises Limited, stated to Mackenzie on 18 November 1941, "No aspect of the technical side of our war effort is more vulnerable to criticism than the arrangements made by the British to ensure technical information reaching those of us here who are dedicated to producing essential war material."[22]

The reasons behind the British lack of action are unclear, but they were undoubtedly connected with the failure to appreciate the special needs of Canadian science and industry. The lack of any central coordination of British wartime science caused problems in Ottawa, as it did in Washington, because it was impossible for any one ministry to establish in Ottawa an office responsible for all technical liaison. Instead of being offered guidance, the Canadians either were not kept advised of technical developments or were confused by contradictory advice and information. Such dubious advice came from visiting experts from any of half a dozen different British government departments.[23] Finally, after the passage in March 1941 of the Lend-Lease Act, which opened American industry to large-scale British orders, the British lost much of their interest in nurturing Canadian advanced-technology production.[24]

One quite unexpected consequence of the Tizard Mission was that Canada did acquire a small portion of the managerial expertise it required for administering its advanced-technology weapons program. Colonel F.C. Wallace, the British army representative to the mission, did not return to the United Kingdom; he settled permanently in Canada. Wallace arranged to be seconded to the National Research Council in the winter of 1941, and he soon became the most important scientific administrator in the country, after Mackenzie. In January 1942, Wallace was placed in charge of the National Research Council's radar research program. Then, in the fall of 1943, he took control of Research Enterprises' radar production division. But this was too late. Until then, Wallace had had only limited ability to influence the Canadian scientific mobilization, and by 1943 the Canadian radar program was fatally flawed.[25]

One other long-term effect of the Tizard Mission was the legacy of the personal contact which Canadian scientists fostered with their American and British counterparts. The British decision to send its nuclear research team to Canada in 1943 was the direct result of the Tizard Mission's observations of Canadian research resources. Cockcroft's appointment to head the Anglo-Canadian nuclear program in 1944 was made partly because he had established close relations with leading Canadians such as Mackenzie, Howe, and Ralston in the autumn of 1940. Similarly, his friendship with senior American scientists, such as Bush, made Cockcroft a suitable candidate in American eyes. Atomic energy, of course, became one of the major areas of Canadian research and development in the postwar period, but it owed its origins to the Tizard Mission.

The effect of the contacts Canadian scientists opened with their American counterparts was even greater than that of their relationship with British scientists. The legacy of American and Canadian cooperation on military scientific and advanced-technology projects continued long after the war. While it can, of course, be argued that Canada would ultimately have become reliant on American military technology with or without the mission, there can be no doubt that the roots of this cooperation were planted in the late summer of 1940 when Tizard arrived in North America.

Wallace's unplanned permanent sojourn in Canada and the personal connections made with American and British scientists did not, however, provide the expertise needed in Canada to make up for the shortfalls in its scientific industrial structure. While members of the Tizard Mission had seen Canada's scientific potential, they had failed to consider the absence of adequate resources for development. Engineering development expertise was necessary if a highly sophisticated piece of military hardware was to be successfully taken from the laboratory to the factory floor and then placed into operational service. Adequate Anglo-Canadian technical liaison was not established until 1943, when the National Research Council's liaison office in London was significantly expanded. The Canadians had come to realize that they could not proceed without British guidance. By 1943, however, it was too late to salvage many of Canada's high-technology programs.

The radar program provides the best example of the consequences of the failure to establish adequate liaison. Initially, the Canadians were successful in manufacturing long-wave radar sets such as the ASV Mark II. Most of these sets were based on British designs using North American components. But when attempts were made to design, develop, and manufacture short-wave radar independently in Canada, the results were disastrous. The gun-laying set, the GLC Mark III, was obsolete before it entered service, and it saw only limited operational use. The RX/C radar, built for the Royal Canadian Navy, was withdrawn, because of fatal technical faults, just a few months after it entered service in early 1944. Not until early 1943 did British radar experts finally play the role that members of the mission had envisioned, for it was then that British Admiralty radar experts began to guide Canadian efforts to design and build excellent sets, such as the type 268 motor-torpedo-boat radar. But by mid-1944, when the 268 entered full-scale production at Research Enterprises, the Canadian radar production was no longer required; it had been eclipsed by the far more successful American program. At the end of the war Canada dismantled its huge industrial investment in radar and scrapped it.

Thus, the mission's legacy to Canada was to launch Ottawa on a course that led to an expensive short-term failure. This was because the Canadian government did not correctly assess Canada's economic potential in the first place and because the British government did not follow through with policies implemented by Ottawa as a result of the advice of Tizard, Cockcroft, and others. This stands in stark contrast to the long-term positive impact that the mission had on the United States. Canadians were certainly in part to blame, but theirs was the fault of ignorance not culpable negligence. By the time Howe, Mackenzie, and Phillips were aware of the shortcomings in Canada's economic structure, it was too late to change course.

Despite the difficulties experienced by Canada, the international system of technical collaboration begun by the Tizard Mission had important consequences far beyond the Second World

War. Right at the end of the conflict, the United States drew away from international defence cooperation. Congress passed several acts that limited the exchange of information with any foreign power, especially in the area of nuclear research. This return to isolationism did not last long. The beginning of the Cold War led to the founding of the North Atlantic Treaty Organization in 1949. One component of NATO was the mandate to foster defence technical cooperation. Although much more work is required on the subject, it appears that the model used by NATO was the system of technical exchanges begun by the Tizard Mission. Only when more studies are done on this and other aspects of war and postwar technical cooperation will the full ramifications of what was begun by the Tizard Mission be understood.

Notes

INTRODUCTION

1 For more on the German scientific war, see Beyerchen, *Scientists under Hitler*, and Walker, *German National Socialism*.

CHAPTER ONE

1 For more information on the war work of German chemists, see Haber, *The Poisonous Cloud*.

2 Hartcup, *The War of Invention*, 21–43.

3 Robert Millikan, *Autobiography*, 140. The other members of the Ames Committee were Dr George Burgess, metallurgist at the Bureau of Standards; Professor George Hulett, chemist at Princeton University and the Bureau of Mines; Professor Harry Reid, geologist at Johns Hopkins University; Dr R.P. Strong, professor of tropical medicine at Harvard University; Dr Lindsey Williams, assistant health commissioner of New York; and Dr H.D. Dakin, director of the Herter Laboratory, New York. See "The Official Bulletin," 7 June 1917, Archive of the National Academy of Sciences (NAS), NAS-NRC, IR, Inter-Allied Exchange of Information, French and British Scientific Mission to U.S., 1917 (hereafter French and British Mission, 1917).

4 Ibid.

5 André Tardieu to Hale, 25 June 1917, and George Hutchinson to asst. secretary, 30 June 1917, NAS, NAS-NRC, IR, Inter-Allied Exchange of Information, Italian Military Mission to the U.S., 1917–18.

6 Millikan, *Autobiography,* 153.

7 Untitled report, 17 June 1917, NAS, NAS-NRC, IR, French and British Mission 1917.

8 Ibid.; Millikan to P.G. Lamme, 11 June 1917, Lamme to Millikan, 13 June 1917, letter to Edward D. Adams, 11 June 1917, chairman of Submarine Committee to Wm. L. Saunders, 11 June 1917, and H.T. Barnes to Millikan, 20 June 1917, NAS, NAS-NRC, IR, French and British Mission, 1917. The Canadian scientist was H.T. Barnes of McGill University. See also Kevles, *The Physicists,* 120–1, and Hackmann, *Seek and Strike,* 42–3.

9 Millikan, *Autobiography,* 153. Notes of at least part of Rutherford's brief to the conference have survived. See Notes Dictated by Sir Ernest Rutherford, 4 June 1917, NAS, NAS-NRC, IR, French and British Mission, Notes on British Subdetecting Work, 1917.

10 Millikan, *Autobiography,* 146, 154; Hackmann, *Seek and Strike,* 89–92; Hale to W.W. Campbell, 2 August 1917, NAS, Ex. Com., Committee on Physics, Subcommittee on Subdetection, General.

11 Lee De Forest to Gen. George Squier, 9 July 1917, and "Memorandum on the Organization of Work on the Location of Guns by Sound: The Result of the Conference with Majors Fabry and Abraham and Captain Owens," 30 June 1917(?), NAS, NAS-NRC, IR, French and British Mission, 1917.

12 "NRC Executive Committee Meeting," 12 July 1917, NAS. See also "Memorandum for Secretary of War, Subject Gas Warfare," 2 July 1917, NAS, NAS-NRC, IR, French and British Mission, 1917.

13 Adj. Gen. to chairman, NRC, 6 July 1917, NAS, NAS-NRC, IR, French and British Mission, 1917.

14 "Report by Professor Sir Ernest Rutherford, FRS, and Commander Cyprian Bridge, RN, on visit to the United States of America in Company of the French Scientific Mission, 19 May to 9 July 1917," Public Record Office (PRO), ADM 137/1436, as quoted in Hackmann, *Seek and Strike,* 43.

15 Vice-Adm. R.H. Pierse, BIR, to Hale, 20 July 1917, NAS, NAS-NRC, IR, French and British Mission, 1917.

16 Letter to the secretary of war, 9 November 1917, NAS, NAS-NRC, IR, Inter-Allied Exchange of Information, General, 1916–18. See also Rutherford to Millikan, 14 October 1917, ibid. This letter contains

information on the latest anti-submarine developments and personal details on Rutherford's family.

17 "Scientific Liaison with America," 8 July 1917. Names of the authors were not provided, but one was certainly Horace Darwin, and the other may have been A.V. Hill. See Darwin to Hale, etc., 16 July 1917, and Millikan to Lawrence Lowell, 5 September 1917, PRO, AVIA 8/3.

18 Millikan, 170, 297–8; letter to the secretary of war, 9 November 1917, Military Committee to chairman, Executive Committee, NAS, NAS-NRC, IR, Inter-Allied Exchange of Information, General, 1916–18. See also Hartcup, *The War of Invention*, 43.

19 Hackmann, *Seek and Strike*, 257.

20 See the correspondence on postwar patent disputes with the United States in PRO, AVIA 8/16 and 8/23.

21 Guerlac, *Radar in World War II*, 2:43–4. See also Allison, *New Eyes for the Navy.*

22 Ibid., 59–121.

23 *Times*, 8 August 1934.

24 Wimperis to Londonderry, Ellington, Dowding, and Sir Christopher Bullock, 12 November 1934, as quoted in Clark, *Tizard*, 110–11.

25 Tizard, as quoted in Faren, "Henry Thomas Tizard," 324.

26 Snow, *Science and Government*, 6.

27 Tizard, as quoted in Faren, "Henry Thomas Tizard," 320–1.

28 Faren, "Henry Thomas Tizard," 330.

29 For more details on Tizard's early career, see Clark, *Tizard*, 1–104.

30 Ibid., 105–92.

CHAPTER TWO

1 Tizard to CAS, 24 October 1939, Public Record Office (PRO), AIR 2/4209.

2 Kevles, *The Physicists*, 287–301.

3 As quoted in Dupree, *Science and the Federal Government*, 367.

4 Ibid.

5 For more details on Anglo-American diplomatic relations in the prewar period, see Macdonald, *The United States, Britain and Appeasement*, Reynolds, *The Creation of the Anglo-American Alliance*, and Offner, *American Appeasement*.

6 Macdonald, *The United States, Britain and Appeasement*, 180.

7 Leutze, *Bargaining for Supremacy*, 21–7.

8 "Minute on Technical Exchanges" [n.d. but probably May 1938], and permanent secretary to Captain Wilson, 24 May 1938, PRO, ADM 116/4302.

9 Wilson to Alan G. Kirk, 22 September 1938, Naval Historical Center, Washington (NHC), Kirk Papers, Attaché's Correspondence, box 2.

10 Guerlac, *Radar in World War II*, 1:175–83.

11 Minute, 8 March 1938, PRO, ADM 116/4302.

12 Minute, 12 March 1938, PRO, ADM 116/4302.

13 "Minute on Technical Exchanges" [n.d. but probably May 1938]; see also minute by S.V. Goodall, 29 March 1938, PRO, ADM 116/4302.

14 Board minutes, 12 May 1938, PRO, ADM 116/4302.

15 Wilson to Sir R.H. Archibald Carter, 8 August 1940, PRO, ADM 116/4302; list of enclosures, 8 August 1940, ibid.; permanent secretary to Wilson, 24 May 1940, ibid.

16 Minute by director of plans, 30 May 1940, minute by DNI, 2 June 1938, minute by DCNS, 15 June 1938, minute by first sea lord, 17 June 1938, minute by DCNS, 20 June 1938, and minute by DNI, 20 May 1938, PRO, ADM 116/4302.

17 Naval attaché to DNI, 29 September 1938, PRO, ADM 116/4302.

18 Minute by DNI, 2 December 1938, PRO, ADM 116/4302.

19 Minute by DNI, 9 January 1939, PRO, ADM 116/4302.

20 Minute by John Godfrey, DNI, 8 March 1939, PRO, ADM 116/4302.

21 Minute by Backhouse, 27 March 1939, PRO, ADM 116/4302.

22 Visit of aircraft representatives to USA sponsored by AII through AA Washington, PRO, AIR 2/3949. This document lists visits by private British aviation concerns. Seven visits were sponsored in 1935, eleven in 1936, thirteen in 1937, twenty-three in 1939, and six through to July 1939.

23 See the correspondence in the file on Harris's visit in PRO, AIR 2/3335.

24 Craven and Cate, *The Army Air Forces in World War II*, 1:598–9; chief of Bureau of Ordnance to under-secretary of the navy, 26 September 1941, National Archives, Washington (NARS), RG 80, F41–6; see also the various documents and historical summary in NARS, RG 18, Army Air Forces assistant chief of air staff, chief of Material and Service Research and Development Branch case histories, 1941–46, box 27, Norden bombsight.

25 W/C W. Sanderson for Air Chief Marshal C-in-C Bomber Command to secretary, Air Ministry, 17 June 1938, PRO, AIR 2/3339.
26 Boyle to H.M. air attaché, 20 July 1938, PRO, AIR 2/3339.
27 Pirie to AI1, 9 August 1938, PRO, AIR 2/3339.
28 Boyle to AA Washington, 8 March 1938. See also "Tactical Note: Bombing Methods in the USA," September 1938, on the Air Ministry's appreciation of American doctrine, PRO, AIR 2/3339.
29 *Time*, 6 February 1939, 9–10. See also Haight, *American Aid to France*, 94–102.
30 Pirie to A.R. Boyle, 30 March 1939, PRO, AIR 2/3339.
31 Ibid.
32 "Report by Air Commodore A.T. Harris on Certain Aspects of American Aviation," spring 1939, PRO, AIR 2/3335. For information on RAF bombsight research and development, see the various documents in PRO, AIR 14/234 and 237.
33 G.C. Pirie, "Visit to Infantry School, Fort Benning, Columbia, Georgia on April 13th to Witness Air Demonstration," 18 April 1939, PRO, AIR 2/3339.
34 W.S. Douglas, ACAS, to DCAS, 24 April 1939, PRO, AIR 2/3339.
35 DDI to DOR, 19 April 1939, PRO, AIR 2/3339.
36 "Report on Visit to the United States of America, May–June 1939, by W/C D.F. Anderson," PRO, AIR 2/2912.
37 "Report by Air Commodore A.T. Harris on Certain Aspects of American Aviation," spring 1939, PRO, AIR 2/3335.
38 Air attaché, Washington, to director of air intelligence, 6 June 1939, PRO, AIR 2/3339. The American navy's attitude towards the British request for the Norden bombsight can only be inferred indirectly from contemporary British sources. However, U.S. naval documents from early 1941 support this interpretation. See senior member, Joint Air Advisory Committee, to chief of naval operations, 25 April 1941, NARS, RG 80, F41–6.
39 AA Washington to Air Ministry, 11 May 1939, PRO, AIR 2/3339.
40 For the influence of RAF strategic bombing policy on British foreign policy in this period, see Smith, "The Royal Air Force and British Foreign Policy, 1932–37."
41 W.S. Douglas, ACAS, to CAS, 5 June 1939, PRO, AIR 2/3339.
42 Kennedy, "Strictly Confidential for the President and Secretary of State," 1 May 1939, NARS, RG 59, 811.21.
43 Green to Secretary of State, 2 May 1939, ibid., emphasis added.

44 Sir Kingsley Wood, secretary state for air, to Lord Halifax, foreign minister, 17 August 1940, PRO, AIR 2/3339.

45 Chamberlain to Roosevelt, 25 August 1939, PRO, AIR 2/3339.

46 Roosevelt to Chamberlain, 31 August 1939, PRO, AIR 2/3339.

47 Lothian to Halifax, 8 September 1939, PRO, AIR 2/3339.

48 Halifax to Wood, 18 September 1939, PRO, AIR 2/3339.

49 For Roosevelt's political situation on the amendment of the Neutrality Act, see Reynolds, *The Creation of the Anglo-American Alliance*, 65–6.

50 Secretary of state to first lord, 8 November 1940, PRO, AIR 2/3339.

51 "Secret and Personal for the President. The following from Naval Person, 16 October 1939," in Kimball, *Churchill and Roosevelt Correspondence*, 1:28.

52 Anderson to Kirk, 20 October 1940, NARS, RG 80, A8-3/EF13.

53 Kirk to Anderson, 9 November 1939, ibid.

54 Quotation from a memo by Posseller, Bureau of Aeronautics, 11 November 1939, NARS, RG 72, F41-8, vol. 5. See also C.C. Bloch, C-in-C U.S. Fleet, to CNO, 31 October 1939, and "Release of Confidential Information" [n.d. but early November 1939], ibid.

55 W.R. Furlong to CNO, "Subject: Recent Publicity on Bombsights," 6 November 1939, ibid.

56 Foreign Office to Lothian, 5 December 1939, PRO, ADM 116/4302.

57 Air attaché, Washington, to DIR, Air Ministry, 20 December 1939, and Lothian to Foreign Office, 14 December 1939, PRO, AIR 2/3339.

58 W.J. Mackenzie to J.V. Perowne, 20 May 1940, PRO, ADM 116/4302.

59 Kirk to Anderson, 5 January 1940, NHC, Kirk Papers, Attaché's Correspondence, box 2.

60 Kirk to Anderson, 6 February 1940, ibid.

61 DNI, 26 February 1940, PRO, ADM 116/4302.

62 See the memoranda of the PAS(S), 28 February 1940, and others through to the memorandum of the DSR, C.S. Wright, 2 May 1940, in PRO, ADM 116/4302.

CHAPTER THREE

1 The best account of Hill's scientific career is found in Katz, "A.V. Hill."

2 Hartcup, *The War of Invention*, 161–2.

3 Hill, "Science in the War."

4 Clark, *Rise of the Boffins*, 136.

5 Snow, *Science and Government*, 39. See also Blackett, *Studies of War*, 107, and E.G. Bowen, *Radar Days*, 150–1.
6 Tizard to CAS, 24 October 1940, CAS to secretary of state for air, 30 October 1940, and Tizard to Hill, 2 December 1939, Public Record Office (PRO), AIR 2/4209.
7 Tizard to Newall, 5 January 1940; for this bureaucratic dispute between the three ministries, see the correspondence in PRO, AIR 2/4209.
8 Ibid. See also Katz, "A.V. Hill," 115–17.
9 Clark, *Tizard*, 250.
10 The list can be found at Churchill College, Cambridge (CC) in the A.V. Hill Papers (AVHLI), 217.
11 F.G. Bartlett to Hill, CC, AVHLI 217.
12 Hill to Tizard, 5 November 1957, Imperial War Museum (IWM), (HTT) 766.
13 Reynolds, "Lord Lothian and Anglo-American Relations," 1–4.
14 Ibid., 4.
15 A.V. Hill, "RDF in Canada and the United States; and a Proposal for a General Interchange of Scientific and Technical Information, and of Service Experience, between the Defence Services of Great Britain and Those of the United States," 18 June 1940, PRO, AVIA 22/2286.
16 Ibid. See also "Letters from A.V. Hill," IWM, HTT 706.
17 See "Letters from A.V. Hill," IWM, HTT 706.
18 Lord Lothian, telegram 595, PRO, FO 371/24255.
19 Ibid.
20 Ibid.
21 "WM (40), 58th Conclusion, min. no. 6," 2 March 1940, and "WM (40), 67th Conclusion, min. no. 7," 13 March 1940, PRO, CAB 65/6.
22 J. Balfour to F.H. Sandford, Air Ministry, 24 April 1940, PRO, FO 371/24255.
23 Excerpt from "WM 104 (40)," 26 April 1940, PRO, ADM 116/4302.
24 Ibid.
25 "Notes on Mission to America," IWM, HTT 706.
26 "Summary of File S4471" and "Notes on Mission to America," IWM, HTT 706.
27 Tizard to CAS, 30 April 1940, IWM, HTT 251.
28 Tizard Diary, 3 May 1940, IWM, HTT 16.
29 Ibid.
30 Ibid.

31 "Notes on a Meeting Held in Air Ministry, Whitehall, on 3 May, 1940," PRO, ADM 116/4302.

32 "Notes on the Relative Advantages and Disadvantages of the Exchange with the USA of Information on RDF and Other Radio Developments," n.d., PRO, ADM 116/4302.

33 Ibid.

34 Admiralty to J.J. Balfour, 1 May 1940, PRO, ADM 116/4302.

35 J.H. Peck to J.J. Balfour, 11 May 1940, PRO, FO 371/24255.

36 Memo, John Godfrey, 4 May 1940, PRO, ADM 116/4302; Kirk to Anderson, 24 April and 15 June 1940, Naval Historical Center, Washington (NHC), Kirk Papers, Attaché's Correspondence, box 2.

37 Memorandum by C.S. Wright, 2 May 1940, PRO, ADM 116/4302, emphasis added.

38 Ibid.

39 Ibid.

40 Tizard Diary, 3 May 1940, IWM, HTT 16.

41 Minute by Tizard to ACAC, 8 May 1940, "Summary of File S4471," IWM, HTT 706.

42 Memorandum to the first lord, 18 May 1940, PRO, ADM 116/4302, Leutze, *Bargaining for Supremacy*, 76; minutes of the chiefs of staff meeting, 18 May 1940, IWM, HTT 251.

43 Memorandum to first lord, 18 May 1940, PRO, ADM 116/4302.

44 Marginal note by Alexander, 19 May 1940, on memorandum to the first lord, 18 May 1940, ibid.

45 Alexander to Churchill, 20 May 1940, PRO, FO 371/24255 (also found in PRO, ADM 116/4302).

46 Churchill to Alexander, 21 May 1940, PRO, FO 371/24255.

47 Tizard to Sinclair, 19 June 1940, House of Lords Record Office (HLRO), Beaverbrook Papers, D406. See also Tizard to Sinclair, 21 June 1940, ibid.

48 Jones, *Most Secret War*, 92–110. In his account, Jones states that he met with Churchill, Sinclair, Joubert, Lindemann, Beaverbrook, Tizard, and many senior RAF officers on 21 June to discuss the beam question. Churchill ordered further investigations, disregarding Tizard's advice. Tizard, according to Jones, resigned that afternoon, but his letter of resignation is dated two days earlier. Undoubtedly Tizard knew in advance that his advice would be ignored and he had already tendered his resignation.

49 Minute dated 5 June 1940, PRO, PREM 3/475/11.

50 Churchill to Mackenzie King, 5 June 1940, as quoted in Gilbert, *Finest Hour*, 473.
51 Note of 6 June 1940, PRO, PREM 3/475/1.
52 Tizard to Hill, CC, AVHLI 2/7; Hill to Aydellotte, 29 May 1940, Swarthmore College Library, Aydellotte Papers, "Personal, Misc. Correspondence," RG6/3.
53 Frankfurter's role in developing the plan is contained in Hill to Aydellotte, 29 May 1940, ibid.
54 A.V. Hill, "RDF in Canada and the United States; and a Proposal for a General Interchange of Information of Scientific and Technical Information," 18 June 1940, and "Research and Development for War Purposes in Canada," 18 June 1940, PRO, AVIA 22/2286.
55 C.J. Mackenzie to Hill, 22 May 1940, CC, AVHLI 2/7; Hill, "Research and Development for War Purposes in Canada," PRO, AVIA 22/2286.
56 Hill to Lindemann, 18 June 1940, and Hill, "Proposal for the General Interchange of Scientific & Technical Information between the Defence Services of Great Britain and the United States," Nuffield College, Lindemann Papers 57.3.
57 PS to S of S, 26 June 1940, PRO, AIR 2/7193.
58 Joubert to private secretary to PM, 15 June 1940, PRO, AIR 2/7308.
59 "Air Ministry Scientific Intelligence, Monthly Summary," no. 2, May 1940, PRO, CAB 63/169. See also R. Peck, ACAS(G), to VCAS, 14 May 1940, PRO, AIR 2/7193.
60 Minute by G. Slessor, 15 June 1940, PRO, AIR 2/7193.
61 Sinclair to Churchill, 25 June 1940, PRO, FO 371/24255. See also Sinclair to Hill, 22 June 1940, IWM, HTT 58.
62 Churchill to Sinclair, 30 June 1940, PRO, FO 371/24255.

CHAPTER FOUR

1 Lord Lothian to the president, 8 July 1940, National Archives, Washington (NARS), RG 59, 811.24, Ei/1.
2 Lothian to Foreign Office, 27 June 1940, Public Record Office (PRO), FO 371/24255.
3 See J. Balfour to Peck, 1 July 1940, PRO, FO 371/24255. It was also not sent until three days after Sinclair's memo, which directly influenced Churchill's endorsement.
4 See, for instance, Tizard to Hill, 6 May 1940, Churchill College, Cambridge (CC), Hill Papers (AVHLI), 2/7: "I am in favour of the

interchange of information you suggest, but there is some difference of opinion and the policy is now being discussed on a high plane, I will see that the people concerned get your most recent information."

5 Lothian to Foreign Office, 1 July 1940, PRO, FO 371/24255.

6 Memo by B. Sendall, 4 July 1940, PRO, ADM 116/4302; Foreign Office to Lothian, 6 July 1940, PRO, FO 371/24255.

7 Lothian to Foreign Office, 18 July 1940, ibid.

8 Lothian to Foreign Office, 22 July 1940, ibid.

9 Reynolds, *Creation of the Anglo-American Alliance*, 109.

10 Acting secretary of state to secretary of the navy and war, 19 July 1940, NARS, RG 59, 811.24, Ei/1.

11 A.V. Hill, "RDF in Canada and the United States; and a Proposal for a General Interchange of Scientific and Technical Information, and of Service Experience, between the Defence Services of Great Britain and those of the United States," 18 June 1940, PRO, AVIA 22/2286.

12 GP to YE [Your excellency, Lothian], 8 July 1940, PRO, FO 371/24241.

13 Director, Naval Research Laboratory, to chief of naval operations, 26 July 1940, NARS, RG 80, A8-3/EF13.

14 Memo, Gen. Strong, AC of S, WPD, for C of S, 19 July 1940, as quoted in Terrett, *The Signal Corps*, 192.

15 CNO to bureau chiefs, 21 May 1940, NARS, RG 19, C-A8-3(1), 1; Kirk to Anderson, 24 April and 15 June 1940, Naval Historical Center, Washington (NHC), Kirk Papers, Attaché's Correspondence, box 2.

16 Stimson to acting secretary of state, 22 July 1940, NARS, RG 165, box 2193, 9771-249/177A. See also Stark to secretary of state, 21 July 1940, NARS, RG 65, 811.24 Ei/4.

17 Sumner Wells, acting secretary of state, to Lothian, 29 July 1940, NARS, RG 59, 811.24 Ei/1.

18 Hill, as quoted in Clark, *The Rise of the Boffins*, 137.

19 Notes by ACAS(R) [n.d. but found with Joubert to Hill, 6 July 1940], Imperial War Museum (IWM), Tizard Papers (HTT) 58.

20 Joubert to Rear Adm. Tom Phillips, 3 July 1940, PRO, ADM 199/1156.

21 "Notes on Conclusion of a Meeting held in Air Marshal Joubert's room at 12PM on 9 July 1940," IWM, HTT 58.

22 Marginal note by DSR on memo by B. Sendall, 4 July 1940, PRO, ADM 116/4302.

23 Leutze, *Bargaining for Supremacy,* 134–5.
24 Bailey to VCNS, 5 July 1940, PRO, ADM 199/1156.
25 Memorandum by T.S.V. Phillips, VCNS, 5 July 1940; also marginal note on same by AVA, 5 July 1940, PRO, ADM 199/1156.
26 See "Interchange of Information with United States Naval Authorities" [n.d. but found with memorandum by assistant controller, 24 April 1940, and memorandum by C.S. Wright, DSR, 5 May 1940], PRO, ADM 116/4302.
27 H. Phillips, DTM, to VCNS, 7 July 1940, PRO, ADM 199/1156.
28 Memorandum by TSVP, 7 July 1940, ibid.
29 Memorandum by BAF, 13 July 1940, ibid.
30 Memorandum by BAF, 18 July 1940, ibid. See also BAF to first lord, 20 July 1940, ibid.
31 Churchill to Ismay, 17 July 1940, PRO, PREM 3/475/1, folio 33–4.
32 E.I.C. Jacobs, War Cabinet Office, "Exchange of Secret Technical Information with the United States of America," 20 July 1940, PRO, FO 371/24241.
33 Minute by J.V. Perowne, 18 July 1940, PRO, FO 371/24255.
34 See, for instance, Beaverbrook to Churchill, 27 June 1940, PRO, PREM 3/475/1; Beaverbrook to Knox, 21 July 1940, House of Lords Record Office (HLRO), Beaverbrook Papers.
35 Memorandum by sec. of state for foreign affairs to the war cabinet, WP (40) 276, 18 July 40, PRO, FO 371/24256.
36 Minute by Perowne, 23 July 1940, PRO, FO 371/24241.
37 Halifax to prime minister, 25 July 1940, PRO, FO 371/24241.
38 "Meeting of Ministers and Advisers held at 10 Downing Street, Thursday, 25 July 1940, 6:00PM," PRO, AVIA 22/2286.
39 "Notes on Professor Lindemann's ideas for Air Defence by Sir Henry Tizard," 23 July 1940, HLRO, Beaverbrook Papers.
40 Beaverbrook to Churchill, 12 July 1940, PRO, PREM 3/475/1.
41 Cockcroft, "American Liaison," 24 June 1940, PRO, AVIA 22/2286; note of 26 April 1940, IWM, HTT 706.
42 See, for instance, memorandum by DSR, Admiralty, 21 July 1939, 22 April 1940, and 22 October 1940, PRO, ADM 1/10860. It should also be noted that in July 1939 Chatfield had supported the Royal Society's proposal; see Chatfield to Stanhope, 19 July 1939, ibid.
43 Clark, *Tizard,* 244–5.
44 H.J. Gough to Joubert, 6 July 1940, PRO, AIR 2/7193. Information on Chatfield's relationship with Churchill was provided by Eric Grove in a conversation with the author, 10 May 1992.

45 Tedder, as quoted in Clark, *Tizard*, 256.
46 Tizard Diary, IWM, HTT 16/68.
47 Sinclair to prime minister, 26 July 1940, and C.G. Garrett to E.I.C. Jacob, 27 July 1940, PRO, ADM 199/1156.
48 Minute of 27 July 1940, PRO, PREM 3/45/1, folio 26.
49 Joubert to CAS, 13 July 1940, PRO, AIR 2/7308; minute by W.M. Mackenzie, 12 July 1940, PRO, AIR 2/7193.
50 Ibid.; P.S. Mackenzie to PVS, 5 July 1940, PRO, AIR 2/7193.
51 Tizard Diary, 31 July 1940, IWM, HTT 16/68
52 Tizard, "American Mission Suggested," 1 August 1940, PRO, PREM 3/475/1.
53 Tizard Diary, 1 August 1940, IWM, HTT 16/68.
54 Minute of 1 August 1940, PRO, PREM 3/475/11, folio 24.
55 Tizard Diary, 6 August 1940, IWM, HTT 16/48; Tizard to Churchill, 6 August 1940, PRO, PREM 3/475/1.
56 Cockburn and Ellyard, *Oliphant*, 84–9; E.G. Bowen, *Radar Days*, 152–3.
57 Director of naval intelligence to chief of naval operations, 23 and 25 July 1940, NARS, RG 80, A8-3/EF13.
58 Lt. Col. H.C. Minton, Ordnance Department, to assistant chief of staff, G-2, 2 August 1940, NARS, RG 165, box 2193; Miles to assistant secretary of war, chief of ordnance, Air Corps, engineers, signals officer, and chief of chemical warfare, ibid.; Lt. Col. K.T. Blood to assistant chief of staff, G-2, 12 August 1940, ibid.; Maj. Gen. J.L. Schley, chief of engineers, to Miles, 27 July 1940, ibid.
59 Minton to assistant chief of staff, G-2, 2 August 1940, ibid.
60 Hartcup and Allibone, *Cockcroft and the Atom*.
61 E.G. Bowen, *Radar Days*, 1–149.
62 Tizard Diary, 6 August 1940, IWM, HTT 16/68.
63 Halifax to Churchill, 7 August 1940, PRO, ADM 199/1156; Perowne to secretary of state, 5 August 1940, PRO, FO 371/24241.
64 Ismay to PM, 8 August 1940, PRO, PREM 3/475/1.
65 Minute to Halifax, 9 August 1940, PRO, PREM 3/475/1, folio 15.
66 "British Technical Mission to the USA, 1940: Notes on Meeting held at Thames House, Millbank on August 10th 1940," IWM, HTT 252.

CHAPTER FIVE

1 Strong to chief of staff, 24 August 1940, National Archives, Washington (NARS) RG 165, box 1294. See also "Military Attaché Report,

Great Britain, Subject: British Fire Control," by Colonel Raymond E. Lee and Major R. Stadler, 15 August 1940, and "Subject: Radio Detection," 26 August 1940, ibid.

2 CNO to chief of bureaus, etc., 5 August 1940, NARS, RG 80, A8-3/EF13; also see Lt. Cl. H.C. Minton, Ordnance Bureau, to assistant chief of staff, G-2, 2 August 1940, NARS, RG 165, box 2193; Lt. Col. K.T. Blood, Coast Artillery Corps, to assistant chief of staff, G-2, 12 August 1940, ibid.; chief of naval operations to chief of bureaus, etc., 13 August 1940, NARS, RG 80, A8-3/EF13.

3 Chief of naval operations to bureau chiefs, 5 August 1940, ibid.

4 Col. J.A. Crane, acting assistant chief of staff, G-2, to assistant chief of staff, WPD, G-4, chief of ordnance, etc., 21 August, NARS, RG 165, box 2193.

5 Tizard Diary, 22 August 1940, Imperial War Museum (IWM), Tizard Papers (HTT), 16.

6 Tizard Diary, 23 August 1940, ibid.

7 Tizard Diary, 26 August 1940, ibid.

8 Tizard Diary, 27 August 1940, ibid.; Henry Stimson Diary, 27 August 1940, Yale University Library.

9 Tizard Diary, 27 August 1940, IWM, HTT 16.

10 Robert P. Patterson, assistant secretary of war, "Memorandum for the Chief of Arms and Services," 29 August 1940, NARS, RG 165, box 2193; Tizard Diary, 28 August 1940, IWM, HTT 16.

11 Ibid.; for more on Purvis and the British Purchasing Mission, see Hall, *North American Supply*.

12 Tizard Diary, 28 August 1940, IWM, HTT 16.

13 Extracts from the diary of Miss Doreen Geary, IWM, HTT 706.

14 Gilbert, *Finest Hour*, 797–9.

15 For more information on the BATM and Pew, see Zimmerman, *The Great Naval Battle of Ottawa*, 30–2, 85–6, 127.

16 W.L. Pryor, Jr, "Memorandum for Chief of Bureau, Subject: Underwater Sound – British Asdic," 31 August 1940, NARS, RG 80, A8-3/EF13.

17 Tizard Diary, 30 August 1940, IWM, HTT 16.

18 Tizard Diary, 7 September 1940, ibid.

19 "Conference at Navy Department," 29 August 1940, Public Record Office (PRO), AVIA 10/1. For information on the duplexor, see Guerlac, *Radar in World War II*, 1:80–3.

20 "Visit to the Naval Research Laboratory," 30 August 1940, PRO, AVIA 10/1.

21 "Meeting with Officials at War Department," 29 August 1940, PRO, AVIA 10/1.

22 Tizard Diary, 5 September 1940, IWM, HTT 16. See also "Notes on a Visit to Wright-Patterson Field and Patterson Field, Dayton, Ohio, September 4," and "Notes on Visit to Fort Monmouth, 6 September 1940," PRO, AVIA 10/1.

23 Anderson to chiefs of Bureau of Ships, Ordnance, etc., 4 September 1940, NARS, RG 80, A8-3/EF13.

24 Mauborgne to assistant chief of staff, G-2, 10 September 1940, NARS, RG 165, box 1294. See also Miles, "Memorandum for the Chief of Staff," 10 September 1940, ibid.

25 Miles to chief of staff, 12 September 1940, NARS, RG 165, box 383.

CHAPTER SIX

1 E.G. Bowen, *Radar Days*, 152–4.

2 Ibid., 154–5.

3 Ibid., 150.

4 "Meeting of the British Technical Mission," 10 September 1940, Public Record Office (PRO), AVIA 10/4; Tizard Diary, 9 September 1940, Imperial War Museum (IWM), Tizard, Papers (HTT) 16.

5 "List of Representatives on Various Subcommittees of British Technical Mission," 10 September 1940, National Archives, Washington (NARS), RG 165, box 418. This list has been somewhat modified. Richard Fairy of the Ministry of Aircraft Production was also listed as being a possible member on committees 4 and 7, but there is no indication that he ever served. Also listed on number 4 was a Mr Fletcher, and Wallace and Pearce were listed on number 8 but did not actually sit on this committee.

6 Tizard to Gough, 29 August 1940, PRO, AVIA 22/2281.

7 Lt. Col. T.D. Finley to Tizard, 9 September 1940, NARS, RG 165, box 394, 300-T139/5; Miles to Surgeon General, 10 September 1940, NARS, RG 165, box 2193, 9771-249/198.

8 Tizard Diary, 16 September 1940, IWM, HTT 16; Maass and Flood, "Chemical Warfare," 20 October 1940, PRO, AVIA 10/2; Lt. Col. C.M. Busbee to Surgeon General, 16 September 1940, NARS, RG 165, box 2193, 9771-249; Busbee to chief of the Chemical Warfare Service, 16 September 1940, ibid.; Miles to the surgeon general, 20 September 1940, ibid.; Finley to Tizard, 23 September 1940, ibid.; Col. L.B. McAfee to the

surgeon general, 26 September 1940, ibid.; Tizard to Finley, 28 September 1940, ibid.; "Conversation with Representatives of the Canadian Chemical Warfare Service," 9 October 1940, ibid.; "Memorandum for the Chief of the Chemical Warfare Service," 11 October 1940, ibid.

9 Faulkner, "Visit to the Naval Research Laboratory to Inspect Watch Buoy," 18 September 1940, PRO, AVIA 10/2.

10 Bennett and Stuart, "Diary of a Visit to Wright Field and the Eastman Kodak Comp., Rochester, NY, 23 September 1940 – 10 November 1940," PRO, AVIA 10/1.

11 Lt. Comm. Ormsby, "Report on US A/S Measures (III)," 20 September 1940, PRO, AVIA 10/1; director of naval intelligence to naval attaché, Ottawa, 13 September 1940, NARS, RG 80, 8-3/EF13; H.C. Hayes and P.N. Arnold, "Underwater Sound: Echo-Ranging Equipment (British)," 14 October 1940, NARS, RG 80, 8-3/EF13.

12 Col. R.C. Candee, chief, Information Division, to chief of Air Corps, 24 September 1940, NARS, RG 18, 350.05.

13 Tizard Diary, 10 September 1940, IWM, HTT 16.

14 Maj. Gen. J.O. Mauborgne to assistant chief of staff, G-2, 21 September 1940, NARS, RG 165, box 394.

15 Tizard to T.D. Finley, 23 September 1940, and Finley to Tizard, 25 September 1940, NARS, RG 165, box 2193.

16 Memo from John Foster to Tizard, 20 September 1940, PRO, AVIA 10/2.

17 Francis H. Vanderwerker, "Memorandum for the Assistant Chief of Staff, G-2, Subject: Report on the Meeting of the Commercial Committee on the Interchange of Secret Technical Information with Representatives of the British Government," 25 September 1940, NARS, RG 165, box 2193.

18 A complete listing of all meetings can be found in "Activities of British Technical Mission from 9 September 1940," IWM, HTT 706.

19 E.G. Bowen, *Radar Days*, 157.

20 Tizard Diary, 19 September 1940, IWM, HTT 16.

21 Hall, *North American Supply*, 191. The design of the Merlin engine was supplied by the British to the Americans on 13 June 1940.

22 For more details on the adoption of the Bofors gun and the Kerrison predictor, see Green, Thomson, and Roots, *The Ordnance Department*, 407–10.

23 Bush to Arnold, 7 July 1941, as quoted in Dawson, *Engines and Innovation*, 46.

24 Woodward-Nutt, "Information Given to U.S. Authorities," 28 October 1940, IWM, HTT 706. See also Maj. J.G. Moore, U.S. Army Air Corps, "Reports on Conferences with British Mission," 28 October 1940, NARS, RG 18, Secret 337 Conference.

25 Senior member, Navy Department AA Board, to chief of naval operations, NARS, RG 80, A8-3/EF13.

26 Miles to the director of naval intelligence, 19 September 1940, NARS, RG 165, box 2193. This list included the bombsight, interchangeable percussion and time fuse system, Mark X base detonating fuses, self-destroying anti-aircraft ammunition relays, bomb ballistic tables, details of manufacturing of the auto frettage and centrifugal casting of guns, and details of the production of armour plate. By 26 October only the bomb ballistic tables remained on the restricted list. See Stimson and Knox to Vannever Bush, 26 October 1940, NARS, RG 80, A8-3/EF13.

27 Extract of letter of the secretary of the navy, 28 September 1940, NARS, RG 165, box 2193; chief of naval operations, "Subject: British Observers in the United States Fleet," 19 September 1940, NARS, RG 80 A8-3/EF13. Lord Lothian's comment was reported by Vannevar Bush in an interview on 20 August 1944 (NARS, Boston Branch, Radiation Laboratory Records, box 49, historians' files).

28 Director, Naval Research Laboratory, to chief of naval operations, 26 July 1940, NARS, RG 80 A8-3/EF13.

29 H.G. Bowen, technical aide to the secretary of the navy, to the secretary of the navy, "Current Visit of British Technical Mission to the United States: Important Matters in Radio and Underwater Sound Brought to Light During," 4 October 1940, NARS, RG 80, A8-3/EF13. Another more detailed report on British asdic equipment can be found in the same file. It was written by H.G. Hayes and P.N. Arnold, and was completed on 14 October. This report has similar conclusions to that of Pryor and Bowen's but was based on first-hand observation of asdic equipment in Ottawa, Montreal, and Halifax.

30 Capt. H.D. Bode, ONI, to Cockcroft, 16 October 1940, and CNO to secretary of the navy, 1 November 1940, NARS, RG 80, A8-3/EF13.

31 Radiogram from Lee for Major Edwards to War Department, 22 October 1940, NARS, RG 165, box 1173.

32 Radiogram, military attaché, London, to War Department, 8 November 1940, ibid. See also Miles to military attaché, London, 29 October 1940, ibid.

33 Vose to chief of Material Division, Air Corps, 19 October 1940, NARS, RG 165, box 383.

34 Brig. Gen. Crane to Sperry, 21 October 1940, ibid.

35 "Practice Results: US Navy – Visit by Captain Faulkner to Fleet Training Section of Navy Department, 17 September 1940," PRO, AVIA 10/1.

36 Captain H.W. Faulkner, "Visit to the U.S. Fleet Based in Honolulu, 22–9 September 1940," PRO, AVIA 10/1.

37 Wallace, "Notes on Visit to Aberdeen, 3 October 1940," ibid.

38 Fowler, "Report on a Visit to Aberdeen Proving Ground, 28 November 1940," PRO, AVIA 10/2.

39 H.F.G. Letson, "Memorandum: Centrifugal Casting of Guns," 5 October 1940. See also Letson, "Notes on Visit to Watertown Arsenal, 5 October 1940," (PRO, AVIA 10/1; Fowler, "Report on Visit to Watertown Arsenal, 5 October 1940," ibid.; Wallace, "Notes on Visit to Watertown Arsenal, October 5, 1940," written on 16 October 1940, ibid.

40 "Memorandum for the Chief Signals Officer, Chief of Ordnance etc.," 28 November 1940, NARS, RG 165, box 421; Brig. John J. Kingman, assistant chief of engineers, to assistant chief of staff, G-2, 4 December 1940, ibid.; Maj. John H. MacArthur, Chemical Warfare Service, to ACS, G-2, 4 December 1940, ibid.; Lt. Col. M.K. Barrol, Jr, Ordnance Department, to ACS, G-2, 4 December 1940, ibid.; Capt. E.R. Quesada, Air Corps foreign liaison officer, to ACS, G-2, 16 December 1940, ibid.; Mauborgne to ACS, G-2, 4 December 1940, ibid.

41 E.G. Bowen, *Radar Days*, 178–81.

CHAPTER SEVEN

1 Baxter, *Scientists against Time*, 142.

2 Kevles, *The Physicists*, 293–6.

3 Bush, *Pieces of the Action*, 74.

4 Interview with Vannevar Bush, 20 August 1940, National Archives (NARS), Boston Branch, Radiation Laboratory Records, box 49, historians' files.

5 Kevles, *The Physicists*, 296–7.

6 Roosevelt to Bush, 15 June 1940, Massachusetts Institute of Technology (MIT), President's Office, AC4 230/18. In his memoirs, Bush claims that it was his idea not to compete with the military's

research program, an idea found in most secondary sources on the formation of the OSRD. The above letter makes it clear that Bush was ordered by Roosevelt not to create a rival research program.

In an interview given in August 1944, Bush stated that in 1940 "the atmosphere was not hospitable in the services for cooperation with civilians. The Army and Navy even kept things from one another" (interview with Vannevar Bush, 20 August 1940, NARS, Boston Branch, Radiation Laboratory Records, box 49, historians' files).

7 Some of the early correspondence on Loomis's work can by found in the Vannevar Bush papers at the Library of Congress in the Loomis file. These indicate that Loomis was conducting research well before Roosevelt's approval of the NDRC and that he had an experimental microwave radar using a klystron in operation before the end of June 1940. For early navy, army, and civilian microwave radar research, see Guerlac, *Radar in World War II,* 204–10.

8 Bush interview, 20 August 1940, NARS, Boston Branch, Radiation Laboratory Records, box 49, historians' files.

9 Ibid.

10 Ibid.; Tizard Diary, 28 August 1940, Imperial War Museum (IWM), Tizard Papers (HTT) 16.

11 "Visit to the Naval Research Laboratory, Anacostia Station," 30 August 1940, Public Record Office (PRO), AVIA 10/1.

12 Tizard to H.G. Bowen, NARS, RG 19, C-A8-3(1), box 1.

13 Robert Patterson, assistant secretary of war, to Bush, 12 September 1940, NARS, RG 277, civilian files, Tolman files, box 2; Anderson to Bush, 16 September 1940, NARS, RG 19, C-A8-3(1), box 1.

14 E.G. Bowen, *Radar Days*, 159.

15 Ibid., 162; Cockcroft, "Notes on Visit to Loomis Laboratory, Tuxedo Park, 28 and 29 September 1940," PRO, AVIA 10/1.

16 Stimson Diary, 2 October 1940, Yale University Library.

17 As early as 10 October, Bowen's indispensability to the American microwave program was recognized by Bush, Loomis, and others associated with the Microwave Committee. Bush had already asked Fowler that Bowen stay on in the United States for an indefinite period (Bush to Loomis, 10 October 1940, Library of Congress, Bush Papers, Loomis file). Note: In this letter, Bowen is incorrectly identified as Bown.

18 E.G. Bowen, *Radar Days*, 165–6.

19 Ibid., 167–8.

20 Guerlac, *Radar in World War II*, 257.

21 Bush to Loomis, 10 October 1940, Library of Congress, Bush Papers, Loomis file.

22 "Notes on Meeting of Micro-wave Sub-committee of NDRC", 11 October 1940, PRO, AVIA 10/1.

23 E.G. Bowen, *Radar Days*, 172.

24 "Meeting of Micro-wave Sub-committee of NDRC," 12 October 1940, PRO AVIA 10/1.

25 Clark, *Rise of the Boffins*, 184. Gee was first tested in the autumn of 1940.

26 E.G. Bowen, *Radar Days*, 173. See also the untitled report dated Sunday, 13 October, PRO, AVIA 10/1.

27 Ibid., 174; untitled report, 14 October 1940, PRO, AVIA 10/1.

28 The fundamental difference between Loomis's proposal and the final production model of LORAN was the substitution of medium-frequency transmitters for the high-frequency types originally proposed. Development work was undertaken by the special navigation group under the direction of Melville Eastham. The basic design was completed in September 1941 (E.G. Bowen, *Radar Days*, 174; Guerlac, *Radar in World War II*, 283–5).

29 Guerlac, *Radar in World War II*, 258; R.H. Fowler, "Three Visits to Sperry, 10–17 October 1940," PRO, AVIA 10/1; Cockcroft, "Visit to Sperry, 17 October 1940," ibid., and "Visit to Bell Laboratory, 18 September 1940," ibid.

30 Untitled report, 18 October 1940, PRO, AVIA 10/1; Loomis to Bush, 24 October 1940, PRO, AVIA 10/2; Guerlac, *Radar in World War II*, 258, 666; E.G. Bowen, *Radar Days*, 175, 215–16.

31 Bush to members of the NDRC, 26 October 1940, NARS, RG 277, Compton files, 1940–41 correspondence; "Memorandum on Interchange of Scientific Information between the National Defense Research Committee and Great Britain and Canada," 25 October 1940, ibid.; "Memorandum: On Operation of Proposed Information Interchange Procedure with Great Britain and Canada..." [n.d. but likely 25 October 1940], ibid.

32 Ibid., 26–40.

33 O.R. Frisch and R. Peierls, "On the Construction of a 'Super-Bomb' Based on a Nuclear Chain Reaction" [n.d. but February 1940], PRO, AB 1/9.

34 "Second Meeting of the Subcommittee of the Committee for the Scientific Survey of Air Defence on the U Bomb," 24 April 1940, PRO, AB 1/8.

35 Hewlett and Anderson, *The New World, 1939/1946*, 15.

36 Ibid., 17–25.

37 A.V. Hill, "Uranium-235," 16 May 1940, PRO, AB 1/9.

38 Minutes of the MAUD committee, 10 July and 7 August 1940, PRO, AB 1/8.

39 E.G. Bowen, *Radar Days*, 155. See also Hartcup and Allibone, *Cockcroft and the Atom*, 99.

40 "Report on the Meeting with Committee of U.S. Scientists Working on Uranium at Bureau of Standards," 7 October 1940, PRO, AVIA 10/1.

41 Hewlett and Anderson, *The New World, 1939/1946*, 40.

42 "Notes on a Discussion with Fermi," 16 November 1940, PRO, AVIA 10/2.

CHAPTER EIGHT

1 British Technical Mission to Canadian Defence Council, 24 October 1940, Public Record Office (PRO), AVIA 10/1; Cockcroft to the assistant chief of staff, Canadian Army [n.d. but late October 1940], ibid.

2 No other Canadian industrial undertaking required that Canada create an industry capable of undertaking all facets of research, development, and production. Most other manufacturing involved the adaptation of British designs to Canadian industrial standards and were usually a comparatively well-understood and unsophisticated technology. For instance, Canadian shipyards built Flower-class corvettes rather than sloops because they could be built using mercantile standards rather than the far more rigorous Admiralty requirements for true warships. Trucks were built in large numbers in the factories of General Motors and Ford of Canada, though attempts to build tanks failed. The only industry that approached radar in its complexity was the manufacturing of aircraft. But unlike radar, the most complex component (namely, the engines) was not manufactured in Canada. For more on Canadian industrial production during the war, see Stacey, *Arms, Men and Governments*, and Bliss, *Northern Enterprise*.

3 Zimmerman, *The Great Naval Battle of Ottawa*, "Radar and Research Enterprises," and "The Royal Canadian Navy and the National

Research Council, 1939–45," 203–21; Bothwell, *Nucleus*, 54–105; Fortier, "Le rôle de l'Etat fédéral dans le développement de l'industrie aéronautique canadienne, 1901–1984"; Bryden, *Deadly Allies*. Less critical but still useful in tracing Canada's participation in advanced-technology research, development, and production are Middleton's *Physics at the National Research Council, Radar Development in Canada* and *Mechanical Engineering at the National Research Council*.

4 For more on Canadian business before the Second World War, see Bliss, *Northern Enterprise*.

5 "History of the British Admiralty Technical Mission," unpublished monograph (copy at the Directorate of History, Department of National Defence, Ottawa), 110; Hall, *North American Supply*, 1–38, 224–8; Hall and Wrigley, *Studies of Overseas Supply*, 46–65; Stacey, *Arms, Men and Government*, 485–528.

6 Tizard Diary, 23 January 1940, Imperial War Museum, (IWM), Tizard Papers (HTT) 16.

7 Research and development for War Purposes in Canada, 17 June 1940, PRO, AVIA 22/2286.

8 A.V. Hill Report, 18 June 1940, National Archives, (NARS), New England Branch, Waltham, Radiation Laboratory Records, box 49.

9 Notes by ACAS(R) [undated but found with Joubert to Hill, 6 July 1940], IWM, HTT 58. See also Cockcroft, "American Liaison," 24 July 1940, PRO, AVIA 22/2286; Sinclair to Hill, 22 June and 1 July 1940, Joubert to Hill, 6 June 1940, and Sinclair to Hill, 1 July 1940, IWM, HTT 58; "Notes on Conclusion of Meeting Held in Air Ministry, 9 July 1940," ibid.

10 Tizard Diary, 8 August 1940, IWM, HTT 16; telegram to Halifax and Lothian, 11 August 1940, in C.J. Mackenzie Diary, National Archives of Canada (NAC), MG 30, B122, vol. 1.

11 Tizard Diary, 16 August 1940, IWM, HTT 16. According to King's diary, Tizard did not impress the importance of the mission on the Canadian prime minister. King remembered only a description of radar and of future long-range bombers, which could be based in Canada in order to strike at Europe and Asia. There is no record that King talked to Roosevelt about the mission (Mackenzie King Diary, 16–20 August 1940, NAC, MG 26).

12 Fowler to Appleton, 16 August 1940, IWM, HTT 58; Tizard Diary, 16 August 1940, IWM, HTT 16.

13 "RDF Work in Canada," 5 June 1940, NAC, RG 77, Acc. 85–86/178, NRC file, S45-7-16, vol. 2.

14 H. Rowley, memo to DPD, 16 July 1940, NAC, RG 24/8086.

15 Pew to DSD Bath and Captain A/S, 21 July 1940, PRO, CAB 115/166.

16 Tizard Diary, 19 July 1940, IWM, HTT 16.

17 "Daily Meeting of Members of the British Technical Mission," 12 September 1940, PRO, AVIA 10/4.

18 Tizard Diary, 14 September 1940, IWM, HTT 58.

19 "Memorandum on Interchange of Scientific Information between the National Defense Research Committee and Great Britain," 25 October 1940, NARS, RG 277, box 37; Bush to Knox and Simpson, October 1940, ibid.; Bush to Mackenzie, 30 October 1940, and Mackenzie to Bush, 4 November 1940, ibid., box 32; "Memorandum for Chief of Staff," 14 November 1940, NARS, RG 165, War Plans Division 4340.1.

20 Mackenzie to McNaughton, 6 December 1940, in Thistle, *The Mackenzie-McNaughton Wartime Letters*, 55–6.

21 Fowler to Mackenzie, 30 September 1940, and Cockcroft to Jackson (Ministry of Aircraft Production), 29 October 1940, NAC, RG 77, Acc. 85–86/178.

22 Tizard Diary, 25 September 1940, IWM, HTT 16.

23 Mackenzie to McNaughton, 28 September 1940, in Thistle, *The Mackenzie-McNaughton Wartime Letters*, 49; Cockcroft to Gough, 30 September 1940, PRO, AVIA 22/2286.

24 Tizard Diary, 27 September 1940, IWM, HTT 16.

25 British Technical Mission to Canadian Defence Council, 24 October 1940, PRO, AVIA 10/1.

26 Cockcroft to the assistant chief of staff, Canadian Army [n.d. but late October 1940], PRO, AVIA 10/1. Cockcroft also advised the NRC on its research priorities in the coming years (see Cockcroft, "Memorandum on the Radio Research Program of the National Research Council," 11 November 1940, in Mackenzie Diary, NAC, MG 30, B122, vol. 1).

27 Other sources state that the Radio Valve Company managed the plant (Mackenzie Diary, 25 November 1940, NAC, MG 30; Kennedy, *History of the Department of Munitions and Supply*, 1:425).

28 Canada Wire still has a large operation on the REL site; memorandum report by Professor Edward L. Bowles, 6–8 August 1941, Howe Papers, NAC, MG 27, vol. 43, folio 5-9-85-7(2); *War History of the Radio Branch*, 45.

29 Cockcroft, "Report on a Discussion on Uranium with Dr. G.C. Laurence and Stedmann," 22 November 1940, PRO, AB 1/171.

30 G.C. Laurence, "Nuclear Fission Research in the United States," 6 December 1940, PRO, AB 1/171.

CHAPTER NINE

1 Telegram, Monet to Salter and Purvis, 20 November 1940, Public Record Office (PRO), AVIA 22/2281.

2 For an example of American policy on technical cooperation in early 1941, see War Department Air Corps Material Division, "Office Memorandum 41-3," 10 February 1941, National Archives, Washington (NARS), RG 18, 350.051.

3 Secretary of war to secretary of the Treasury, 15 October 1940, NARS, RG 65, War Plans Division 4340; memo by Maj. Frederick Hopkins, 20 September 1940, NARS, RG 18, 334.82. Maj. F.M. Hopkins, recorder, Army-Navy British Purchasing Commission Joint Committee, to chief of ordnance, NARS, RG 18, 334.8.

4 Reynolds, *The Creation of the Anglo-American Alliance*, 145–68. The quotation is from WSC to FDR draft, 28 December 1940, PRO, PREM 3/462/1, as quoted in Reynolds, 159.

5 Tizard to prime minister, 19 October 1940, PRO, PREM 3/475/1.

6 "Summary of Important Policy Decisions to be Obtained by Sir Henry Tizard on Arrival in England" [n.d. but late September 1940], PRO, AVIA 10/2.

7 Clark, *Tizard*, 272–92.

8 Gough to secretary, 7 October 1940, PRO, AVIA 22/2286.

9 "Notes of a Meeting in Connection with Sir Henry Tizard's Mission to America (1940)," 14 October 1940, PRO, AVIA 22/2286.

10 Watson-Watt to Gough, 18 October 1940, ibid.; see also Pye to Gough, 18 October 1940, ibid.

11 Tizard to prime minister, 19 October 1940, PRO, PREM 3/475/1.

12 Gough to department secretary, 30 October 1940, PRO, AVIA 22/2286; "Minutes of a Meeting for the Arrangement for the Exchange of Technical Information Concerning Scientific Research Work in North America," 29 October 1940, ibid.; Tizard Diary, 29 October 1940, Imperial War Museum (IWM), Tizard Papers (HTT) 16.

13 "Recent Visit of Sir Henry Tizard to Canada and the United States," 4 November 1940, IWM, HTT 306.

14 "Memorandum by the Chairman of the North American Supply Committee," 13 November 1940, PRO, CAB 66/13.
15 "WM (40), 293rd Conclusions," 21 November 1940, PRO, AVIA 22/2286. Lothian was so instructed on 25 November (Foreign Office to Lothian, PRO, AVIA 22/2286).
16 "Statement Regarding Practice Hitherto Followed by Departments in Regard to the Disclosure of Information to the USA by the Joint Secretaries of the War Cabinet Committee on the Disclosure of Information to the U.S.," 3 December 1940, PRO, AVIA 22/2286.
17 Lothian to Foreign Office, 3 December 1940, ibid.
18 Reynolds, *The Creation of the Anglo-American Alliance*, 155.
19 Brig. Gen. Martin Scalon to Lt. Gen. H.H. Arnold, 13 December 1940, NARS, RG 18, 350.05.
20 Memo by Halifax, 5 December 1940, PRO, FO 371/24263.
21 Halifax to Walker, 18 December 1940, ibid.
22 W.L. Gorell Barnes, "Committee on Disclosure to United States of America of Secret Information [in] Relation to Supply Matters," 21 December 1940, House of Lords Record Office (HLRO), Beaverbrook Papers.
23 Gough to secretary, 7 January 1941, PRO, AVIA 22/2286.
24 Beaverbrook to Tizard, 29 October 1940, IWM, HTT 262.
25 Interview with Air Commodore Leedham, 26 September 1940, National Archives of Canada (NAC), RG 77, NRC, S45-2-16, vol. 3; Leedham to McKinley, 27 September 1940, ibid.; McKinley to Cockcroft, 17 December 1940, NAC, RG 77, NRC, S45-2-16, vol. 4; "Memorandum to Mr. Banks," 30 December 1940, ibid.; McKinley to Howe, 1 January 1941, ibid.; Howe to Beaverbrook, 2 January 1940, ibid.; McKinley to Mackenzie, 19 December 1940, NAC, RG 77, NRC, B45-2-30, vol. 1.
26 "DSA (41), 1st Meeting War Cabinet Committee on Disclosure to USA of Secret Information Relating to Supply Matters," 15 January 1941, PRO, ADM 199/1156.
27 "Memorandum on Interchange of Scientific Information between the National Defence Research Committee and Great Britain and Canada," 10 October 1940, PRO, AVIA 10/2.
28 Gough to department secretary, 15 November 1940, and "Note on Scientific Liaison with the USA through Directorate of Scientific Research, Ministry of Supply," 28 November 1940, PRO, AVIA 22/2286.

29 Cockcroft, "Memorandum to Sir Henry Tizard on the Future of Work Arising out of the British Technical Mission," 29 November 1940, PRO, AVIA 22/2286.

30 Duncan to Purvis, 20 December 1940, PRO, ADM 199/1156; Supply Council in North America to Supply Committee, 12 January 1941, ibid.

31 Knox to British Purchasing Commission [sic], 9 January 1941, NARS, RG 165, 9771-49.

32 James Forestal, acting secretary of the navy, to the secretary of state, 27 January 1941, and Cordell Hull to the secretary of the navy, 4 February 1941, NARS, RG 59, 811.24, E1/5; "Proposed Negotiations with British Commonwealth Governments in Respect of Reciprocal Use of Patents and Secret Processes," 8 February 1941, ibid., 811.24, E1/6.

33 "Minutes of the 2nd Informal Discussion on Exchange of Scientific and Technical Information with the USA," 21 February 1941, IWM, HTT 255.

34 Conant, *My Several Lives*, 248–71. See also Hershberg, *James B. Conant*, 142–6.

35 Goldberg, "Inventing a Climate of Opinion," 429–52.

36 Gowing, *Britain and Atomic Energy*, 67–9.

37 Goldberg, "Inventing a Climate of Opinion," 436–7.

38 Conant, *My Several Lives*, 266.

EPILOGUE

1 W.L. Webster, personal memo on BCSO, 26 June 1942, Public Record Office (PRO), AVIA 38/918.

2 "Report of OSRD Activities in the European Theatre during the Period March 1941 through July 1945. Part I: Summary," National Archives, Washington (NARS), RG 277, box 128, Liaison Office.

3 Zimmerman, *Great Naval Battle of Ottawa*, 159.

4 See Guerlac, *Radar in World War II*, 341–52, 414–19.

5 For more on the American jet engine industry, see Constant, *Origins of the Turbojet Revolution*.

6 "Visit of Wing Commander C.D. Dunn of the Royal Air Force to Wright Field on 19, 20, 21, 24 February 1942," NARS, RG 18, Norden Bombsight History. See also John J. McCloy to Mr Lovett, 1 January 1942, ibid.

7 For more on the Norden bombsight in the war, see the Norden Bombsight History in NARS, RG 18, and Robert Vance Brown's "History of the Norden Bombsight," part IV, Naval Historical Center microfilm.

8 Tizard Diary, 30 August 1940, Imperial War Museum (IWM), Tizard Papers (HTT) 16.

9 Cohen and Gooch, *Military Misfortunes*, ch. 4, "Failure to Learn: American Antisubmarine Warfare in 1942," 59–94.

10 See, for instance, Carroll Pursell, "Science Agencies in World War II: The OSRD and Its Challengers"; Dupree, "The Great Insat-uration of 1940."

11 The author wishes to make it clear that in no way is he referring to the historians given in the note above. This statement is directed instead at several incompetent individuals, best left unnamed, who have dismissed the influence of the mission on the United States out of hand. Unfortunately, this led to the refusal by the journal *Technology and Culture* to publish an article based on the findings presented in this book.

12 Meigs, *Slide Rule and Submarines*, 26.

13 Ibid., 28.

14 Ibid., 29.

15 For more on the BCSO, see the files in PRO, AVIA 38/917 and 7/2796.

16 Guerlac, *Radar in World War II*, 697.

17 For more on the breakdown of Anglo-American cooperation, see Gowing, *Britain and Atomic Energy*, 147–78.

18 Hinsley, *British Intelligence in the Second World War*, 1:311–13.

19 Mackenzie Diary, 23 January 1941, NAC, MG 30.

20 "Memorandum on the Procedure for Co-operation between the British Central Scientific Office and Representatives of Dominion Scientific Effort for War Purposes," 30 June 1941, NARS, RG 277, box 29.

21 "Memorandum on Interchange of Scientific Information between the National Defense Research Committee and Great Britain and Canada," 24 October 1940, PRO, AVIA 10/2.

22 Phillips to Mackenzie, 18 November 1941, NAC, RG 77, NRC, B45-2-30, vol. 3.

23 There are many examples of Canadian frustration with the inability of the British scientific and engineering personnel to coordinate their activities. In one case, in February 1942, Robert Watson-Watt,

representing the Ministry of Aircraft Production, unsuccessfully attempted to change all the production priorities of the radar program because top priority had been given to Admiralty and Ministry of Supply projects (Mackenzie Diary, 3 February 1942, NAC, MG 30).

24 The documentary evidence and the official historians seem to suggest that after the passage of the Lend Lease Act, Canada was viewed, at best, as a minor player in the war of science and advanced technology. Renewed interest in Canadian resources began only when the Americans refused to cooperate, as in the case of atomic energy, or when serious planning for the postwar period began in late 1943.

25 Middleton, *Radar Development in Canada*, 30–3, 44–5.

Bibliography

PRIMARY SOURCES

Canada

DIRECTORATE OF HISTORY, NATIONAL DEFENCE HEADQUARTERS, OTTAWA
Chiefs of Staff minutes and papers
Naval Board minutes
Naval Staff minutes

NATIONAL ARCHIVES OF CANADA, OTTAWA
MG 26, W.L. Mackenzie King papers
MG 27, C.D. Howe papers
MG 30, C.J. Mackenzie diary and papers
RG 2, War Cabinet Committee papers and minutes
RG 24, Air Force Central Registry files
Army Central Registry files
Atlantic Command files
Canadian Naval Liaison files
Naval Council minutes
Naval Directorate of Operations Research files
Naval Headquarters Registry files
Pacific Command files

RG 28, Records of the Department of Munitions and Supply Records of the Department of Reconstruction and Supply
RG 77, Records of the National Research Council
John Henderson Papers (consulted at the National Research Council before transfer to NAC)

NATIONAL RESEARCH COUNCIL OF CANADA, OTTAWA
Central Registry files
Coordinating and Management Committee minutes
Heads of Groups Meeting minutes
Papers of the Head of the Division of Physics and Electrical Engineering
PRA and PRB reports

Great Britain

CHURCHILL COLLEGE, CAMBRIDGE
S.V. Alexander papers
E.G. Bowen papers
J.D. Cockcroft papers
Charles Goodeve papers
A.V. Hill papers
S.W. Roskill papers

HOUSE OF LORDS RECORD OFFICE, LONDON
Papers of Lord Beaverbrook

IMPERIAL WAR MUSEUM, LONDON
HTT, Papers of Sir Henry Tizard

NUFFIELD COLLEGE, OXFORD
Lindemann papers

PUBLIC RECORD OFFICE, LONDON
AB 1, U.K. Atomic Energy Authority, War of 1939–45, correspondence
ADM 1, Admiralty and Secretariat papers, general subject files ADM 116, Admiralty and Secretariat cases
ADM 137, War of 1914–18, Admiralty Historical Section, packs and miscellaneous
ADM 199, War History cases
ADM 204, Admiralty Research Laboratory reports

ADM 205, First Sea Lord's papers
ADM 215, Records of the Admiralty Signals Establishment
AIR 2, Air Ministry, registered files
AIR 14, Bomber Command files
AVIA 7, Telecommunications Research Establishment files
AVIA 8, Air Ministry's Inventions and Research and Development files
AVIA 10, Ministry of Aircraft Production, unregistered papers
AVIA 22, Ministry of Supply, registered files
AVIA 38, North American Supply papers
CAB 63, Hankey papers
CAB 65, War Cabinet minutes
CAB 66, War Cabinet memoranda for WP and CP series
CAB 101, Historians' papers, military
CAB 102, Historians' papers, civil
CAB 115, Central Office for North American Supplies
PREM 3, Prime Minister's Office, operational papers

United States

LIBRARY OF CONGRESS, WASHINGTON
Vannevar Bush papers

MASSACHUSETTS INSTITUTE OF TECHNOLOGY ARCHIVES, BOSTON
President's Office papers

NATIONAL ACADEMY OF SCIENCES, WASHINGTON
Records of the National Research Council

NATIONAL ARCHIVES, BOSTON BRANCH
Records of Division 10, the Radiation Laboratory

NATIONAL ARCHIVES, WASHINGTON
RG 18, U.S. Army Air Corps, central decimal files
RG 19, Naval Research Laboratory, general files
RG 59, Department of State, central decimal files
RG 72, Bureau of Aeronautics files
RG 80, Secretary of the Navy/CNO files
RG 165, Military Intelligence Division files
– War Plans Division files

RG 277, Records of the Office of Scientific Research and Development

NAVAL HISTORICAL CENTER, WASHINGTON
Papers of Admiral N.H. Kirk

SWARTHMORE COLLEGE ARCHIVES, PENNSYLVANIA
Papers of Frank Aydellotte

YALE UNIVERSITY LIBRARY
Henry Stimson diary

SECONDARY SOURCES

Allison, David Kite. *New Eyes for the Navy: The Origin of Radar at the Naval Research Laboratory.* Washington: Naval Research Laboratory, 1981.

Baxter, James Phinney, 3rd. *Scientists against Time*. Boston: Atlantic/Little Brown, 1946.

Baylis, John. *Anglo-American Defence Relations 1939–1984*. 2nd ed. London: Macmillan, 1984.

Beyerchen, Alan D. *Scientists under Hitler*. New Haven: Yale University Press, 1977.

Blackett, P.M.S. *Studies of War*. London: Oliver and Boyd, 1962.

Bliss, Michael. *Northern Enterprise*. Toronto: McClelland and Stewart, 1987.

Bothwell, Robert. *Nucleus*. Toronto: University of Toronto Press, 1988.

Bothwell, R., and W. Kilbourn. *C.D. Howe*. Toronto: McClelland and Stewart, 1979.

Bowen, E.G. *Radar Days*. Bristol: Adam Hilgar, 1987.

Bowen, Harold G. *Ships Machinery and Mossbacks*. Princeton: Princeton University Press, 1954.

Brown, Anthony Cave, and Charles B. MacDonald, eds. *The Secret History of the Atomic Bomb*. New York: Dial Press, 1977.

Brown, Robert Vance. *History of the Norden Bombsight*. Washington: Naval Historical Center microfilm.

Bryden, John. *Deadly Allies*. Toronto: McClelland and Stewart, 1989.

Bush, Vannevar. *Modern Arms and Free Men*. New York: Simon and Schuster, 1949.

– *Pieces of the Action*. New York: William Morrow, 1970.

Clark, R.W. *The Rise of the Boffins*. London: Phoenix House, 1962.

– *Tizard*. London: Methuen, 1965.

Cockburn, Stewart, and David Ellyard. *Oliphant*. Adelaide: Axiom Books, 1981.

Cohen, Eliot A., and John Gooch. *Military Misfortunes: The Anatomy of Failure in War*. New York: Vintage Books, 1991.

Compton, Arthur Holly. *Atomic Quest*. New York: Oxford University Press, 1956.

Conant, J.B. *My Several Lives*. New York: Harper and Row, 1970.

Constant, Edward W., II. *The Origins of the Turbojet Revolution*. Baltimore: Johns Hopkins University Press, 1980.

Craven, Wesley F., and James Lea Cate. *The Army Air Forces in World War II*. Vol. 1. Chicago: University of Chicago Press, 1948.

Davis, Nuel Pharr. *Lawrence and Oppenheimer*. New York: Simon and Schuster, 1968.

Dawson, Virginia. *Engines and Innovation*. Washington: NASA, 1991.

"A Discussion on the Effects of the Two World Wars on the Organization and Development of Science in the United Kingdom." *Proceedings of the Royal Society*, A342 (1975): 441–5.

Drury, Alfred T. "War History of the Naval Research Laboratory." Unpublished monograph. Washington: U.S. Naval Historical Division, 1948.

Dupree, A. Hunter. "The Great Insaturation of 1940: The Organization of Scientific Research for War." In *The Twentieth-Century Sciences*, ed. Gerald Holton. New York: W.W. Norton, 1972.

– *Science in the Federal Government*. Cambridge: Harvard University Press, 1957.

Dziuban, Stanley. *Military Relations between the United States and Canada, 1939–1945*. Washington: Office of the Chief of Military History, 1959.

Eggleston, Wilfrid. *National Research in Canada*. Toronto: Clarke Irwin, 1978.

– *Scientists at War*. Toronto: Oxford University Press, 1950.

Faren, W.S. "Henry Thomas Tizard." *Biographical Memoirs of Fellows of the Royal Society* 7 (1961): 324.

Fisher, David E. *A Race on the Edge of Time*. New York: McGraw-Hill, 1988.

Fortier, G. "Le rôle de l'Etat fédéral dans le développement de l'industrie aéronautique canadienne, 1901–1984." PH D thesis, Université Laval, 1985.

Friedman, Norman. *Naval Radar*. Annapolis: Naval Institute Press, 1984.

Furer, Julius A. *Administration of the Navy Department in World War II*. Washington: GPO, 1959.

Gilbert, Martin. *Finest Hour*. London: Heinemann, 1983.

Goldberg, Stanley. "Inventing a Climate of Opinion: Vannevar Bush and the Decision to Build the Bomb." *Isis* 83 (1992): 429–52.

Gowing, Margret. *Britain and Atomic Energy, 1939–45*. London: Macmillan, 1964.

Granatstein, J.L. *Canada's War*. Toronto: Oxford University Press, 1975.

Green, C.M., H.C. Thomson, and Peter C. Roots. *The Ordnance Department: Planning Munitions for War*. Washington: Office of the Chief of Military History, 1955.

Guerlac, Henry E. *Radar in World War II*. 2 vols. New York: American Institute of Physics, 1987. (Note: First publication of secret official history of radiation laboratory completed in 1946.)

Haber, L.F. *The Poisonous Cloud: Chemical Warfare in the First World War*. Oxford: Clarendon Press, 1986.

Hackmann, Willem. *Seek and Strike*. London: HMSO, 1984.

Haight, John McVicar, Jr. *American Aid to France, 1938–1940*. New York: Atheneum, 1970

Hall, H. Duncan. *North American Supply*. London: HMSO, 1955.

Hall, H. Duncan, and C.G. Wrigley. *Studies of Overseas Supply*. London: HMSO, 1956.

Hartcup, Guy. *The Challenge of War*. Newton Abbot: David & Charles, 1970.

– *The War of Invention: Scientific Development, 1914–18*. London: Brassey's, 1988.

Hartcup, Guy, and T.E. Allibone. *Cockcroft and the Atom*. Bristol: Adam Hilgar, 1984.

Heilbron, J.L., and Robert W. Seidel. *Lawrence and His Laboratory*. Berkeley: University of California Press, 1989.

Hershberg, James G. *James B. Conant: Harvard to Hiroshima and the Making of the Nuclear Age*. New York: Alfred A. Knopf, 1993.

Hewlett, Richard, and Oscar Anderson. *The New World, 1939/1946*. University Park: Pennsylvania State University Press, 1962.

Hezlett, Arthur. *The Electron and Sea Power*. London: Peter Davies, 1975.

Hill, A.V. "Science in War: Co-operation with Canada and the United States." *Cambridge Review*, May 1941.

Hinsley, F. *British Intelligence in the Second World War*. Vols. 1–3A. Cambridge: Cambridge University Press, 1979–83.

"History of the British Admiralty Technical Mission." Unpublished monograph, 1946. (Copies at NAC, PRO, and the Directorate of History.)

Howeth, L.S. *History of Communications-Electronics in the United States Navy*. Washington: GPO, 1963.

Jay, K.E.B., and J.D. Scott. "History of the Development and the Production of Radio and Radar." Unpublished monograph. London: Public Record Office (PRO, CAB 102/63–4).

Jones, R.V. "Churchill and Science." In *Churchill*, ed. Roger Blake and William Roger Louis, 427–42. New York: W.W. Norton, 1993.

– *Most Secret War*. London: Hamish Hamilton, 1978.

Jones, Vincent C. *Manhattan: The Army and the Atomic Bomb*. Washington: Center for Military History, 1985.

Katz, Sir Bernard. "A.V. Hill." *Biographical Memoirs of the Royal Society* 24 (1978): 70–149.

Kennedy, J. de N. *History of the Department of Munitions and Supply*. 2 vols. Ottawa: King's Printer, 1950.

Kevles, Daniel J. *The Physicists*. New York: Alfred A. Knopf, 1978.

Kimball, William, ed. *Churchill and Roosevelt: The Complete Correspondence*. Vol. 1. Princeton: Princeton University Press, 1984.

Lasby, Clarence. "Science and the Military." In *Science and Society in the United States*, ed. D.D. Van Tassel and M.G. Hall. Homewood, Ill.: Dorsey Press, 1966.

Lash, Joseph. *Roosevelt and Churchill, 1939–41*. New York: W.W. Norton, 1976.

Leutze, James R. *Bargaining for Supremacy*. Chapel Hill: University of North Carolina Press, 1977.

– ed. *The London Journal of Raymond E. Lee, 1940–1941*. Boston: Little Brown, 1971.

Macdonald, C.A. *The United States, Britain and Appeasement, 1936–1939*. London: Macmillan, 1981.

Meigs, Montgomery. *Slide Rules and Submarines*. Washington: National Defense University Press, 1990.

Mellor, D.P. *The Role of Science and Industry*. Canberra: Australian War Memorial, 1958.

Messinger, Charles. *Bomber Harris*. London: Arms and Armour Press, 1984.

Middleton, W.E.K. *Mechanical Engineering at the National Research Council of Canada, 1929–1951*. Waterloo: Wilfrid Laurier University Press, 1984.

– *Physics at the National Research Council of Canada, 1929–1952*. Waterloo: Wilfrid Laurier University Press, 1979.

– *Radar Development in Canada: The Radio Branch of the National Research Council of Canada, 1939–1946*. Waterloo: Wilfrid Laurier University Press, 1981.

Millikan, Robert. *The Autobiography of Robert A. Millikan*. New York: Prentice-Hall, 1950.

Murfett, Malcolm. *Fool-Proof Relations: The Search for Anglo-American Naval Cooperation during the Chamberlain Years, 1937–1940*. Singapore: Singapore University Press, 1984.

Offner, Arnold. *American Appeasement: American Foreign Policy and Germany, 1933–1938*. Cambridge, Mass.: Belknop Press of the Harvard University Press, 1969.

Phillipson, D.J.C. *International Scientific Liaison and the National Research Council of Canada, 1916–74*. Ottawa: NRC, 1985, 26–30.

Postan, M.M. *British War Production*. London: HMSO, 1964.

Postan, M.M., D. Hay, and J.D. Scott. *The Design and Development of Weapons*. London: HMSO, 1963.

Pursell, Carroll. "Science Agencies in World War II: The OSRD and Its Challengers." In *The Sciences in the American Context: New Perspectives*, ed. Nathan Reingold, 359–78. Washington: Smithsonian Institution, 1979.

Reynolds, David. *The Creation of the Anglo-American Alliance 1937–41*. London: Europa Publications, 1981.

– "Lord Lothian and Anglo-American Relations, 1939–1940." *Proceedings of the American Philosophical Society* 73, pt. 2 (1983): 1–4.

Roskill, S.W. *Churchill and the Admirals*. London: Collins, 1977.

– *Naval Policy between the Wars*. 2 vols. London: Collins, 1976.

– *The War at Sea*. 3 vols. London: HMSO, 1954–61.

Sapolosky, Carroll. "Academic Science and the Military: The Years since World War Two." In *The Sciences in the American Context: New Perspectives*, ed. Nathan Reingold, 379–99. Washington: Smithsonian Institution, 1979.

Sapolsky, Harvey M. *Science and the Navy*. Princeton: Princeton University Press, 1990.

Smith, Malcolm. "The Royal Air Force and British Foreign Policy." *Journal of Contemporary History* 12 (1977): 153–74.

Snow, C.P. *Science and Government*. Cambridge: Harvard University Press, 1961.

Stacey, C.P. *Arms, Men and Government*. Ottawa: Department of National Defence, 1970.

Stewart, Irvin. *Organizing Science for War*. Boston: Little Brown, 1948.

Swords, Sean S. *A Technical History of the Beginnings of Radar*. Dublin: Trinity College, 1983.

Taylor, A.J.P. *Beaverbrook*. London: Hamish Hamilton, 1972.

Terrett, Dulany. *The Signal Corps: The Emergency*. Washington: Office of the Chief of Military History, 1956.

Thistle, Mel. *The Inner Ring*. Toronto: University of Toronto Press, 1966.

– ed. *The Mackenzie-McNaughton Wartime Letters*. Toronto: University of Toronto Press, 1978.

Waddington, C.H. *OR in World War II: Operational Research against the U-Boat*. London: Elek Science, 1973.

Walker, Mark. *German National Socialism and the Quest for Nuclear Power*. New York: Cambridge University Press, 1991.

War History of the Associate Committee of the Radio Branch. Ottawa: NRC, n.d.

War History of the Division of Physics and Electrical Engineering. Ottawa: NRC, 1949.

War History of the Radio Branch. Ottawa: NRC, 1948.

Woodward, Sir Llewellyn. *British Foreign Policy in the Second World War*. Vol. 1. London: HMSO, 1970.

Zimmerman, David. *The Great Naval Battle of Ottawa*. Toronto: University of Toronto Press, 1989.

– "Organizing Science for War: The Management of Canadian Radar Development, 1939–45." *Scientia Canadensis* 10, no. 2 (1986): 93–108.

– "Radar and Research Enterprises: A Case Study of Wartime Industrial Failure." *Ontario History*, June 1988.

– "The Royal Canadian Navy and the National Research Council, 1939–45." *Canadian Historical Review*, June 1988.

Index